Catharsis in Psychotherapy

Čatharsis
in Psychotherapy

Michael P. Nichols
Albany Medical College of Union University

Melvin Zax
University of Rochester

GARDNER PRESS, INC. New York

Distributed by Halsted Press

A Division of JOHN WILEY & SONS, INC.

New York • London • Sydney • Toronto

GARDNER PRESS, INC.
19 Union Square West
New York, New York 10003

Distributed solely by the HALSTED PRESS
Division of John Wiley & Sons, Inc., New York

Library of Congress Cataloging in Publication Data

Nichols, Micheal P
    Catharsis in psychotherapy.

    Includes index.
    1. Psychotherapy. 2. Catharsis. I. Zax,
Melvin, joint author. II. Title.
RC480.5.N5   616.8'914   76-30468
ISBN 0-470-99064-3

Printed in the United States of America
1 2 3 4 5 6 7 8 9

For Melody

Preface

*E*motional catharsis is currently enjoying a renaissance in several innovative approaches to psychotherapy. Unfortunately, the growth of these therapies has not been matched by careful theoretical analysis or systematic research. In the complex realm of psychotherapy it is easy to overlook the need to measure results, but therapists neglect their responsibility by doing so and patients sacrifice their rights by letting them. Believing that psychotherapy is best used when most understood, we set out to examine the literature on catharsis.

We were surprised and disappointed to find too few rigorous studies to constitute a body of empirical evidence, so we branched out to include historical accounts and non-empirical descriptions of catharsis in a variety of contexts that relate to psychotherapy. After chronicling the history of catharsis in behavior change, we described and critically examined modern cathartic therapies. Then, after assembling the meager research evidence, we went on to add some speculation about the process of emotional catharsis. Our hope is that this systematizing and criticizing will inspire students, researchers and therapists to improve the conduct of psychotherapy.

This project took nearly six years to complete; work on it had to compete with teaching, research, and practice for our time and energy. We are grateful to several people who were kind enough to help along the way.

The most important contributions were made by three

therapists who generously shared their experiences and ideas. Foremost among these is Bob Pierce, a brilliant and talented clinician, whose work inspired this project and whose support sustained it. James F. Smith taught us a great deal about emotive techniques and theories, and Joyce DuBrin helped us to learn that techniques are no substitute for warmth and persistence.

Jay Efran read and critiqued several sections of the manuscript. Jay's criticism is always sharp; submitting something to him is a trial by fire, but what emerges is the better for his having had a hand in it. Jon Allen, Steve Nowicki and Dave Freides also read segments of the manuscript and made useful suggestions about how to improve it.

Several typists worked on the project and we thank all of them, especially Rita Thomas and Jean Fletcher.

Finally, thank you, Barbara Fried for a thorough and professional job of copy editing.

M. P. N.
M. Z.

Atlanta, Georgia
Rochester, New York

Contents

Preface   vii

Chapter 1
Catharsis: Its Meaning and Nature   1

Chapter 2
Catharsis in Religious and Magic Healing Rituals   13

Chapter 3
Psychoanalysis and the Cathartic Technique   29

Chapter 4
Hypnotherapy and Traumatic Neuroses   39

Chapter 5
Catharsis in Group Treatment   65

Chapter 6
Bereavement   89

Chapter 7
Recent Emotive Approaches to Psychotherapy   103

Chapter 8
The Empirical Evaluation of Catharsis   155

Chapter 9
Summary and Implications for Clinical Practice   197

References   235

Index   255

Catharsis in Psychotherapy

Catharsis:
Its Meaning and Nature

Catharsis is a widely used but vaguely defined term. It is generally understood to mean "a process that relieves tension and anxiety by expressing emotions,"—emotions that have been hidden, restrained, or unconscious. However, this is not an operational definition, and many disagreements about the value of catharsis result from the varying usage of the term.

In chapters that follow we shall describe Freud as having abandoned the use of catharsis on the grounds that it was ineffective, Berkowitz and Bandura as concluding that catharsis of aggression leads to more aggression, and Alexander Lowen as highly prizing catharsis in psychotherapy. These apparently discrepant views can be clarified and partially resolved merely by describing what each meant by catharsis. The conclusions of these scientists are not about words and concepts, but about specific events and behaviors. Freud referred to the recall by hysterical patients of single instances of previously forgotten memories. Berkowitz and Bandura referred to children engaging directly or vicariously in hostile and destructive behavior toward other children. Lowen referred to expressive physical movements. To understand what is meant by *catharsis* as the

1

word is used in psychotherapy and other forms of behavior change we must be more specific.

Etymologically, *catharsis* derives from the Greek *katharsis*. The essential meaning of *katharsis* was "to clean or purify", but it had shades of other meanings as well. In a medical context, the word meant purgation, or the elimination of offensive humors. In a religious context, it referred to rebirth or initiation; and in a moral and spiritual context, meant relief of the soul and spirit by purification. Thus, its semantic origins suggest that catharsis has always included two ideas: purgation or purification; and rebirth or initiation into a new state. Greek mythological heroes, for instance, were thought to be reborn into a more exalted state following the successful completion of purifying sacrifices and trials. Also, the admission of guilt was apparently associated with rituals in Greek religious sanctuaries.

In writing of catharsis achieved through art, Aristotle emphasized its aspect of purgation. Music and drama are worthwhile, Aristotle said, because of their cathartic, purgative function. These art forms drive the passions to a peak and then exorcise them. Tragedy arouses pity and fear, and purges these emotions; it is therefore of value despite the attacks of certain moralists and philosophers. In the *Poetics* (1) he wrote, "Tragedy, then is a representation of an action that is serious, complete, and of a certain magnitude; in language pleasurably and variously embellished suitably to the different parts of the play; in the form of actions directly presented, not narrated; with incidents arousing pity and fear in such a way as to accomplish a purgation (katharsis) of such emotions." Emotions are aroused and then purged because the audience is able to identify with the tragic hero to the extent that his pain has relevance and meaning to them.

This Aristotelian concept of tragedy is thus not simply a passive intellectual exercise. It is a profound upheaval, charged with emotion generated through similarities between the tragic hero's experience and the audience's experiences. The shock of the emotional arousal and purgation helps to rearrange perceptions and so leads to a modification of the audience's self-concept and world view. Aristotle believed that the powerful intellectual and affective experience of having anxiety dissolve in tears fosters personal exploration and development.

Breuer and Freud (2) used *catharsis* to describe the process of a sudden recall of a previously forgotten memory, together with the expression of the feeling associated with it, when this event was accompanied by a release of repressed psychic energy and followed by a feeling of relief. This definition subsumes other psychoanalytic metaphors—psychic energy, hypercathexis, repression, and discharge. This extra baggage creates two difficulties. First it can be argued that the concept of catharsis is used by many who reject the psychoanalytic model and that it should be defined independently of that model. The second shortcoming of the psychoanalytic definition of catharsis is that it is vague and unclear because it rests on these other concepts that are themselves vague and ill-defined. We have chosen to present the psychoanalytic definition of catharsis, despite its surplus meaning, because when the term is used, the psychoanalytic model *is* often invoked, if only implictly. In common usage *catharsis* refers not only to a specific event, but to an elaborate explanatory model as well.

This psychoanalytic model, however useful it may be, contains certain nonverifiable and misleading assumptions. For one thing, it suggests that emotions are somehow stored up before they are discharged. They must, therefore, have a container. In his "Project for a Scientific Psychology," Freud (3) attempted to create a neurological model to explain the phenomena of emotional behavior. He postulated that both external and internal stimulation is transformed into Q (psychic energy). This energy affects the nervous system by filling up (cathecting) neurons, which in turn discharge when they become completely filled (hypercathected). Freud eventually abandoned this neurological model, because he believed that without knowing more about the nervous system it was impossible to provide a thorough and coherent mechanistic explanation of behavior. Nonetheless, he continued to assume that a neurological explanation was possible, so that even when he described emotions in psychological terms, he still thought of them as things rather than processes, and they still required a container. Some of his metaphors involve a concept of an "inner space" (4) that acts as a repository for affects, for the unconscious, and for memories. His explanation of catharsis also is typically based on a hydraulic model. When emotions are not discharged, he said, they reside in inner space, incrementally accumulating tension. Affect must be ventilated and drained off, or pressure builds to a point where it becomes destructive.

That is, affects are like water boiling in a kettle. If the kettle is not allowed to blow off steam, it will explode.

A variant of this view is Freud's safety-valve theory of emotion (5), in which he considers emotions to be the subjective experience of drives—their affective charge. Emotional expression provides partial discharge of drive energy when the object of a drive is out of reach. When action to satisfy an instinctual drive is impossible or dangerous, catharsis permits internal discharge and the reduction of tension. Fenichel (6) modified this idea by positing that emotion breaks through only when ego control fails. Hence, according to Fenichel, full emotional expression, as in catharsis, is a regressive phenomenon. As a child matures, increased ego mastery results in modification of the character of the affect. Affect is "tamed" by the ego, and used to anticipate the arousal of instincts.

One problem with this Freudian hydraulic model is that it implies a closed system of psychic energy. However, the value of catharsis rests neither on the hydraulic model of emotion nor on the belief that psychic energy exists within a closed system. Emotion has long thought to be related to action, and different theorists have expressed this relationship in different ways. Darwin, for instance, viewed emotion as a vestige of instinctual response patterns. McDougall described emotion as accompanying instinctual action in an integrated pattern. Furthermore, emotions are not related only to action, but also to motivation, appraisal of the environment, and evaluation of bodily state. However, emotions are organized toward action. Magda Arnold (7) describes emotions as action tendencies, and points out that acting on emotions brings relief from the physical tension engendered by their arousal.

> Anger brings an urge to strike and tear, to use the muscles poised for action, to express the tension that threatens to smother us. To act as anger prompts us to act, so that we crush or destroy what annoys us, not only removes the obstacle but also brings relief from the unbearable physical tension. Similarly with other emotions. Their physiological effects are such that action must follow under pain of considerable discomfort.

This statement seems to support the idea that catharsis is therapeutic. However, according to Arnold, the expression of emotion brings relief *only* when action removes the source of the emotion. If the cause of an emotion remains, according to her, emotional expression will only intensify the emotion, so that clearly she does not endorse the value of catharsis in psychotherapy. We may, however, accept the idea that emotions are part of an action sequence and then draw different conclusions.

Freud's hydraulic model implies that if the action sequence is not completed—for example, if an angry child does not yell at his father—the subjective feeling component somehow collects into a pool. An alternative explanation would be that the undischarged affect is restimulated by thoughts of the object (father); the undischarged affect would then leave a residual tension, and this tension is associated with the memory. In psychoanalytic terms, the "internal object" carries an affective charge, and the affect is associated with thoughts that may be out of awareness. Thus, undischarged affects may persist (or be capable of being restimulated) as part of the internal representation (or memory) of persons or experiences. Cathartic discharge can then be viewed as a partial completion, without the undesirable consequences (retaliation from the father) of the original disposition to act. One reason why it is important to discharge the affect is that it is felt as tension, and thus may disturb the relationship to the person involved (father) or interfere with conflict-free rationality. That is, appropriate and efficient thinking may be impaired by the disruptive impact of strong, though vaguely understood, feelings.

We can also explain catharsis in terms of learning theory. When a child is subject to a distressing experience, such as being beaten up by an older child, a strong emotional reaction occurs. The defeated child may suffer feelings of shame and humiliation as well as physical pain. Such an encounter may have two results. First, there is a powerful feeling of hurt and upset, or conditioned emotional reaction (CER). This reaction carries a strong negative valence, and the child typically avoids a rematch. The second result may be generalization; that is, he may avoid not only this particular situation, but also a whole host of situations with some components similar to the original.

The CER may be restimulated by any of a variety of cues from the original traumatic event—for instance, being struck, seeing a threatening bully, or even seeing any older children. Because the CER causes avoidance and withdrawal, the unhappy child may not get a chance to learn to discriminate real from imagined situations of danger once he finds he can quickly reduce the restimulated CER by flight. To compound his difficulties, the child may not be aware of this sequence. The CER requires no conscious participation on his part. The instrumental act or avoidance response may or may not be consciously chosen, but in either case the reasons behind it are likely to be unknown.

If the pain from the fight was severe or the humiliation intense—in other words, if the CER is powerful—the incident may have far-reaching consequences. Though weeks, months, and even years may pass, the child or adult still continues his pattern of avoidance, which is regularly reinforced by a temporary abatement of the CER. This pattern of avoidance may seriously interfere with his life style if it leads him to withdraw from all situations that involve confrontation.

By making a strong effort, he may be able to overcome his impulse to withdraw, and hence decondition the CER to some situations. However, unless the CER to the original stimulus configuration is extinguished, it is liable to be restimulated by new situations. To unlearn or extinguish the original reaction requires a replication of its cues. The strong emotional response attendant on the traumatic scene serves both as a cue that the original scene is being restimulated (in imagination) and also as one of the original stimuli. If the response is repeated without avoiding the re-imagination of the scene, the response may be extinguished if it is not followed by the feared unpleasant consequences. In this way the unpleasant reaction and the subsequent avoidance of a variety of similar situations can be eliminated with one stroke.

According to this explanation, then, emotional catharsis is merely an epiphenomenon. It is merely one facet of the original stimulus-response configuration in the process of extinguishing a CER. This explanation appears to fit some, but not all of the facts. Emotional ventilation itself seems to have a beneficial impact even without (apparent) recapitulation of early learning situations. Admittedly, this point is speculative. Testing it requires evaluating the differential improvement in patients who can re-imagine a distressing incident without further signs of distress—that is, they have extinguished it—versus those who may still show signs of upset, but have experienced a greater amount of emotional discharge.

The idea that cathartic expression is not the emotion, but a phenomenon that follows it, however, naively assumes that emotions are simple events that, once elicited, remain in pure form until discharged or suppressed. In fact, however, emotions are quite complex processes involving a neurophysiological component, a behavioral-expressive component, and a phenomenological or experiential component. Catharsis itself may also be analyzed into these three components as well as being considered a part of the expressive aspect of emotions.

For the sake of simplicity, we will sometimes here distinguish cathartic discharge from the experience of emotional arousal, in part to underscore the fact that discharge is not always a part of the experience of emotion. Such an artificial separation of catharsis and emotion does, in fact, fit the facts of common experience. Most people have experienced emotional arousal and tension without the relief of ventilation and discharge often enough to believe them to be two separate processes. However, although this certainly happens, we consider it to be an abortion of the natural sequence of emotional experience.

It seems that in the absence of any interference, emotional expression is a spontaneous aspect of the experience of affect. This expression serves both a therapeutic and communicative function. The therapeutic function consists of discharge of the tension—"psychological" as well as physical—of an incompleted action tendency. The communicative function announces the affect, and, by implication, the nature of the action that is wished for. How others respond to these two aspects of emotional expression is critical in determining the future of complex emotional arousal-response sequences. However, not all emotional expression is part of a natural sequence in the complex experience of emotions. Instead, because emotional expression serves a communicative function, at times it may be aimed primarily at influencing others.

The child who is permitted to stay up late if she cries at bedtime soon learns that crying can be used as a device to manipulate her parents in other situations as well. Thus, what was at first a spontaneous response to distress becomes an operant behavior. Where crying was originally a respondant, serving both to communicate and relieve the tension of distress, it may become turned on in an attempt to control others. Often it is this second, operant, aspect of emotional expression that serves as a stimulus to cause others to discourage all—even respondant—signs of emotional expression. When a child's crying is recognized as a command to change things, parents typically respond by discouraging crying. However, if the respondant and operant functions of crying can be distinguished, it is possible to permit the former without being manipulated by the latter. Thus, if a child cries when told to go to bed, her parents may sympathize with her feelings, but still refuse to change their bedtime rule. In this way the child learns that it is permissible to have and express feelings, but not possible to use them to make her own rules.

From what we have said thus far, we see that catharsis has two related but separate components: one is relatively intellectual—the recall of forgotten material; the second is physical—the discharge of emotion in tears, laughter, or angry yelling. The cognitive-emotional aspect consists of the contents of consciousness during the re-experiencing of an emotional event. The somatic-emotional aspect consists of the motoric discharge of emotion in expressive sounds and actions such as the tears and sobbing of grief, *or* the trembling and sweating of fear. It is so usual in psychotherapy for the cognitive and somatic aspects of catharsis to occur together that this distinction has generally been elided. For example, in the case of Anna O. (2), the patient recalled seeing her servant's dog drink from a water glass. As she remembered this scene, the patient gave "energetic expression" to the anger she had long held back. The therapist may regard these concomitant expressions as inseparable; focus on the cognitive, as Freud did; or stress the somatic, like Reich.

In some cases, on the other hand, catharsis consists of a cognitive experience without somatic concommitants; in still others, tension relief is apparently achieved even though the person is thinking of nothing specific or of something that we suspect is not the "real" cause of his distress. People sometimes focus their thoughts on a remote calamitous event and cry about it as a way of justifying tears which in fact may have been provoked by some other event, or by the accumulation of numerous small frustrations "not worth crying over." When President Kennedy was killed, thousands of people wept. They experienced feelings of deep sorrow and loss, and their thoughts were of the slain President. However, it seems unlikely that most of those who wept were attached deeply enough to this particular man to account for their sadness. Rather, his death probably restimulated various losses and frustrations in their own lives, and provided the occasion for, but not the cause of, their tears.

An example more pertinent to psychotherapy can be found in a statement by Arthur Janov (8), who claims that the most important catharsis is that which reaches back to experiences that occurred very early in life.

> . . . trauma seems to be laid down in the nervous system and remembered organismically. The physical system knows it is being traumatized even when there is no accompanying consciousness. And again, it is not enough to know about these occurrences; if they were traumatic, they must be relived and experienced fully in order to be resolved from their continuing effect on the organism.

Janov describes two patients who achieved great catharsis in the process of "re-experiencing" traumatic births. These people, who undoubtedly did achieve a dramatic catharsis, thought they were remembering their births; however, it is much more likely that they were discharging tensions from much more recent hurts and that the image of birth merely served as a way to focus on these other frustrations.

The question whether catharsis in psychotherapy is equally effective when the patient is thinking about some symbolic event, such as birth, while he is crying, rather than thinking about more recent, but less dramatic, events, although fascinating, cannot easily be answered, simply because we cannot know where the energy behind the catharsis comes from. The way that various psychotherapists deal with this question reflects their underlying theories. Those, such as many Reichians, who value the visceral and somatic aspects of emotional discharge do not concern themselves with why their patients cry. That they cry is thought to be sufficient. These therapists de-emphasize the thoughts and memories associated with cathartic discharge; they focus on attacking the mechanisms of emotional constriction, rather than on liberating one or a series of crucial repressed emotional experiences. Janov, on the other hand, considers the decisive aim of therapy to be to uncover and discharge residual emotions from certain key early childhood frustrations. For him the contents of consciousness are all important. Loosening the sinewy fibers of emotional suppression is but a means to achieve this end. Crying about adult concerns is described as derivative of and preparatory to getting back to the earlier and critical experiences.

Another not uncommon example of somatic expression of emotion divorced from the awareness of the cognitive content occurs when we weep without thinking of anything specific. Often this happens after a series of minor frustrations produce unrelieved tension. Such apparently uncaused weeping also can occur when persons have suffered great losses but have not given vent to their grief. Thus, it seems that the residue of many distresses or one major distress may produce an emotional catharsis later on, even though the person is not thinking of the originally distressing events.

Cognitive-emotional catharsis consists of vividly re-experiencing and usually talking about an emotional event without motoric discharge of the emotion evoked. This happens commonly both in psychotherapy and in everyday life. In a social situation, a woman once described the details of the death of her newborn son. She was clearly re-experiencing the event in vivid detail, and spoke in a deeply involved manner, obviously experiencing much pain. Although she did not cry or tremble the retelling apparently afforded her great relief; had the situation been more private, she undoubtedly would have shed tears.

The cognitive aspect of catharsis has components of both recall and confession. The recall component involves the retrieval of memories, a process that is, of course, not unique to catharsis. However, the patient's experience of the memories that accompany catharsis may be quite dramatic. He is often amazed at how vividly he re-experiences something he has not remembered for years. Indeed, tracing a theme in therapy can often be facilitated by asking the patient to recall his experiences of a particular affect, rather than of some content. Watkins (9) uses this approach, which he calls the "affect bridge," in hypnotherapy; and Jackins (10) uses a similar approach in Re-Evaluation Counseling.

This retracing of experiences of affect may lead to productive material when a patient reports experiencing more feeling about a situation than seems appropriate. For example, a patient gave signs of being very uncomfortable about accepting a certain amount of dependency in the therapeutic relationship. She said that it was hard for her to relax her defenses enough to ask for help and accept the position of being a patient. She was then asked to recall experiences in which her trust in people had been violated. She recited a series of such experiences; then she remembered a heretofore "forgotten" event of her childhood, involving a pet rooster of which she was very fond. She once had to leave the house, and had asked her father to look after this pet. When she came home, she found, to her horror, that her father had cut the rooster's head off, and that the poor creature was still running about in the yard with his head hanging off. As she remembered this, she sobbed and wailed for her lost rooster—and for her betrayal. The memory and the crying did not magically erase the patient's fear of dependency. Nor was this technique the only, or necessarily the best, way to deal with her conflict. The point is that a seemingly innappropriate affective experience in the present may often be traced to an event in the past to which the affect was appropriate, but perhaps insufficiently expressed.

There are two related but slightly different explanations for the phenomenon of enhanced recall under catharsis. The first is simply that the emotion experienced in catharsis recapitulates a potent part of the stimulus configuration that was present when the event was stored in memory. Since strong emotional experiences are relatively scarce, the lack of retroactive interference enhances this associational effect. A second explanation, based on state-dependent learning (11), is that the original learning took place while the person's central nervous system was in an aroused state (probably an enhanced level of biogenic amines) so that recall may be possible only when that state is recreated. Penfield's experiments in the early fifties (12), in which affectively charged memories were produced by electrical stimulation of the brain, lend support to this view. Support of a more speculative sort comes from the transactional analysts (13) who treat crying and screaming as emotions in the "Child" (infantile) segment of the personality, which can be *relived* but not *recalled*. Whatever the correct explanation for this phenomenon, it is a common clinical observation that memory retrieval is often facilitated and enhanced when the patient re-experiences strong emotions. This may be particularly true of significant and painful memories, which are commonly "forgotten," perhaps *because* of their attendant painful affect.

Another cognitive or verbal aspect of catharsis is the feature of confession. Not only are events vividly recalled, they are also shared with the therapist. It may be this act which makes the therapist's understanding and acceptance truly meaningful. That which is not communicated can neither be understood nor accepted. The patient who is unable to share his indiscretions with his therapist inevitably finds the therapist's assurances of acceptance meaningless. Until they are brought out in the open, the patient will wonder how the therapist would feel about him if he knew certain things of which the patient is ashamed. However, the therapist's acceptance of the patient as worthwhile after a guilty secret has been revealed affirms and enhances the patient's self-esteem.

The clinical literature and as yet inconclusive research suggests that catharsis is most effective when it consists of both the cognitive and somatic aspects. Grayson's approach (14) which combines emotionally charged cathartic mourning with the development of insight supports this view. Grayson believes that the somatic component of emotional discharge can strengthen the ego sufficiently so that it enhances the patient's ability to achieve a cognitive restructuring of his experience. Jackins (15) holds a similar viewpoint, except that he believes that after somatic catharsis, the patient can form his own reevaluation with no assne from the therapist. This position seems overly optimistic in that it relies heavily on the patient's ability to be rational and objective about his own experience. It also reflects a distrust of therapists, since Jackins seems to imply in part that the therapist will foist a dogmatic, authoritarian interpretation on the patient. The current psychoanalytic position (16) is that catharsis may clear the way for the development of insight. Thus it is thought that interpretation is useless while the patient is in the throes of emotion, but that the patient's reasonable ego is more accessible after the emotion subsides.

If it is true that a combination of the somatic and cognitive aspects of catharsis is best, then the somatic expression of feeling must significantly benefit psychotherapy. How this might occur has never been made clear. In chapters that follow we will consider how this process may operate.

CHAPTER 2

Catharsis in Religious and Magic Healing Rituals

*W*hy include a chapter on religious and magic healing in a book designed to provide an assessment of catharsis in psychotherapy? Surely, many psychotherapists believe that what they do is distinct from other processes resulting in behavior change. Furthermore, they would hardly be content to compare psychotherapy with religious healing and magic rituals. Still, while systematic attempts at psychotherapy are relatively recent efforts on man's part to change behavior are ancient indeed.

Healing rituals in primitive societies were predicated on a belief in magic and supernatural forces. The methods were naturalistic, but they often involved unwitting application of what would today be called therapeutic mechanisms. Religious and magical ceremonies have featured a great variety of rationales and procedures; but in many instances, they are characterized by powerful emotional arousal and catharsis.

Men learn by observing and attempting to predict and control natural events. This is science. But, when men are bewildered and uncertain, they resort to supernatural explanations of their experience. This is magic and religion. As scientists, we may profitably study such pre-scientific practices, for they may produce desirable results and, thereby, be worth testing in more precise and potent forms. Furthermore a survey of the extent played by catharsis in primitive rituals serves to put modern cathartic therapy in a context of ancient historical precedents that may help to generate hypotheses for future confirmation. Although often obscured by fantastical theories, many of these traditions contain insights worth rediscovering. Before presenting sample accounts of specific emotive rituals we shall discuss the prominence given to emotionalism and catharsis in various theories of religion and magic.

Although magic and religion often merge, they can be distinguished. *Magic* describes practices purporting to control or forecast events; religion involves a reverence for, and appeal for help from supernatural beings or forces. Thus, magic is more practical. It is aimed at direct control of nature. Because he claims to be able to predict and control events, the magician's theories have always been subject to confirmation or disconfirmation.

Most primitive magic practices are concerned with emotional tension and methods of releasing or preventing its buildup. As Evans-Pritchard (1) points out, " . . . magic is a substitute activity in situations in which practical means to attain an end are lacking, and its function is either cathartic or stimulating, giving men courage, relief, hope, tenacity." Also, ordinary social living generates emotional arousal which, if not discharged in the situation that evokes it, must be vented in a substitute activity. And for this, magic serves admirably.

Malinowski (2) believed that the essential function of both magical and religious rites is cathartic. They reduce fears and tensions. Furthermore, he pointed out, the mimetic form of many rites suggest the desired ends: "In the magic of terror, in the exorcism directed against powers of darkness and evil, the magician behaves as if he himself were overcome by the emotion of fear, or at least violently struggling against it. Shouts, brandishing of weapons, the use of lighted torches, form often the substance of this rite. Or else in an act, recorded by myself, to ward off the evil powers of darkness, a man has ritually to tremble, to utter a spell slowly as if paralyzed by fear."

Such acts, though rationalized and explained by some principle of magic, are clearly expressions of emotion. If these rituals do provide cathartic release, we would expect them to be followed by a reduction in tension, a conclusion that has been observed to be true in relation to fear. The magician serves as a model by behaving as though he is overcome by fear himself, and in an atmosphere of mystery and ritual, his expression of these feelings may well prove to be contagious. Furthermore, by trembling ritually a man is liable to generate a great deal of genuine emotional arousal and discharge.

Other cathartic rituals have also been recorded. The Corybantes, a magico-medical secret society in primitive Greece, cured mentally disordered persons with rites of excorcism, incantations, and orgiastic dancing (3). Roman as well as Greek physicians recognized the purgative value of restimulating frightening memories (4). Even peoples who abhor violence may express hatred and anger in black magic rites, clenching and shaking their fists, shouting angrily, and even miming imaginary hostile acts. Such behavior provides release and reduction of tension.

Catharsis may thus be one of the basic functional mechanisms of magical rites through which passions are partially spent, even though not gratified. Levine (5) noted the use of ritual for discharging hostile feelings among the Gusii in the highlands of Kenya. In this culture, nonaggression is a social ideal, and afflictions are generally explained by witchcraft and sorcery. The afflicted denounce suspected witches with great venom, and in so doing ventilate much hostile feeling. This practice goes beyond mere affective discharge. It is clearly a means of expressing aggression against personal enemies, and therefore a step in the direction of violence. But, however nasty, the aggression remains fantastic and verbal, rather than actual and physical, and nonaggression is maintained as a social ideal. This fantasy aggression may be partially responsible for the rarity of murder or fighting among this tribe.

Beattie's (6) descriptions of witchcraft and sorcery in East Africa also demonstrate that cult activity in this region has always been markedly expressive. Most rituals and festivals feature elaborate costumes with ornate headresses and masks representing various gods and spirits. Villagers celebrate with considerable histrionics. Ritual rattles are shaken, accompanied by spirited dancing and singing. As Beattie notes "The excitement and colour of these occasions, contrasting vividly with the drab everyday life of agricultural labour, may be presumed to have a strongly cathartic effect on participants, and so to provide at least a partial means to the release of inner tensions. There is evidence, too, that 'cures' by these means of quite serious conditions are not uncommon" (p. 51).

The effects of catharsis on behavior also are important in primitive medicine. Some primitive medical successes can be attributed to effective physical measures—massage, cauterization, surgery, isolating the sick, diet, and the use of herbs and drugs. The ancient Egyptians in particular pioneered in physical medicine (7). Illnesses were systematically traced to organic causes and only when no physical causes could be discovered were occult agencies like evil spirits assumed. Western psychotherapists have been thoroughly ethnocentric about their healing practices and have failed to learn from their counterparts in other cultures, the witchdoctors or shamans. This probably reflects both the low publication rate of witchdoctors and the rejection of their magical theories by which they explained their practice. This is understandable, but unfortunate. If all psychotherapies supported by mumbo jumbo theories were rejected, few would remain (cf. Chapter 7).

Medicine men—magicians, priests, shamans, witchdoctors, diviners, healers, sorcerers, herb doctors, obeah doctors, insangoma, mundunugu—performed several functions, some of which may be called folk psychiatry. Primitive folk psychiatries are substantially psychological, and are practiced by those whose standardized cultural role gives them the power to instill hope, exert suggestion, and modify psychological defenses. Any psychotherapist who has learned how much harder it is to influence family members or friends than patients has some appreciation of the power that a socially sanctioned role conveys. The same subcultures that influence the development and patterning of psychological disorders also shape the world views and practices of its healers.

Shamans are invested with rigid, socially-defined roles and functions. Their apparent effectiveness helps insure high status and material rewards that typically are second only to those of tribal chieftains. Hierarchic professional systems and specializations exist, and many native healers exhibit a high degree of psychotherapeutic skill. Training is long and rigorous, thus insuring a certain amount of selectivity. Furthermore, in societies with limited vocational possibilities, intelligent and ambitious men would be attracted to a profession that provides social prestige, public attention, and wealth. The witchdoctor is thus an important member of his community, embodying insight and wisdom as well as superstition and ignorance.

As a folk psychiatrist, the primitive healer used techniques still practiced in modern psychiatry: rest, removal from stress, relaxation, hypnosis, suggestion, and catharsis. Various examinations of religious healing rituals in primitive societies have shown that catharsis has played a central role. Shamans created highly charged emotional ceremonies in which sufferers were encouraged to re-enact past experiences, their excitement being intensified by rhythmic music, chanting, and dancing.

Various descriptions of primitive healing rituals exemplify the therapeutic application of cathartic procedures. Gillin (8), for example, describes the treatment of a case of "magical fright" that he observed among the Guatemalan Indians in 1946. Magical fright is a disorder that includes depression, anxiety, and withdrawal from social contact, and its accepted cause is loss of soul. To cure a case of magical fright, the shaman must recapture and return the lost soul. The subject of Gillin's description, was a 63-year-old Indian woman, suffering from what we would call agitated depression. She was quite depressed, and neglectful of her household duties; her contact with friends and family was reduced, and she suffered from diarrhea, stomach pains, and loss of appetite. She was also extremely anxious, and alternated rapid, jerky movements with profound lethargy. Magical fright was diagnosed, and a shaman was summoned. The shaman began his treatment by confirming the diagnosis and urging the woman to confess. "After several minutes of fidgeting, the patient 'broke down' and loosed a flood of words telling of her life frustrations and anxieties. . . . During the recital of this story, the curer, Manuel, nodded noncomittally, but permissively, keeping his eyes fixed on her face. Then he said that it was good that she should tell him of her life. . . . She then told about a recent experience. . . . " The woman described the precipitating incident in full detail with much affective ventilation.

After the recital, the patient was noticeably more relaxed. The shaman told her that he could cure her and made an appointment to treat her four days later. By the end of this first session, a great deal of catharsis had occurred; the shaman had offered an explanation for the affliction, and had given his authoritative reassurance that the case could be cured. The four-day wait probably enhanced expectancy, and created an atmosphere of emotional excitement.

The curing ceremony was held before a large social gathering. The shaman offered ritual prayers and fashioned images of spirits from a ball of beeswax. Following this, he led a small group of people through the darkness to the spot where the precipitating event had occurred. Here he addressed the spirits. Then he returned to the village, and walked with the patient into a field where, at his instruction, she removed her clothing and stood naked in the darkness. He offered her a drink of a supposedly magic alcoholic potion. The curer himself took a mouthful of the drink, and after waiting a few seconds, suddenly spewed a fine spray of alcohol all over the patient's face. The shock of the alcoholic liquid in the cold air rocked the patient. He sprayed her entire body, while she stood shivering and crying. Following this, the patient was ordered to lie down, still naked, on the floor of her hut while the shaman massaged her with eggs. His explanation was that evil spirits would leave the woman's body and enter the eggs, but essentially he was giving her a deep muscle massage. Finally, the patient was clothed and told to lie in bed covered with blankets. Next day the woman's anxious depressed state had changed to happiness.

One of the key elements in this successful treatment was confession, which has always been one of the hallmarks of both magic and religious healing. Lebarre (9) compared the procedures used in several different American Indian tribal healing ceremonies, and found a common therapeutic strategy of talking about guilts and worries to an accepting listener. He concluded that this use of cognitive-emotional catharsis in healing rituals reflects an awareness that confession is able to liberate feelings of guilt and anxiety. It is also true that the dramatic procedures used for confessing may also facilitate increased somatic-emotional discharge. Confession has both a cognitive and a somatic component, although the two are never completely distinct. The cognitive aspect of confession, stressed by LaBarre, involves admitting one's sins and hearing from the nonjudgemental listener that he or she isn't horrible. The somatic aspect of confession, which was more apparent in Gillin's account, involves expressing and discharging pent-up feelings. Clearly the cognitive aspect of confession and exoneration has somatic consequences, and vice versa.

Rasmussan (10) notes that the Eskimo culture assigns a central role to confession in the treatment of sickness. In one case he reports, the patient is an Eskimo woman, complaining of sadness, anxiety, and pains. She cries, "the sickness is due to my own fault. I have but ill fulfilled my duties. My thoughts have been bad and my actions evil." In our culture, such self-derogation could be considered a symptom of the depression, and efforts would be made to counteract this confession. In her culture, this litany of self-accusation is considered part of the cure, and she is encouraged to continue, and to relate various offenses in response to the shaman's questioning.

The shaman pressed her about events that she had trouble remembering, while at the same time, many of her family and friends stood by imploring that she be released from blame for her offenses, and thus, giving her emotional support. Each time she confessed a new misdeed, the shaman asked for more. As Rasmussen reports, the shaman said 'There are still offenses, evil thoughts, that rise up like a heavy mass, and she was only just beginning to get clean. The confessions were beginning to help her." This tactic led to the recovery of additional (repressed or suppressed) memories of a very painful nature, until eventually the confession was considered complete, and the patient recovered.

Shamanism, still practiced in widely differing parts of the world, manages to maintain both a fairly rigid tradition within each region and a high degree of similarity between regions. Descriptions of shamanism in Siberia and Central Asia (11), the Malay peninsula (12), Alaska (10), and Central America (8, 13) reveal a great deal of parallelism. Eliade (11) has described a variety of healing seances in northern and central Asia, in several of which those present were brought to tears. He describes a typical Tartar healing thus: "The shaman expatiates on the grief of the family and the sadness of the house. 'Your wife and your dear children, so unexpectedly orphaned, call you, hopelessly weeping and wailing, and cry to you, Father, where are you? Hear and have pity on them, come back to them. . . . Your herd of countless horses longs for you, whinnying loudly and crying pitifully, 'Where art thou, our master? Come back to us?' Among the Abakan Tartars such melodrama may continue for five or six hours. At moments during his incantation the shaman may demonstrate his occult powers by performing such tricks as touching a redhot iron with his tongue, walking through a blazing fire, or striking at his face with a razor without leaving a mark. This behavior enhances the expectancy of success and helps to generate an emotionally-charged atmosphere. The emotional intensity of such occasions is further heightened by drum beating, by chanting, and often by the induction of ecstasy through intoxication from mushrooms, tobacco, or narcotics. During the ecstasy the shaman is thought to be on a journey to the underworld, or the mythical world of spirits, there to recover and return the lost soul. All the while, the shaman dances, leaps, and cries out, while the drums beat and observers sing.

The magic of Southeast Asia is similar to its Siberian counterpart, and also shows the influence of Hinduism and Mohammedanism (12). Disease is thought to emanate from formless spirits. Harmful auras are believed to issue from the bodies of murdered men, slain animals, certain reptiles, and roosters of unusual color. These auras are thought to cause fever, some cases of blindness (perhaps hysterical), and madness. Also blamed for such plights are goblins, gnomes, ghosts, and banshees. The Malay healing seances resemble the Mongolian. An atmosphere of mystery and expectation is created, and feelings are aroused by the sounds of tambourines, frantic incantations, voices of invisible beings relayed by the shaman. The shaman dances deliriously, chants, and whirls around, uttering piercing cries. Sacrificial offerings are made to expel spirits of disease, tapers are lit, incense is burned, and food is offered to appease the spirits. The shaman leaps about convulsively, shrieking in unintelligible spirit language. Participants perform mime and ritual dancing designed to provoke an emotional reaction and to relieve tension in the patient and audience alike. This performance is repeated on three successive nights. The shaman may brush or sprinkle the sick person with fluids and massage him with medicinal leaves. In addition, he may try to coax the evil spirits to leave the sick person and enter his own body, where his familiar (often a tiger) can dispel them; or he may coax the spirits onto a model boat which is then set adrift in the river. While these activities are going on, patients experience a hysterical delirium. They scream, cry out, and utter a jumble of meaningless words.

All these various shamanistic practices are probably based

on trial and error. The most successful were probably used repeatedly, and spread from tribe to tribe until eventually some became almost universal. The fact that cathartic rituals are so widely known suggests that they were among the most successful. Some highly cathartic elements of shamanism, for instance, were part of a great mystical movement known as the Ghost Dance religion that spread through North American Indian tribes in the nineteenth century (11). To prepare for the coming of salvation, members of a tribal group danced continuously from five to six days, and went into trances during which they were thought to converse with the dead. Participants sang and danced in rings around fires. They wore "ghost shirts," ritual costumes bearing designs of stars and mythological beings. While not designed specifically for healing the sick, these cathartic rituals provided an opportunity for great emotional discharge in a colorful social setting. The Ghost Dancing movement was a kind of shamanism for the masses, and provides a link between magic healing rituals and religious ceremonies.

The origins of religious healing—and psychotherapy—can be traced to astrologers, sorcerers, and magicians in ancient Egypt, Babylonia, Judea, Chaldea, Arabia, Greece, and Rome. In the book of Psalms, Hebrew poets encouraged the expression of feelings, and implied that unrecognized feelings will have their revenge. Job's story also contains the idea that repressed guilt can cause physical ailments. Jews early developed some rudimentary ideas about psychotherapy related to primitive beliefs in demons, sorcerers, and witches (14), and to a great extent, had the idea that illness was the will of God. Calestro (15) has pointed out that early Christian healing rites consisted of a good deal of emotional release, mixed with some features of physical mortification and reduction of guilt.

Among other primitive cults, West Indian voodoo practices are also based on a combination of religions and magical traditions. Voodoo is most prevalent in Haiti, although it is also very much alive in other parts of the Carribean including Trinidad and Brazil. This cult mixes African beliefs and rites with some features of Catholicism, and was brought to Haiti by the slaves in the second half of the seventeenth century.

Voodoo cultists recognize God, Jesus Christ, the Virgin Mary, and most of the Catholic saints; however, the Catholic pantheon is less important than spirits, ancient African gods, supernatural beings, and *loa* (mysteries) (16). This strange and colorful cult has captured the imagination of writers and film makers; most of us are likely to have heard about its belief in zombies (the walking dead), and its idea that it is possible to inflict injury on enemies by sticking pins in dolls. Most of its practice is far more benign, however; indeed, although it is not primarily a healing art, much voodoo ritual is probably therapeutic. At the heart of most voodoo ceremonies is the belief in and acting out of mystical possession.

Voodoo ceremonies are social in nature. The sympathetic concern of the crowd makes it safe for the person being possessed by a loa to abandon himself to a trance; further license is granted by the belief that after the trance, he or she will be amnesic for what occurred. Therefore, when possessed, voodoo cultists can thus act out feelings and other suppressed aspects of their personalities with impunity. The possessed person can rage verbally at his enemies, or act out benign charity, since whatever he does will be attributed to the loa who was "riding him." However, unlike the hysteric whose symptoms can reflect only his personal needs and fears, the ritually possessed person must act in a manner that corresponds to some mythical personage.

Voodoo ceremonies provide both the possessed and the observers with the opportunity to experience and express a great deal of emotion. The audience participates by yelling, laughing, and crying. The person in the trance may express even more intense taboo feelings, because he is in no way responsible for his deeds or words. When the possessed expresses opinions or gives free reign to aggressions, indiscretion is sometimes shocking; if this happens, the crowd shows its disapproval by imploring the god to shut up. In this respect possession has much in common with drunkenness which in other cultures is often used to excuse outbursts of frankness in the same way.

Metraux points out that not uncommonly a voodoo devotee is possessed by loa whose character is the very opposite of his own. This suggests that it is the unexpressed and unacceptable aspects of emotions and character that are being ventilated. Furthermore, even though much trance behavior is prescribed by mythology, acting out a prescribed part can be cathartic if the emotions expressed are truly felt. What begins as simulation of a loa may end as an expression of hidden aspects of the self as the person in a trance becomes emotionally involved in the ritual.

As in so many emotion-oriented religious and magical rites, music and dancing enhance the excitement. Indeed, drumbeating may be considered the driving force of every voodoo ceremony. The drummers, or tambouriers, stimulate the dancers to feverish emotional fervor, excite emotions, heighten suggestibility, impair restraint, and promote catharsis. Metraux reports, "The tambouriers are endowed not only with a delicate sense of rhythm and a vast musical expertise but also with exceptional nervous stamina. For nights on end they made their instruments speak with a passionate violence which at times attains frenzy. To see them with their eyeballs turned back, their faces taut, to hear the rattling gasps in their throats, you might easily suppose them to be possessed."

Medicine in the urban areas of Europe continued to be a blend of naturalism and spiritualism until well past the seventeenth century. Popular emphasis was placed on faith healing and witchcraft, and those who were mentally ill were treated by priests who tried to expel the devil.

The ideas of witchcraft and demoniac possession led to untold suffering, the result of organized witch hunts in which thousands of people were killed (17). Hunting and killing witches however, was only one of many responses to psychopathology and deviancy; Zilboorg (4) points out that the care and treatment of deranged individuals involved a broad range of practices. Disturbed persons tended to be left at liberty as long as they were not a public nuisance, and custody, when deemed necessary, was relegated to family and friends.

One common treatment for a troubled individual was to make a pilgrimage to a healing shrine. Of all the Christian healing shrines, perhaps the most renowned is Lourdes. Frank (13) alludes briefly to the use of emotional arousal and catharsis in the healing rites at Lourdes. A much more thorough description is provided by Weatherhead (14), who himself made a pilgrimage there in order to study the healing rites.

The story of Lourdes is fairly well known. Briefly, it is a small town in the South of France at the foot of the Pyrenees where, in 1858, a devoutly religious Catholic girl, fourteen-year-old Bernadette Soubirous, was walking by a cave with her younger sister and a friend. Just at the entrance to a grotto, Bernadette, who had become separated from her two companions, had a vision of the Blessed Virgin Mary. Later, Bernadette returned to the same spot and discovered a spring that still flows today. When Bernadette reported her vision to the church authorities, they were at first skeptical; eventually, however, her vision was declared to be a miracle and a shrine was erected on the site where throngs of pilgrims, many of them sick and crippled, come in hope of a miraculous cure. Apparently many of these suffering individuals have benefited by their pilgrimage, and many dramatic cures have been reported.

A pilgrimage to Lourdes engenders hopeful expectations in the believing, besides generating emotional arousal and ventilation. Patients who travel to Lourdes attend very colorful masses; they bathe in the cold water from the spring; and they either take part in or witness magnificent evening processions by candlelight which are apparently both beautiful and intensely moving. Thousands of pilgrims kneel in the square, illuminated by the candles they carry, while reciting the Apostle's Creed. These mass devotions in an atmosphere of optimistic expectation and religious excitement doubtless produce a great ventilation of feeling. However, catharsis is not the only remedial force operating at Lourdes; the enormous power of suggestion, stemming from the belief that a supernatural power will produce a miraculous recovery, must certainly also play a major role in the cures that occur there.

Modern church services are typically calming experiences, where ministers offer reassurance and gentle persuasion in the hope of guiding parishioners toward increased self-control over impulses and emotions. Religious revival meetings, on the other hand, are anything but subdued occasions. They feature intense emotional excitement, and dramatic conversion experiences, and have always been directed at the heart and the emotions rather than at the head and the intellect.

From a psychological perspective, we may say that revivals appeal to emotional mechanisms for disrupting old behavior patterns and implanting new ones. A religious explanation for revivals was offered by Charles Finney, a nineteenth-century revivalist: "God has found it necessary to take advantage of the excitability there is in mankind to produce powerful excitements among them before he can lead them to obey" (18). Revivalism invariably includes intense emotional excitement and discharge of feelings. Revival meetings are conducted by a minister, skilled in oratory and in the ways of inciting high-pitched emotionalism; preaching to a crowd that is primed to anticipate an intensely emotional experience; and end with conversions, often dramatic and not infrequently involving long-lasting behavior changes.

In *Battle for the Mind*, William Sargant (19) compares the techniques of revival ministers and practitioners of political brainwashing. Both build high emotional levels of tension and fear in people, and then point to a new ideology as the path of salvation. The greater a person's emotional involvement, the greater the likelihood of being converted. Of one eighteenth-century revivalist, Eleazar Wheelock, Loud (20) wrote, "Large assemblies burst into sobbing and outcries under his preaching and the converted went to the floor as if under sledgehammer blows." John Wesley was able to make his audience start " . . . trembling, weeping and swooning away, till every appearance of life was gone, and the extremities of the body assumed the coldness of a corpse. At one meeting not less than a thousand persons fell to the ground apparently without sense or motion" (19).

Revivalist styles have varied with the times. Early American revivalists favored a threatening approach—blistering condemnation of sin peppered with references to hellfire and brimstone. Emotional browbeating was used to threaten and frighten people into changing their ways. Later, in the Victorian era, Dwight L. Moody relied on a more staid approach to reach his audiences (18), but with William A. "Billy" Sunday theology took a back seat and revivals became unabashedly dramatic performances (20, 21). Audiences laughed, cried, and cheered in response to Sunday's humorous, slangy, florid rhetoric and acrobatic gyrations. He admonished his audiences not to "sit in their pews and become mildewed," and rattled off denunciations of " . . . those ossified, petrified, mildewed, dyed-in-the-wool, stamped-in-the-bottle, horizontal, perpendicular Presbyterians" (18). One sympathetic biographer described a typical Sunday performance (21):

People understand with their eyes as well as their ears; and Sunday preaches to both. The intensity of his physical exertions—gestures is hardly an adequate word—certainly enhances the effect of his preacher's earnestness. No actor on the dramatic

stage works so hard. Such passion as dominates Sunday cannot
be simulated; it is the soul pouring itself out through every pore
of the body.

Some of the platform activities of Sunday make speculators
gasp. He races to and fro across the platform. Like a jack-knife
he fairly doubles up in emphasis. One hand smites the other.
His foot stamps the floor as if to destroy it. Once I saw him
bring his clenched fist down so hard on the seat of a chair that I
feared the blood would flow and the bones be broken. No
posture is too extreme for this restless gymnast. Yet it all seems
natural. Like his speech, it is an integral part of the man. Every
muscle of his body preaches in accord with his voice."

Obviously parallels exist between revivalist ministers like
Sunday and psychotherapists, especially cathartic therapists.
Both stress the value of personal experience and emotional intensity, and provide a dramatic emotional release that can be
very rewarding for people who live in dread of their feelings.
What therapists call discharge of repressed affect, preachers
call cleansing of unspiritual nature by the Holy Spirit. Furthermore, in religious uncertainty, as in psychological distress, confusion and fear of the unknown lend great weight to the
pronouncements of any authoritative figure, be he preacher or
therapist. Descriptions of nineteenth-century revivals (22, 23,
24) suggest that it would be hard to overestimate the excitement they aroused. Imagine thousands of people wailing,
shouting, falling to the ground overcome by emotion, or singing, dancing and laughing uncontrollably. Many revival
meetings featured "exercises"—jerking, rolling on the ground,
and sometimes barking to tree the devil. These violent
muscular spasms—also called "falling out"—served to let out
supercharged emotional arousal, and were explained as
evidence of divine grace and conversion. Another manifestation of the presence of supernatural forces was speaking in
tongues—Glossolalia; this hysterical babbling of gibberish is
still thought to be a prerequisite to the baptism of the Holy
Spirit by many Pentacostalists.

Revivalists typically add clapping, singing, and rhythmic
dancing to their hell-fire and damnation preaching to stir their
followers to devotional delirium, very much like primitive
religious rites. "At many of the 'big quarterlies' and the

'protracted meetin's,' which are held in the South, there are
scenes of frenzy, of human passion, of collapse, of catalepsy,
of foaming at the mouth, of convulsion, of total loss of inhibition, compared with the scorching heat of which the Indian
ghost-dance seems at times only a pale moon'' (23).

In certain North Carolina cults a striking refinement has
been added to rhythmic singing, dancing, and hand-clapping
as a means of generating wild emotional excitement. Poisonous
snakes are handled and passed from person to person. Apparently, by flirting thus with death these cultists become
highly aroused emotionally. Revivalists have not typically
made use of alcohol and other drugs (19) to enhance their excitement as has been done in other religious rituals. They have
occasionally used lengthy protracted meetings to intensify
emotional arousal, similar to marathons and weekend encounter workshops.

The literature on religious revivalism (23, 22, 20, 18) contains many reports of genuine and lasting behavior changes
resulting from these emotional orgies. As William James (25)
said, "Emotional occasions, especially violent ones, are extremely potent in precipitating mental rearrangements."
Furthermore, startling affective experiences greatly increase
the power of religious conversions to alter behavior.

Religious conversions sometimes involve changes in
seriously disturbed persons. The observations of Mr. Swan, an
early nineteenth century revivalist, provide such an example
(20). " 'She was in a rocking chair, with her hands clasped upon
her breast, and gnashing her teeth as though she would take
them out of her head, and was past speaking,' says Swan. 'As I
stood before her, I gained a view of the finally lost in hell'.''
This woman was subsequentntly baptized and saved by the
revivalist, following which she apparently led a normal life.
Evidently, the pathology dealt with by faith healers may be the
same as that dealt with by psychotherapists, although their explanatory model is quite different.

Most people regard the treatment of psychological disorders prior to the eighteenth century as a litany of horrors,
only briefly interrupted by the enlightened Greeks. Stories of
cruelty and torture fill the bulk of historical sections in most
textbooks of abnormal psychology. Such atrocities are undoubtedly a major if not predominant trend in prescientific at-

tempts to deal with madness. However, there is an equally significant, though less often recognized, history of therapeutic endeavors by religious healers and magicians.

In general, then, we can say that primitive magic and religion include what today are called nonspecific psychotherapeutic healing mechanisms—the power of suggestion, faith, hope, support, and cathartic ventilation. Certainly the religious rites described above all use catharsis. Some of these religious rites were consciously designed to heal; the healing caused by others may be considered a byproduct of spiritual purpose. On the basis of this anecdotal material, it is only possible to conclude that catharsis *may* have been beneficial in alleviating *some* human problems, although we cannot say to what extent. Even when positive effects seem immediately obvious, we have no way of knowing how enduring such effects may be, for scientific and systematic studies on this matter do not exist.

Furthermore, religious rites contain a mixture of many elements that may play a significant role in behavior change. One powerful force in all such rites is the effect of suggestion. The afflicted individual is clearly given to believe that he is in the hands of a supernatural power who is capable of working miracles, an idea that is enhanced to an unknown degree by the elaborate ceremony, the strength of belief of those who participate in the ceremony, and the expectations for change by the family and friends of the afflicted individual.

The effectiveness of any method aimed at changing behavior is also affected by the specific characteristics of the persons involved. As far as psychotherapy is concerned, we know that no single system is effective with all clients. What then can we say about the sort of people who might be drawn to the cathartic religious rituals examined above? One thing is that they were and are typically less intellectually sophisticated than modern psychotherapy patients. Another is that most of these rites were, and to some extent still are directed at nonliterate clients, who may be more amenable to emotive, affective interventions than to insight-enhancing, cognitive ones. In short, cathartic procedures may be more appropriate for the primitive nonintellectual who lacks the sophistication to profit from insight-oriented treatments.

CHAPTER 3

Psychoanalysis and
the Cathartic Technique

*T*he early psychotherapeutic
efforts of Freud and Breuer, and the therapeutic theory and
system that evolved with psychoanalysis placed heavy reliance
on the use of catharsis with hysterical patients (1). Freud was
first introduced to the cathartic approach by Breuer's account
of the treatment he had carried out with Anna O., who suffered
a myriad of hysterical symptoms. Breuer spent a great deal of
time with this patient trying to alleviate her symptomatology,
and learned that she experienced two markedly different states
of consciousness. In one she was entirely cognizant of her surroundings, and, though downcast and somewhat anxious, she
was generally normal. In the other she hallucinated, and was
"naughty"—that is, she was abusive to others, threw pillows at
people, tore the buttons off her clothing and bedclothes, and
was generally unpleasant. This latter state was characterized by
her as a "cloudy" period. Breuer noted that if she were hypnotized during this second state and was able to describe hallucinations or fantasies that she had experienced in the course
of the day, she would awaken with a clear mind and be relatively calm and cheerful. Sometime later, however, the whole
process would have to be repeated.

At first her fantasy productions emphasized the tragedies

in her life, or were examples of poetic compositions. After the death of her father, they changed into very frightening, even terrifying impressions. While recounting them she shook with fear and described altogether frightful images, following which she would awaken from hypnosis quite relieved.

Breuer's treatment consisted of visiting the patient in the evening to help her relieve herself of the fantasies accumulated since his last visit. When this was done thoroughly, the patient generally became quite calm and for some time after would be manageable and comfortable. Gradually her symptoms would return, however, and it would become necessary for Breuer to encourage the cathartic process once more. After hearing Breuer's account of this case, Freud attempted cathartic treatment himself, and in 1893 the two wrote a paper describing this therapeutic process as well as their theory of the psychic mechanisms underlying hysterical neuroses.

Symptomatic treatment required that the patient be hypnotized, and then encouraged to recall the events which provoked the symptom in the first place, along with the aroused emotions that had accompanied these events when they occurred. If the patient could describe the event in as much detail as possible and put the feelings it evoked into words, the symptom invariably cleared up.

After describing this relatively straightforward and simple treatment procedure, Breuer and Freud then tried to explain the reasons why this patient continued to suffer the effects of emotions stimulated much earlier in life—that is to say, they were asking why some traumatic memories remain troublesome, and others do not. First, they theorized, the fading of a memory or the dissolution of an emotion must depend on at least three factors, the most significant of which seems to be the intensity of the affect provoked by the event. A feeling retained over a long period in the psyche must have been extraordinarily intense; its long-lived nature may be due to the fact that it could not originally have been readily expressed. A second reason why psychical traumas cease to be troublesome is that even a very unpleasant memory must exist alongside a large number of other, positive associations. Not uncommonly such associations contradict the feelings aroused in the upsetting situation and help to correct the emotions engendered by the trauma. The memory of an accident, for example, and the associated fright are mitigated by the recollection of a rescue and the feelings of comfort and safety that follow. The normal individual can thus dispel many disquieting emotions through a process of association. A third reason why affective impulses fade is what we call "forgetting": whatever ideas are no longer significant in the life of the individual simply wear away.

Breuer and Freud observed that the hysteric memories which are significant determinants of hysterical symptomatology persist for long periods of time and retain an astonishing freshness. Another remarkable feature about these traumatic affects is that, unlike other memories, they are outside the patient's conscious awareness. For this reason, Breuer and Freud thought that only in a hypnotic state could traumatic memories be retrieved with the appropriate vividness.

Breuer and Freud classified their hysterical patients into two groups on the basis of etiology. The first group consisted of patients who failed to react appropriately to psychical trauma because the trauma occurred in conditions where a full reaction was not possible. Either social circumstances barred complete emotional expression, or the trauma involved situations which the patient desperately wished to forget and therefore intentionally pushed out of his conscious awareness. In the second group, the hysterical condition was determined less by the content of a particular set of memories than by the patient's psychic state at the time of the crucial experience. Sometimes the causes of the symptoms were themselves not particularly significant; but nonetheless they persisted because they were provoked at a time when the patient was in one of the psychic states—the semihypnotic twilight state in which daydreaming occurs, for instance—that allow hysterical symptoms to develop. The first type, *psychically acquired hysteria*, can befall anyone who experiences intense affect under conditions precluding full emotional release. The second type, *dispositional hysteria*, is restricted to individuals prone to hypnoid, or daydreaming, revery states. Breuer and Freud considered they had developed a psychotherapeutic procedure to alleviate hysterical symptomatology by releasing "strangulated affect" through speech. They did not think that they had achieved a true cure for dispositional hysteria, for in such cases they could only treat the symptoms, not the condition—the patient's psychic constitution—that predisposed the development of symptomatology.

Breuer and Freud both believed that affect was basic to the

hysterical symptom, but they dealt with it differently. Breuer's approach is described in the case of Anna O.

> It was in the summer during a period of extreme heat and the patient was suffering very badly from thirst; for, without being able to account for it in any way, she suddenly found it impossible to drink. She would take up the glass of water she longed for, but as soon as it touched her lips, she would put it away like someone suffering from hydrophobia. As she did this, she was obviously in an *absence* for a couple of seconds. She lived only on fruit, such as melons, etc., so as to lessen her tormenting thirst. This had lasted for some six weeks, when one day during hypnosis she grumbled about her English lady-companion whom she did not care for, and went on to describe, with every sign of disgust, how she had once gone into that lady's room and how her little dog—horrid creature! had drunk out of a glass there. The patient had said nothing, as she had wanted to be polite. After giving further energetic expression to the anger she had held back, she asked for something to drink, drank a large quantity of water without any difficulty and woke from hypnosis with a glass at her lips; and thereupon the disturbance vanished, nevermore to return.

Breuer's way of dealing with this symptom was a very passive one. Beyond encouraging the patient to begin to associate to the origins of her symptom, he did not interrupt her descriptions, and made no efforts to stem the flow of unleashed feelings. He would visit Anna in the morning and hypnotize her; he would then ask her to concentrate on the symptom being treated and describe previous occasions when it had appeared. While Anna elaborated on these events, Breuer took notes. He returned in the evening to hypnotize her again, and using the notes he had made in the morning, he would encourage her to give a more detailed account of how the symptom had developed. Thus, Breuer's only directions to the patient were to concentrate her thoughts on a particular topic.

Freud's technique on the other hand, as described in his account of the case of Frau Emmy von N., was considerably more active, and actually seems to discourage complete catharsis.

I asked her the origin of her stammering and she had replied, I don't know. I had therefore requested her to remember it by the time of today's hypnosis. She accordingly answered me today without any further reflection but in great agitation and with spastic impediments to her speech: How the horses bolted once with the children in the carriage; and how another time I was driven through the forest with the children in a thunderstorm, and a tree just in front of the horse was struck by lightning and the horses shied and I thought: "You must keep quite still now, or your screaming will frighten the horses even more and the coachman won't be able to hold them in at all." It came on from that moment. She was quite unusually excited as she told me this story. I further learned from her that the stammer had begun immediately after the first of these two occasions, but had disappeared shortly afterwards and then came on for good after the second, similar occasion. I *extinguished* her plastic memory of these scenes, but asked her to imagine them once more. She appeared to try to do this and remained quiet as she did so; and from now on she spoke in the hypnosis without any spastic impediment.

Later on Freud describes the way in which he encouraged affective expression only to seal it over and suggest it away once it had appeared.

Under hypnosis I asked her what event in her life had produced the most lasting effect on her and came up most often in her memory. Her husband's death, she said. I got her to describe this event to me in full detail, and this she did with every sign of deepest emotion but without any clacking or stammering. . . . And she then went on to say how the baby, which was then a few weeks old, had been seized with a serious illness which had lasted for six months, during which she herself had been in bed with a high fever. And there now followed in chronological order grievances against this child, which she threw out rapidly with an angry look on her face, in the way one would speak of someone who had become a nuisance. This child, she said, had been very queer for a long time; it had screamed all the time and did not sleep, and it had developed a paralysis of the left leg of which there had seemed very little hope of curing. When it was four it had visions; it had been late in learning to walk and to talk, so that for a long time it had been believed to be imbecile. According to the doctors it had had encephalitis and inflammation of the spinal cord and she did not know what else besides. I interrupted her here and pointed out to her that this same child was today a normal girl and in the bloom of health, and I made it impossible for her to see any of these melancholy things again, not only by wiping out her memories of them in their plastic form but by removing her whole recollection of them, as though they had never been present in her mind.

Freud obviously was much more interested in unraveling the sequence of events leading up to the development of a hysterical symptom than he was in how well catharsis would help get rid of it. In a later paper (2) written on the psychotherapy of hysteria, he expressed considerably less confidence in catharsis as a cure than he had in *The Studies on Hysteria*. He remained convinced that catharsis had some efficacy in dealing with certain kinds of hysterical symptomatology, but he also had found it was limited. He apparently believed that in order to provoke true catharsis it was necessary to hypnotize the patient, which presented a problem for him, since he could not hypnotize all his hysterical patients. By necessity, therefore, he had begun to treat many patients in a normal state of consciousness, and he found that by urging these patients to recall what they felt they could not recall, and by encouraging them to "free associate," he was able to get them to retrieve from the depths of their memory many etiologically significant recollections. Another reason that he found the cathartic method a problem was that the approach dealt with symptoms rather than the factors that predisposed patients' to develop hysterical symptoms.

Freud's reservations about the cathartic method by no means meant that he rejected it, but only that he thought that it should be retained for alleviating symptomatology, for which it was useful, while other techniques, more cognitive in nature, should be used to discover the underlying causes of hysterical symptomatology. These other techniques involved bringing to conscious awareness an understanding of etiological factors, and allowing the ego to deal realistically with the hitherto unconscious forces that had been directing behavior. His respect for cathartic treatment as one approach to therapy is apparent in the following statement from *The Studies:* "When I have promised my patients help or improvement by means of a cathartic treatment I have often been faced by this objection: 'Why, you tell me yourself that my illness is probably connected with my circumstances and the events of my life. You cannot alter these in any way. How do you propose to help me then?' And I have been able to make this reply: 'No doubt fate would find it easier than I do to relieve you of your illness. But you will be able to convince yourself that much will be gained if we succeed in transforming your hysterical misery into common unhappiness. With a mental life that has been restored to health you will be better armed against that unhappiness'."

As Freud and his followers gained more experience using the psychoanalytic technique they were led to further criticisms of the curative powers of catharsis. One drawback frequently cited (3, 4), was the assertion that although catharsis does relieve symptomatology, the symptoms do tend to recur, so that the cathartic process must be used again and again. The reason for this is that neurotic symptoms are generally determined by multiple causes, and since catharsis tends to relieve only the affect associated with a single cause, other determinants remain active and account for the return of the symptom (5, 6). As a result, psychoanalysts came to believe that the symptom-by-symptom attack on the neurotic disorder which characterized the cathartic approach was not fruitful. Instead the symptoms themselves were ignored, and all efforts were concentrated on uncovering the unconscious memories the forces of which combined to generate symptomatology. Thus, psychoanalysis changed from an approach of exposing affect to one largely concerned with an intellectual exploration of hidden memories, and of unconscious inner conflicts and the train of events leading up to them.

This change in emphasis led to downgrading the role of catharsis in psychoanalysis. Its detailed exploration of the psyche was directed at dissolving the usual mechanisms of defense against the uncovering of hidden memories, and at a pace slow enough to permit the ego to assimilate the memories and feelings that were liberated in the process. The cathartic approach, on the other hand, forced the patient to give up repressions suddenly by the use of hypnosis, and precluded the exploration of intrapsychic dynamics necessary for a true assimilation of the unconscious material. Furthermore, according to some analysts (3), the cathartic process encourages the patient to remain passively dependent on his doctor and not to engage in active self-exploration. Freud himself (2) was also concerned that when catharsis is used, there is no opportunity to understand the development of the resistance which helps to account for the symptoms. Since the patient is encouraged only to release feelings and not to talk about the events of his life which led up to the development of resistance, he learns little of his own inner workings.

Finally, the cathartic process was objected to because it was seen to act as a form of resistance itself, impeding the analytic process (6), because it brings symptom relief, albeit temporary. The relief experienced through catharsis robs the patient of the motivation to continue his arduous, but necessary, exploration into the causes, the history, and the meaning of his neurotic symptoms.

Although they are sensitive to its many potential pitfalls, psychoanalysts still regard the process of catharsis as having a potentially useful role in psychoanalysis. Fenichel (3), for example, points out that abreaction demonstrates to the patient "the existence and intensity of his emotions." Greenson (6), similarly feels that catharsis has value in that it provides the patient with "a sense of conviction about the reality of his unconscious processes." Thus, catharsis has the potential for breathing life into the details of experiences which might otherwise seem unreal to the patient.

Greenson also feels that catharsis has a significant role to play in connection with symptoms that are derived from particularly traumatic experiences. In such cases he recommends that patients be encouraged to express as much feeling as they can bear, since the relief that this provides enables the patient to cope with the remaining unexpressed affect. He describes, for example, a chronically depressed patient of his who spent part of each therapy hour "sobbing uncontrollably" before being able to participate in an analytic exploration of his depression.

Another positive aspect of catharsis has been pointed up by Ferenczi (4). He was surprised to find that toward the end of the psychoanalytic exploration many of his patients experienced considerable catharsis. He was at first puzzled by this, and wondered if all the deep inner exploration was necessary if it terminated with a process that could be provoked very early in treatment. On reflection, however, Ferenczi recognized this "neo-catharsis" as being qualitatively different from the kind of catharsis typically seen in the early work with hysterics, in that it appeared to be a very dramatic reliving of a buried event characterized by a freshness of detail that was part of the original experience. Ferenczi concluded that this neo-catharsis was only possible after deep psychoanalytic exploration, and that its appearance verified that unconscious resistance had truly been broken down and that an "aetiological reality" had been laid bare.

Catharsis held a central role early in the evolution of psychoanalytic therapy but has since receded in importance. This diminishing regard for the significance of catharsis and the hypnotic procedure occurred as interest developed in understanding the etiology of symptoms, the process of resistance, and the way resistances could be overcome to allow conscious ego forces to be applied to the troublesome unconscious.

CHAPTER 4

Hypnotherapy
and Traumatic Neuroses

*H*ypnotherapy is of manifest historical interest to students of catharsis in psychotherapy, since it was by using hypnotism that Breuer and Freud hit upon the cathartic method. Pierre Janet also relied on hypnotism to unlock affect-charged memories. Somewhat later, but still in the infancy of psychotherapy, hypnotism was used extensively for abreactive therapy with psychological casualties of World War I. However, there is apparently an even more significant relationship between hypnotism and catharsis than an occasional overlap of their separate histories. In fact hypnosis and cathartic psychotherapy have always been so intimately related as to suggest an inherent affinity. Hypnosis was the tool that first enabled therapists to systematically tap their patients' deepest layers of emotions. The observation that significant discoveries follow closely on the heels of advancements in methodology is a commonplace in the history of science. Apparently, the altered frame of mind attending hypnosis was a key that allowed psychotherapists to unlock cathartic reactions in their patients.

In a normal—or typical—state of mind, most people do not spontaneously discharge their emotional feelings. They do so

only when either the intensity of the feelings is increased by
some emotionally upsetting experience, or when their usual
defenses against emotional expression are overcome. Indeed,
for many people, even quite distressing experiences are insufficient to conquer these psychological defenses. Hypnosis apparently helps such people temporarily to defy the cultural
prohibitions against emotional display. The fact that catharsis
is associated with hypnosis suggests that emotional discharge
may occur spontaneously once the defenses against it are
breached. Suggestion undeniably plays a role in hypnotherapy;
but catharsis may be due to the fact that suggestion breaks
down the defenses against emotional discharge. Suggestion
does not directly elicit such discharge.

We shall briefly review the history of hypnosis here, and
show how frequently hypnotism has been associated with
catharsis. This chronicle sheds light on some of the specific
questions involved in cathartic therapy.

Mesmer and Animal Magnetism

Altered psychic states akin to hypnotism have been
recorded from earliest times. Priests, mystics, fakirs, and
charlatans in Egypt, Persia, Greece, India, and the Far East
practiced various forms of hypnotic influence (1, 2); Oriental
practictioners, for instance, instructed subjects to gaze steadily
at precious stones to induce hypnotic trances. Likewise, Indian
yogis and fakirs were able to put themselves into a hypnotic
state by fixating their gaze. Various other religious rites, such
as the Indian Ghost Dance, also have an autohypnotic
character.

In the sixteenth century, Theophrastus Paracelsus
(1493—1541), a Swiss alchemist and physician, advanced the
theory that heavenly bodies exert an effect on mankind
through magnetism, especially on diseases, and his ideas
became widely accepted. Prominent among those who believed
in them was the Scottish physician, William Maxwell. Maxwell
assembled ancient beliefs concerning the curative powers of
magnetism into a doctrine according to which disease resulted
from a loss of vital fluid from various bodily organs (5).
Therapy, he wrote, consists of restoring the requisite amount
of magnetic force. Maxwell's theory was extended by Santa-
nelli in Italy, who asserted that all material things possess a

radiating atmosphere which operates magnetically. Van Helmont (1577—1644) originated the doctrine of animal magnetism by proclaiming that a magnetic fluid radiates from all men and may be guided by willpower to influence others (4).

Whether or not Anton Mesmer was familiar with these ideas is unclear. However, it is likely that he was influenced by the work of friar Athanasius Kircher, who explained forces of attraction and repulsion as emanating from the lodestone (5). Another influence may have come from Sydenham, an English physician who explained convulsive diseases as due to Animal Spirits, which he said accumulated in or were displaced from various parts of the body. While Mesmer's ideas were probably not original, what he did do was combine the theory of magnetic vitalism with the induction of soporific trances, and presented his treatment in a dramatic and flamboyant manner that generated spectacular popular and scientific attention.

Born in Baden in 1734, Mesmer trained as a physician. He became interested in phenomena involving mutual influence between various bodies when a Jesuit priest, Father Hell, showed Mesmer his observations of an apparently curative force emanating from the lodestone. Mesmer was fascinated and decided to pursue the matter. He became convinced that Father Hell was mistaken in attributing his results to the force of the magnet itself; instead, he thought, the magnetic effluvia could be transmitted to whatever object, animate or inanimate, that the magnetizer chose. He modified his original observations later to include the notion that a mysterious fluid, animal magnetism, emanated from his own person, and that potentially it could emanate from any living being (6). Mesmer believed that the human will could control animal magnetism; it could be withdrawn from one point and concentrated in another, thus producing remarkable effects on living creatures. Human beings resembled magnets containing poles of opposite forces and disease occurred when the harmonious distribution of magnetic fluids is disturbed. According to Mesmer, therapy consisted of re-establishing harmony by applying magnetism to the sick.

Mesmer had little success in either Germany or Switzerland, countries in which the intellectual climate was too austere for his theatrical approach. Eventually, his efforts to heal the sick by manipulating magnetic fluid antagonized the faculty of medicine in Vienna, and he was obliged to leave for

Paris in 1778. There he founded a clinic and began to practice and promulgate his theories. His clinic was elaborately decorated, with every effect designed to enhance patients' expectations that something dramatic and mysterious would happen. The rooms were dimly lit and hung with mirrors. The floors were thickly carpeted, the windows curtained, and the walls were painted with weird astrological signs. Music also was played to add to the ethereal effect (7, 3) and to enhance suggestion and expectancy. Furthermore, the clinic gave the impression of being a private and quiet place where patients could safely experience the arousal and discharge of their emotions. This careful attention to setting and atmosphere make it obvious that although Mesmer maintained that he was manipulating a strictly physical force, on some level he must have been aware of using induced expectancy and suggestion in his procedure.

The central feature of Mesmer's treatment room was the *baquet.* This contraption, considered to be the focal point for the magnetic fluid, consisted of a large oaken tub filled with iron filings, water, and powdered glass. Its lid was pierced with holes, through which jointed iron rods protruded. The baquet was said to have been magnetized by Mesmer; it was able to transmit this magnetic force through the rods to the patients. Patients sat around the baquet, linked hands, touched the rods, and waited until eventually Mesmer, the great magnetizer, would appear, wearing a fantastic lilac-colored silk robe and carrying a wand. He passed among the patients, touching some, making passes at others with his wand, and occasionally fixing patients with a stare and commanding them to sleep. Gradually, individual patients became restless and agitated until a "crisis" occurred. One patient would scream, break into a sweat, and convulse. Others soon followed suit, until hysterical convulsions had seized most of those present (3, 4). After these violent episodes, tension subsided, patients felt calm and relaxed, and many experienced remission of their symptoms.

It was natural for Mesmer, in the Age of Enlightenment, to seek a rational and scientific explanation for this profound influence over his patients. Furthermore, any such scientific explanation had to postulate physical forces. Mesmer therefore said that a physical fluid, animal magnetism, produced the crises; but he attributed the cure of his neurotic clients to the crisis itself. Some of these shattering somatic-emotional discharges involved piercing cries and tears; in others the patients went into gales of laughter. Mesmer believed that he himself caused some force to produce the crisis. In the same way, cathartic psychotherapists today are sometimes described as "making their patients cry." However, in both techniques what actually happens is that patients are helped to relax their defenses so that discharge is free to occur. Patients aren't made to cry, they are helped to stop defending against crying. Furthermore, the form of such discharge is partially a matter of suggestion. That is, Mesmer's patients may have channeled their emotional discharge into thrashing, wailing, and screaming in part because that is what they expected to do and that is what they saw those around them doing. In the same way, if Janov's patients are led to expect they will scream, and they see others in groups screaming, they too may scream. However, patients who are thoroughly overcome by their feelings but not exposed to a subtle demand that it take a particular form, will be more likely to express them in profound sobbing and crying.

Mesmer began by working not with groups, but with individual patients. He first established rapport with his patients and engaged them intimately and intensely, a relationship that is especially important for cathartic therapy where the involved concern of a trustworthy person creates an atmosphere in which the patient feels safe enough to risk emotional discharge. Mesmer himself must have possessed great charisma, and undoubtedly used his charm and forceful personality to help patients suspend their habitual defenses against emotional discharge. Perhaps the same is true of all great therapists. Because of this they may be like the ancient magicians who were able to cure people more by using the force of their personalities than by a technique which could be exported.

Mesmer placed himself *en rapport* with his patients by sitting close enough so that his knees touched theirs, often holding their hands and focusing his full attention and most intent gaze upon them. As he became increasingly popular, Mesmer switched to working with large groups of patients. In part he may have done this for economic reasons, but in addition, he may have recognized that one patient's crisis was helpful in stimulating others. His group approach thus capitalized on the fact that an emotional display stimulates affective arousal in observers.

Mesmer's theory of animal magnetism seemed to be borne

out by the fact that he was indeed able to cure many patients of a variety of complaints (4, 7). Actually, to many of his contemporaries his miraculous fluid may have seemed no more magical than Newton's gravity or Franklin's electricity; nevertheless, his work generated a storm of controversy mainly because he himself was so flamboyant. Had Mesmer been satisfied only to quietly investigate animal magnetism, there would have been no uproar. His temperament was such, however, that he could not help but exploit its apparent therapeutic possibilities, which inevitably led to public attention. Few men can resist the pressure of popular acclaim, and it may be that Mesmer was taking advantage of the public's love of mystery by surrounding the baquet with so much hocus-pocus. On the other hand, he may have discovered that expectations of magical power were an important prerequisite for inducing the "magnetic" effects. Whether his success provoked jealousy, or whether Mesmerism's similarity to sorcery provoked scientific opposition, in any case, despite his converting many distinguished doctors and physicists to his theory, the opposition eventually overwhelmed him.

A Royal Commission was appointed to investigate animal magnetism—or, as Mesmer and his followers believed, to crush it. The Commission was a prestigious group representing established medicine and science, and was made up of such luminaries as Lavoisier, Benjamin Franklin, and Dr. Guillotin (2). Its final report was negative, and had the effect of a condemnation from the Academy of Science (8). It is interesting, however, that the Commission did not evaluate the curative effects of animal magnetism; rather it questioned Mesmer's theory of the physical mechanism by which such effects were obtained. That is to say, the commission was not concerned with whether Mesmer cured his patients, but only whether he had discovered a new physical fluid. Furthermore, not Mesmer himself, but Charles Delson, Doctor Regent of the Faculty of Paris, championed animal magnetism before the committee (5). Clinicians are probably more concerned with the outcome of therapies than with the theories supporting them. Thus if a modern day commission were to discredit the theories behind cathartic therapies, many would ask, 'But do they work?'

Two of the commission's tests will illustrate the concreteness demanded of magnetic effluvia. In one test, one of five trees was mesmerized, after which a patient, ignorant of which tree it was, was asked to pass in front of all of them. When the patient fainted before the wrong tree, it was taken as evidence that magnetism did not work. In another test, one of five cups of water was magnetized. When a patient drank from one she was wrongly told was magnetized, she displayed an emotional reaction but not when she drank from the one which actually had been mesmerized (7). The conclusion was that Mesmer's fluid did not exist; the convulsions and the many cures were said to be the result of suggestion and overheated imagination (8). The Commission thus did not investigate the way Mesmer actually practices, and they also failed to note the major role played by emotional excitation and discharge in producing symptom resolution.

Mesmer gradually fell into disrepute, and he eventually moved to Switzerland, where he died in 1815. To the end he was apparently unaware of the psychical nature of animal magnetism. Although his theory of therapy was demonstrably incorrect, his results were real, and for that reason mesmerism spread throughout France and the rest of Europe.

Beginning in the 1780s, Puysegur, Petetin, and Deleuze, following Mesmer's example, produced somnabulistic states and reported therapeutic results of their procedures. These workers still attributed their results to a mysterious magnetic fluid (9), but they also described neuropathic disorders and the various forms of nervous crises in studies which are part of the foundation of modern psychology.

Deleuze's book, *Practical Instruction in Animal Magnetism* (1879) provides a fascinating account of the early theory and practice of magnetism. He described magnetism as a faculty of exercising a salutary influence over men's wills through the medium of magnetic fluid. Deleuze worked mainly with neurotic patients, and he believed (as Charcot did later) that magnetism has no effect on healthy persons. His technique included making several descending passes of light touch along the subject's body in order to distribute magnetic fluid evenly throughout the body.

Deleuze wrote (9), "It often happens that the first impression of magnetism produces a crisis accompanied with convulsive motions, stiffness of limbs, and fits of laughing or crying." Mesmer had said earlier that no cures were possible without the highly emotional crisis but Deleuze asserted that although crises were useful, they were not necessary. This suggests that he was utilizing both suggestion and catharsis to help resolve symptoms. He further advised that when emotional crises do develop, the magnetizer should foster them, because the emotional storm is part of a natural healing process. Thus, despite the fact that their theories of the curative power of magnetism emphasized physical forces, emotional arousal and discharge so regularly attended the relaxation of everyday states of consciousness that even these magnetizers were forced to credit the cathartic release that was so consistently observed.

Deleuze spoke of the force of magnetism as emanating from the magnetizer's will, but he still believed the effect to be physical. In fact, he suggested magnetizing water for the sick to drink. He was, however, particularly aware of the value of catharsis in some cases of psychological disorder, especially "hysterical affections." He wrote, "It [magnetism] produces wonderful effects, and the cure is generally wrought by singular crises, sometimes very violent, and about which we should not be alarmed." Hypochondriacs were also thought to benefit greatly from the cathartic aspects of magnetism. For diseases of a strictly physical nature, however, Deleuze spoke mostly of the calming and soothing effects of magnetism.

Animal magnetism flourished in Germany during the early nineteenth century (1), and was even more popular in France (3), where it was frequently performed on stage. Eventually, however, magnetism, like Mesmer, fell into disrepute, partly because of the extravagances of its proponents and partly because of unfavorable receptions from eminent scientists. Furthermore, the idea that a physical fluid was involved lost its appeal, and practitioners instead turned their attention to the force of the magnetizer's personality, and to the rapport between the healer and his subject. They had discovered that while in "magnetic sleep" patients often were able to confide hidden, embarrassing, and previously forgotten episodes, many of which had been emotionally upsetting. Still there was a failure to have magnetism acknowledged by scientific authorities.

Whatever progress was made toward respectibility was off-set by the notoriety of quacks who used magnetism for frivolous but lucrative stage performances. Science has always been conservative and may owe its slow, but steady progress to an attitude of skepticism toward the new ideas which call prevailing paradigms into question. However, stripped of its flamboyance and theatrics, the phenomenon of magnetism did survive, and, in more sober hands, came to flourish.

Mesmer's seminal ideas about animal magnetism were developed and gradually made respectable by various medical workers. Around 1837, Dr. John Elliotson, a physician at the University College Hospital in London, explored the use of mesmerism to reduce pain during surgery. Dr. James Esdaile also had great success in performing painless surgery using mesmerism; he reported 300 major operations and countless minor ones using mesmerism as his only anesthesia. Investigations into the anesthetic values of mesmerism stopped in 1846, when the discovery of anesthesia by the inhalation of ether occurred; followed in 1847 by discovery of similar effects of chloroform (3). Neither Elliotson nor Esdaile was particularly well-known, and it remained for James Braid to put mesmerism on a truly scientific footing. Braid, a Manchester surgeon, learned mesmerism from the public exhibitions of Lafontaine and began to use it around 1843 for anesthesia and symptom removal. He gave the technique a new name—hypnotism—and he dismissed the idea, that magnetic fluid or current played any part in the induction of hypnosis (10). In fact, he considered hypnosis to be distinct from mesmerism, and his insistence on the difference helped to make hypnotism scientifically respectable. Braid did more, however, than merely relabel. He advanced the theory that hypnotism and its attendant hypersuggestibility are brought about by fixated attention, and his method of induction was to have subjects fix their gaze on the glass stopper of a water bottle. This led to fatigue and to the trancelike phenomena of hypnotism.

Nowhere in Braid's discussion of hypnotism does he report the highly emotional crises that were so much a part of magnetism. This absence of affective upheaval is not surprising, even though some modern practitioners of cathartic therapy—for instance, Jackins and Janov—claim that emotional ventilation occurs automatically in the presence of an attentive listener and in the absence of usual defensive patterns. It seems reasonable to say that hypnotism is a powerful means of relaxing psychological defenses, but then, other variables must be required to produce catharsis. One of these may be a recent history of unhappiness and distress that is apt to distinguish psychotherapy patients. However, as we have already pointed out above, expectancy is an important ingredient in generating emotional ventilation. And Braid did not lead his patients to expect to cry. This fairly obvious, but sometimes overlooked, specific expectancy may be an important aspect of cathartic therapy. That it is not necessary to have such a set is apparent from the frequent occurrence of emotional discharge where none was anticipated. But our clinical experience suggests that catharsis occurs much more easily for patients who expect it to.

After Braid died in 1860, the center of interest in hypnotism again shifted to the continent. In Nancy, a rural physician, Liebeault, opened a public clinic for the poor in 1860 where he practiced hypnosis. Liebeault published his views on hypnotism in 1866, emphasizing the importance of suggestion and pointing out the similarity between ordinary sleep and hypnosis. Consistent with his suggestionist theory, Liebeault used hypnosis therapeutically chiefly as a way to suggest the amelioration of symptoms. Descriptions of his treatment make it apparent that the "suggestions" were offered as gentle persuasion, and also as sharp command. Liebeault was strictly a clinician, and his work might have remained unknown had it not been for Hippolyte Bernheim, a professor of the Nancy Medical School (3), who became the spokesman for the Nancy School.

Meanwhile, Jean Martin Charcot, the pre-eminent neurologist of the era, had begun experimenting with hypnosis at the Salpêtrière Hospital in Paris. He found that his subjects (all hysterical patients) developed the hypnotic state through three successive stages: lethargy, catalepsy, and somnambulism. Each stage showed distinct features (12). Charcot presented his findings to the Academy of Sciences, and its acceptance of his report gave hypnotism a new prestige and stimulated renewed interest in hypnotic phenomena.

Charcot was particularly interested in the relationship between hypnosis and hysteria. Eventually he concluded that both phenomena had an organic basis, and that only neurotic subjects were capable of being hypnotized. Although he experimented a great deal with hypnosis, Charcot used it only for demonstrations and not for therapy. Although he is remembered most for these brilliant demonstrations of the remission of hysterical paralyses under hypnosis, Charcot also pioneered the uncovering of unconscious memories in his studies of "dynamic amnesia," in which he showed that forgotten memories could be recovered under hypnosis. He distinguished these unconscious memories from "organic amnesia," where memories were permanently lost. Among those who attended his lectures on the relationship between hysteria and hypnosis were Alfred Binet and Sigmund Freud.

Although Charcot's conclusions regarding the organic nature of hypnosis were subsequently refuted, his own prestige made the study of hypnosis respectable. In 1890, the British Medical Association recognized the phenomenon and its therapeutic utility with functional disorders (1). Among those who used hypnosis therapeutically were Forel in Switzerland, Krafft-Ebing in Germany, Breuer and Freud in Austria, and Binet and Janet in France. Even Emil Kraepelin spoke favorably of hypnosis.

Nineteenth-century psychiatrists were mainly interested in developing classificatory schemes based on symptom complexes, and searching for the organic pathologies that were assumed to be at the root of most, if not all, forms of psychopathology (13). However, the most significant advances in psychotherapy were made by the hypnotists and magnetizers who were outside and often opposed by the medical establishment, and who investigated the curative power of cathartic crises, discovered the unconscious, and used suggestion to resolve neurotic symptoms.

Some of these practitioners used hypnotism to calm patients; others continued to use Mesmer's techniques of provoking emotional crises in cathartic therapy. Aside from Breuer and Freud the most significant use of hypnotism and catharsis was made by Pierre Janet.

As Freud's ideas became widely known, more and more use was made of hypnotism for the abreaction of traumatic experiences. Pierre Janet, Charcot's pupil and successor at the Salpêtière, investigated the cathartic uses of hypnosis contemporaneously with Breuer and Freud.

Among Janet's procedures, was one he called treatment by "mental liquidation" (3). Janet later went to great pains to point out that Charcot's lectures and his own studies were the starting point for psychoanalysis, and he claimed that much of Freud's work merely duplicated his own. Freud (14) disputed this claim. He was, however, familiar with Janet's work, and he and Breuer refer to it in their *Studies on Hysteria.* In retrospect it appears that Freud and Janet arrived at many similar ideas independently, and that each was a source of inspiration for the other.

Janet observed that neurotic patients are often tormented by disquieting memories. "Again and again psychopathologists have pointed out that a good many neuropathic disorders are induced by an emotion, a disquietude, a grief resulting from some particular happening" (3). Janet had asserted as early as 1886 that traumatic memories played a major role in producing hysterical symptoms. According to his theory of "dissociation," experiences in which very strong emotions were aroused often became split off or dissociated from the rest of the personality. He went on to say that both for the explanation and therapy of many forms of neurosis, traumatic memories must be uncovered, when they exist. He believed that traumatic memories were sometimes, but not always, the cause of neuroses, and suggested that the therapist look for them when nothing can be discovered in the patient's recent history which might explain his neurosis. Because such memories are often hidden in patients' minds without their being aware of them, Janet advised the use of hypnosis and the study of dreams. The persistence of symptoms long after the occurrence of the traumatic events was explained as being due to the inadequacy of the actions taken at the time of the event. Therefore, he reasoned, the patient must be helped to remember the event and to complete the action psychologically.

His early efforts were aimed at suggesting under hypnosis that patients forget traumatic events. He found, however, that the results of this procedure were disappointing. He then hit upon a cathartic procedure which he described as follows: "Just as, in another method of treatment, we dispel symptoms by helping the subject to perform the outwardly directed actions demanded by extant situations, so now we must help them to perform internal actions related to past happenings." This procedure was said to lead to the "liquidation" of the memory and its neurotic sequellae. Janet's theoretical explanation for this is remarkably similar to that of certain contemporary emotive therapists. He asserted that when an event occurs that necessitates action, certain psychological tension is aroused and old tensions from similar events are re-aroused. This tension presses for activation, action, and discharge. The traumatic incident is pathogenic if the aroused emotion and the tendency to action are blocked.

An example will illustrate Janet's method of liquidation. One of his patients was cured of an obsessional dread of syphilis after confessing the actions which exposed him to the risk. "It is plain that, in his absurd and distressing confession, the patient must have expended the energetic charge of the morbid tendency, must have canalised the energy. This immediately relieved him of his distress." In discussing other similar cases, he says that patients may shout, squirm, or go through bodily contortions, and then sob for a long time. The catharsis accompanying vivid recollection of the traumatic incident is illustrated in the following example of a case of severe neurotic obsession: "Two or three consultations are necessary before she can make a fresh avowal of her obsessive idea' . . . While her phrases are being formed with great difficulty, the patient has laughing fits, twitching, and contortions, and in the end she weeps copiously. She then feels bewildered and extremely tired, but is incredibly happy. . . . The transformation is a very rapid one, and (this being rare) it is durable." In such cases, Janet believed that what takes place through catharsis is not merely affective discharge, but a reassimilation or liquidation of the situation. It should be noted that he also considered other sorts of actions, including energetic activity, to be therapeutic.

Janet's work with hysterics led him to conclude that the therapeutic utility of catharsis lay in its ability to reduce tension, for he observed that hysterical patients frequently improved following "convulsive crises in which they will howl and struggle for hours." He also observed similar reductions in tension following violent exercise. Janet did not however advocate a simple tension-reduction model of psychological equilibrium. Instead, he spoke of the desirability of achieving a balance of tension. In some cases, weeping may help reduce tension and restore this balance. In others, treatment by "excitation" is indicated—that is, affective involvement with the events of daily living that may help to free the patient from a morbid preoccupation with himself and his troubles. This emphasis on social activity, he said, may most appropriately be encouraged following the tension-reduction achieved through catharsis. Or, as learning theorists would say, this process involves the shaping of positively reinforcing activities to alleviate depression. Cathartic discharge may lead not to a decrease of tension, but rather to a redistribution of energy. Therefore, following discharge patients may be less agitated and have more usable energy to apply to social behavior and other positively reinforcing activity.

So deeply was Janet convinced of the value of emotional discharge in treating neurotics that he sometimes attempted to stimulate fresh, rather than restimulate previous, emotional reactions. In one case, he purposefully engaged a patient in a heated argument, following which the patient's obsessive symptoms abated. Another example of his confidence in the action of discharge *per se* was his use of exercises such as deep breathing to help reduce neurotic tension.

In 1925, Janet wrote that confession has a strongly exciting effect on the emotions and for that reason seems to be quite therapeutic. As he put it, "The complete expression of the emotions, which is rarely achieved in these patients (who are reserved alike by system and because they are impotent), often has a remarkable effect when it does occur. Many of the patients become unrecognisable if we can only make them cry. After a fit of weeping, which is sometimes very difficult to induce, their obsessive ideas of persecution, the airs they put on, their stiffness, their incessant doubts, and their resistance, will disappear is if by magic." Despite his very strong support of the therapeutic value of catharsis, Janet believed that symptoms may recur and cathartic treatment may need to be repeated.

The histories of hypnosis and cathartic therapy converge in the hypnotic abreaction of traumatic experiences. Breuer and Freud, as well as Janet, used this procedure: however, their results were never as striking as those achieved with cases of traumatic neuroses of war (transient situational reactions).

The overwhelmingly stressful incidents so common in war are paradigms of instances where tremendous feelings are aroused that cannot be expressed because of the necessity for swift action without regard for the dictates of human emotions. With the technological escalation of terror in the first two World Wars the number of psychiatric casualties grew tremendously. At first the prevailing view of such disorders was that although some of the victims were suffering from minute brain lesions caused by concussions from the explosions of shells, most such cases were malingerers. This unsympathetic attitude led to cruel treatment, including painful electric shock designed to be even more unpleasant then returning to combat. Gradually, however, the psychological etiology of "shell shock" was accepted, and its victims were accorded more humane treatment. One procedure that proved effective in treating these traumatic reactions was to hypnotize patients and encourage them to recall and vividly re-experience their battle memories. In the protected environment of the hospital, emotional responses to these terrible incidents, long held in check, could be freely discharged. After this treatment by hypnotic abreaction, many soldiers were able to reintegrate the repressed aspects of their battle experience and eventually to recover.

Prominent among the pioneers of hypnotic abreactive therapy was William Brown, who summarized his treatment experiences in World War I in the *British Journal of Medical Psychology* (15). Working in a neurological treatment center in France from November 1916 to February 1918 he treated from two to three thousand cases of "psychoneuroses of war." Brown's thesis was that the liberation of pent-up feelings (catharsis) produces a resolution of neurotic symptomatology. He hypnotized his patients and told them to remember and to visualize their horrible battle experiences. The patients were frequently seized with emotion, either becoming speechless with horror or screaming out in fear. Brown found that successful treatment demanded that abreaction of these traumatic experiences be repeated several times.

Brown's theoretical orientation was avowedly psychoanalytic, although he explicitly rejected Freud's theory of the sexual origin of neuroses (16). Furthermore, he agreed with Charcot that only hysterics can be hypnotized, and he followed Janet in assigning dissociation a central role in the etiology of psychopathology. In speaking of cases of shell shock from the Western front, Brown said that the patients' condition was always that of dissociation. The term *shell shock* derives from the observation that the typical precipating incident in these cases was the explosion of a shell; however, Brown believed that the pathogenic mechanism was psychological, and not the physical effects of concussion. In the face of overwhelming fear and sorrow, repression was brought to bear in an attempt to control tremendous emotional arousal. The result was that the patient split off the emotion and the memory of the incident. Most also suffered, along with this amnesia, other losses of function, including dumbness, deafness, tremulousness, and paralysis.

Brown's conception of treatment was expressed as follows: "It will be found that such a patient is very easily hypnotized; if it be suggested to him that he will remember the circumstances of his injury with hallucinatory vividness, he will act again the whole circumstances, and in the process his various dissociated functions will return." Thus a process of reintegration or "re-association" occurred when the patient was enabled to recapture those lost incidents. Brown then added, "But we have done more than that, we have given him an outlet for an emotion which was originally experienced by him with too great intensity—with so great an intensity that he could not keep it consciously within bounds, and his mind split in the attempt. The way in which these patients live again through their experiences shows what terrible sensations they must have had. They roll about, gripping at the sides of the stretcher, or rolling on the floor, tearing at their hair with their hands, contorting themselves in every possible way, foaming at the mouth, becoming purple in the face, their eyes starting out of their heads, all their muscles tense."

While under fire, these patients had exerted every effort to suppress their emotions—emotions that otherwise might have impelled them to flee. According to Brown, these attempts succeeded at the expense of dissociating parts of the psyche. As he explained in his plan for treatment, "In curing the patient we bring up the repressed experience once more, we encourage him to work off the emotion involved in it. Just as a person who grieves for someone he has lost finds relief in tears, so we let these patients work off their fear." Once the repression is overcome and catharsis occurs, the blocked mental energy is redistributed and healthy equilibrium is re-established.

Brown was very careful to point out that it is catharsis, not suggestion or expectancy, that accounted for the cures. He did not deny the role of suggestion and expectancy in helping to ameliorate symptoms, but said that catharsis "removes the cause of the symptom." "Abreaction of repressed emotion sweeps away the repression and so frees energy which had been previously needed to hold the repressed memories apart from the rest of the mind and away from clear consciousness.

This freed energy is thus put once more at the general disposal of the personality."

Even in cases of transient situational reactions, however, hypnotically induced cathartic therapy was neither always simple, nor always successful. In many cases of war neuroses, abreaction of wartime incidents was not sufficient to resolve the whole symptom complex. This is not surprising. It is likely that factors in addition to battlefield trauma were responsible for many aspects of the vast number of psychological casualties. War precipitates stress reactions because of certain abnormal demands on the personality, including the demand for blind obedience to military authority, the need for a certain amount of disregard for personal safety, and the need to overcome feelings that killing is wrong. In addition to being a time of great stress, war is therefore a situation that potentiates conflicts within individuals.

Acting in concert, external stresses and restimulated internal conflicts will provoke powerful impulses to act; however, frequently both the behavioral action as well as the affective arousal and readiness to act are blocked. Unlike the usual neurotic conflicts, war-induced impulses are typically destructive rather than erotic, and the counterforces are usually based in reality. The less a soldier is able to react to danger with flight or aggression, the more his autonomic nervous system will be overloaded with affective stimuli. Frequently the consequences involve psychological injury, which often take the form of conversion reactions. Simmel, a German medical officer, described a typical case that exemplifies these dynamics. The soldier suffered from a shaking tremor of the right arm, with peculiar circular movements of the thumb and forefinger, which looked like a one-sided Parkinson. Probing under hypnotism disclosed that during a furious fight with hand grenades, he was just on the verge of setting a grenade fuse with a screw-like movement when suddenly he was blown over. He lost consciousness with his rage undischarged.

Apparently the pressure for discharging affect in these patients was a natural and spontaneous therapeutic tendency. This conclusion is bolstered by Simmel's observations (17) of derivatives of affective discharge during patients' sleep and functional epileptiform seizures. Full discharge of these emotions was not obtained, however, until patients were helped to remember and "relive" these traumatic experiences. For this, hypnosis proved to be a most helpful adjunct. After being hypnotized, war casualty patients were instructed to remember their battlefield experiences and to act out their previously restrained feelings. Props, such as stuffed dummies representing the enemy, served as concrete objects for the outlet of patients' repressed emotions. Under hypnotic treatment, fear of the enemy dummy turned to rage, and produced attacks on the dummy and mutilation. Such discharge of destructive energies toward objects of repressed hatred often brought about a dramatic change in a patient's condition. A great deal of anxiety-producing tension and depression were lifted. Despite these immediate and sanguine results, some cases required additional therapy.

After hypnotically-induced catharses, therapists endeavored to help their patients reconcile emotional experiences with their ideas and values. For example, a patient whose value system did not tolerate murder might be counseled to realize that it was not a man but a dummy, an abstract object of his rage, that he had "murdered" in his hypnotic treatment. In other cases, it might be pointed out that it was not cowardice, but physical injury that prevented a soldier from defending his dead compatriots. A series of supportive interviews usually helped patients understand and reconcile themselves to what had happened under hypnosis, as well as in battle.

Even with this supportive counseling, hypnotic abreaction was not always completely successful. Patients might be helped, but not cured. In such instances, the precipitating battle trauma had apparently revived repressed memories of earlier civilian experiences. Resolution of the neuroses produced by the combination of these events seemed to require longterm treatment. Thus, cathartic treatment bolstered by supportive counseling was successful primarily in the brief treatment of reactions when a lengthy percolating period had not preceded the traumatic incident. However, it seems likely that brief treatment of these cases of whatever sort would not have been enough to cure long-standing neuroses exacerbated in war.

Although the results were often encouraging, the theories about hypnotically induced cathartic theory were usually extensions of Freudian theory, and had some of the same drawbacks, being based on a conception of emotions as pockets of quanta of energy. This was consistent with Freud's 1895 neurological model of the mind (14), in which he suggested an isomorphism between individual neurons and discrete memories and feelings. Freud proposed that once stimulated, neurons filled with a given quantity of energy that remained there until it was discharged. However, it seems apparent that single neurons (or groups of neurons) do not correspond to individual memories, and it also seems unlikely that the affect associated with ideas and memories is stored indefinitely. Indeed, the problem of accounting for the persistence of affect is the most difficult part of explaining the utility of catharsis. We need not claim that affect is a concrete entity, stored in the mind until discharged, in order to account for the beneficial effects of hypnotic abreaction. Instead, it is only necessary to postulate that some incompleted action sequences leave a sense of failure or deficiency. Thus a soldier whose actions were thwarted may have felt guilty or inadequate. Furthermore, it is not necessary to maintain that the emotion associated with these actions is stored, but only that it is capable of being restimulated; and that this restimulation recurs until the memory is recovered and some sense of closure achieved either by an actual completion of the act, or by a vivid discharge of the emotion that impels to action.

During the Second World War, great efforts were made to treat psychological casualties using abreaction under hypnosis (18, 19, 20). In addition, drugs acting on the central nervous system were frequently used to overcome defenses and facilitate abreaction. Most of these were depressants—sodium pentothal (21); a mixture of one part chloroform and two parts ether (22); nitrous oxide, hydrobromide, alcohol, sodium amytal (20) and ether—as well as one stimulant, scopalamine (23). Most of these drugs act to depress highly evolved brain centers and produce a semidrunken state of disinhibition, like that produced by a mild intoxicant.

Although the exact nature of the procedure varied with the practitioner, the basic ingredient was catharsis. Patients were either hypnotized or narcotized, and then encouraged to re-experience their most harrowing encounters in a vivid and melodramatic manner. Shorvon and Sargant (23) noted that simply reciting the experiences brought little or no improvement, but that effective results were usually obtained when the patient reached a pitch of terror, anger, and excitement, often bursting into a flood of tears. Contrary to the predictions of cognitive reassociation theory, the emotional intensity of the therapy was more critical for success than recovering details through remembering. Indeed, Shorvon and Sargant concluded that the discharge of the emotion is critical, not the recall of the details of the traumatic incident, and that remembering details is useful as a means of stimulating cathartic discharge rather than the other way around. Hordern (22) also stressed the affective over the ideational component, and used role-playing techniques to facilitate affective expression of unfinished interpersonal interactions. He might ask a patient, "What do you feel like when he says that? Do you feel angry? How angry? Show me how angry. I'll bring him in. Here he is." The anger is then physically discharged as the patient repeatedly beats his fists against a dummy. Hordern also employed sound effects to facilitate the re-experiencing of the original situation. He worked hard for emotional discharge, and felt that patients obtained a great deal of insight following the release of pent-up feelings.

The general theoretical framework behind these procedures still was primarily psychoanalytic. As Grinker and Spiegel (21) wrote, " . . . the unconscious sources of anxiety should be unearthed and ventilated, and the ego permitted and educated to deal with them rationally and economically." This passage illustrates the nature of the theoretical framework which supported cathartic therapy at that time. However, we need not conceive of consciousness as some sort of deodorizer or antiseptic which magically cleanses the stinking affects raised from the lower depths of the mind in order to evaluate the effectiveness of the therapeutic procedures under consideration.

In *Hypnotherapy of War Neuroses*, Watkins (20) describes the cathartic therapy practiced during the Second World War; his procedures, too, were grounded in psychoanalytic theory. The first step in the treatment of traumatic reactions was to evacuate the victim from the stressful surroundings of battle to a rest area behind the lines. In many cases, a few days of rest in an infirmary was enough to enable soldiers to return to the front. When such rest treatment failed, the victim was taken to a hospital for longer rest and treatment. Cases of reactive depression were treated with insulin injections to increase metabolic activity, promote weight gain, and generally improve physical condition. Anxiety reactions were frequently dealt with by narcosynthetic treatment involving sodium amytal and sodium pentothal. Under the influence of these drugs, repressed material frequently emerged and catharsis occurred. As Watkins put, "Pentothal, commonly called 'walkie-talkie' by the soldiers, seemed to have the effect of bursting 'the dam of the unconscious'." Patients were able to re-enact scenes of great emotional stress and relive painful combat experiences after recalling events for which they were previously amnesic. Like his colleagues, Watkins used simplistic metaphors to explain the effect of abreaction. "The repressed conflict like an infected boil is 'lanced' and the repressed pathogenic material released."

This treatment was apparently particularly effective with acute cases of stress. In some such cases, catharsis seemed to relieve anxiety, disclose unconscious guilt, and resolve symptoms which were most often hysterical conversion reactions. In other cases, however, the predisposing factors were so strong, or the psychological significance of combat stress so great, that although symptoms abated following cathartic treatment, they did return later. In such instances, Watkins recommends deeper and more intensive therapy.

In addition to psychotherapy, rear-echelon hospitals had well-planned programs of rest and relaxation to provide a stable environment and to promote natural forces of recovery. The more severe their breakdowns, the further the patients were removed from combat. Many were transferred back to hospitals in the States. The secondary gain involved must have been an enormous barrier to successful treatment. To recover meant to be returned to the theater of horror, to remain afflicted meant to be removed further from combat and possibly even awarded a generous pension.

Watkins did his work at Welch Army Hospital where cases failing to respond to rest, relaxation, and supportive therapy were sent. Treatment at Welch Hospital lasted from six weeks to several months and included group therapy, recreation and educational activities, physical exercise, and sometimes individual psychotherapy. The cases that failed to respond to this regime were referred to the Special Treatment Company where patients were treated with narcosynthesis and hypnotherapy. The diagnostic categories of the patients referred to this unit ranged from anxiety reactions, to reactive depressions, hysterical conversion reactions, and obsessive-compulsive reactions. Watkins does not distinguish between transient situational reactions and neurotic reactions, but it is reasonable to assume that there was a fair mixture of both. He recommends that abreaction of traumatic disorders not be applied indiscriminately, but only to release blocked emotional tension associated with traumatic experiences, to be followed by intellectual and emotional reinterpretation and insight. He found this treatment to be most effective in cases where reliving some wartime event or family crisis had sufficient emotional impact to produce powerful cathartic expression.

He presents several case studies to illustrate his approach. One case involved a 23-year-old soldier who for thirteen months had suffered from an hysterical paralysis of the right hand. By the time he reached Watkins' Special Treatment Company, the muscles in the hand were beginning to atrophy from disuse. The patient was hostile and belligerent with no insight into the nature of his condition, and he bitterly resented being on a "psycho" ward. Watkins began by being supportive, then hypnotizing the man and giving him direct suggestions to relax and to sleep well at night, but making no attempt to deal with the paralysis. After a few such supportive sessions, Watkins suggested to his patient that he could straighten his hand, which he was able to do, although only feebly and for a short time.

Watkins then decided to try an abreactive session. He placed the soldier in a deep trance and told him to think about the things that were disturbing him. The patient began to breathe heavily; he trembled and squirmed. Tears began to drip from his eyes, but he grimaced and bit his lip to keep from speaking. Watkins urged him to speak.

> Barkley's lips parted and he began to murmur, "My buddy—my buddy—they killed him." This was followed by more thrashing about on the cot. Tears began to flow copiously. Continually the therapist reassured and prodded. Higher and higher mounted the anxiety.
>
> Finally in gasping breaths, snatches of almost incoherent speech began to emerge. "I was in front of him—I couldn't help him. The sons of bitches killed him. I couldn't help him. They would have killed me. Keep going—keep going—keep going."
>
> "That's right, Barkley, keep going."
>
> "Where am I? What's happening? The damn Jerries, the

damn Jerries are coming. The patrol—I'm point man. I'm sup-
posed to stop 'em. I don't see nothing. Where are the Jerries?
There aren't any Jerries!"

"Who is behind you, Barkley?"

"My buddy—the best soldier in the Army. My buddy, he is
right behind me—about twenty feet. A lot of Jerries here. Oh,
damn," and in a tidal wave of agony, Barkley began to paw his
face.

"Kill the sons of bitches. Too late—too late." Rivers of tears
now streamed down his cheeks.

"What's too late?"

"Too late—my buddy is dead. They killed him—they got
behind me. I didn't see them. I didn't see—I want him to come
back. I want him to come back so very bad. Why didn't I see
them first? Why didn't I—Why didn't I throw it?"

"Throw what?"

"The grenade—the grenade I had in my hand. Why didn't I
throw it?"

"Did you have a grenade in your right hand at the moment
your buddy was killed?"

"Yes, I was holding a grenade. I saw the Jerries pass. I could
have knocked them out." (In holding a grenade the hand assumes the same position in which Barkley's hand had become
paralyzed—three fingers around the grenade with the index
finger holding the release.)

"Do you feel as if you were responsible for your buddy's
death?"

Barkley began to kick his feet about. He turned over and
pounded with his fists on the wall—weeping, wailing, crying,
bawling, shouting, "I didn't see them. I didn't see them. I
couldn't help it. It wasn't my fault. If I could have saved him—I
wanted to save him so much."

"Did you think that if you threw the grenade you would
have given away your position to the Germans? Were you
afraid to throw the grenade?"

"Oh, no—they knew our position. I just didn't see 'em is all.
I should've seen 'em." Then he began shouting in a loud voice,
"I didn't kill. I didn't kill." This could have meant either that he
wasn't responsible for the death of his buddy or that he was
castigating himself for not killing the Germans.

This scene continued for another fifteen to twenty minutes.
The sweating, writhing, crying man on the cot poured out every

last ounce of energy—screaming with his whole body that he
was not guilty for the death of his buddy. Like a warehouse full
of fireworks, he was exploding. The abreaction would have to
continue until Barkley was exhausted—until this vast reservoir
of pent-up emotion had been released."

After this tremendous catharsis, the therapist reviewed the
dynamics of what had happened with his patient, and Barkley
was able to open his hand. Because of the atrophy, he had to
have physiotherapy, but eventually recovered the strength in
his fingers.

Hypnotic and drug-induced abreaction procedures are still
being used today. Watkins (25) has described an approach
which he calls "the affective bridge." In this variant of psychoanalysis the patient is moved from present to past incidents,
not by the association of ideas, but of affects. The patient is
told to pay attention only to the affect and to feel it strongly.
Then he traces the affective experience to previous occur-
rences. However, Watkins' goal is clearly to help the patient
achieve insight.

The patient opened her eyes and burst into peals of
laughter: "Now I know why I crave to eat cookies and cakes. I
don't want to *have* a baby. I want to be a baby."

An experimental evaluation of hypnotic abreaction has
been provided by Lipshitz and Blair (26). They reviewed the
literature and concluded that the intellectualizing of experience
has little value, and that the affective experiences of psychotherapy are the most beneficial. They note that (1)
something in the patient frequently changes during abreaction;
(2) repetition of a particular abreaction may be necessary in
order to effect change; and (3) the change may not be lasting.
They conceptualize the process of hypnotic abreaction in terms
of classical conditioning theory. The traumatic incident is the
UCS, the physiological alarm reaction is the UCR, and the associated stimuli are the CS. Thus repeated exposure to the UCS
(under hypnosis) should produce extinction. Extinction,
however, cannot be complete because of spontaneous response
recovery. To test their extinction notion, they performed an
analogue study, using a 23-year-old secretary as the "patient."
She was hypnotized to a somnabulistic level, and encouraged to

"age regress" to some frightening experience. The incident was a near drowning at age ten. Abreaction repeatedly induced over six sessions resulted in a progressive diminution of affective and autonomic responsivity. However, there was a partial return of reactivity during a follow-up session two months later.

This review of the uses of hypnosis and catharsis to treat war-induced traumas leads to a number of conclusions. The first is that hypnosis (as well as certain drugs) facilitates the powerful interruption of inhibition necessary to potentiate catharsis of deeply disturbing and conflictual events.

Hypnosis, conceived of as a special or altered state of consciousness, may be a superfluous explanatory concept. It may be that properly motivated and instructed subjects could undergo experiences and behavior similar to those of hypnotized subjects. But regardless of whether hypnotism produces a unique state of consciousness, its usefulness in achieving catharsis is undeniable. To most people, a hypnotic state, like catharsis, involves unusual, dramatic, and seemingly abnormal behavior. Therefore, patients who believe that they are in a hypnotic trance probably find it easier to overcome their resistance to emotional discharge. Unfortunately, it may also be easier for them to claim that the emotions aroused and discharged are not "real" or actually part of their natural experience. That is, cathartic experiences facilitated by hypnotherapists may be explained away as due to the loss of control, and the involuntary result of the hypnotic process.

Secondly, in order for patients to achieve dramatic emotional catharsis, they have to experience some combination of a traumatic event and a powerful intervention aimed at dislodging their mantle of defenses against the feelings associated with trauma. Most therapists know that patients who come to a session after suffering a loss of some sort are very apt to cry. Such a common occurrence suggests that merely trusting the therapist is enough to permit (some) patients to achieve an emotional discharge. If, on the other hand, patients are well-defended against emotional display, or the precipitating experience was either not very upsetting or too conflictual to acknowledge, extraordinary measures—such as hypnotism or drugs—may be required to achieve catharsis. However, the narcotized or hypnotized patient is less aware of the presence and support of the therapist, and so whatever emotional discharge is achieved in this manner may be seen not as a natural production of the patient, but rather as something wrenched from him, artificially. Therefore, although hypnosis and depressant drugs are apparently effective in facilitating catharsis, they seem to achieve this effectiveness at the cost of interfering with the human qualities of the patient-therapist interaction.

A third conclusion to be drawn from the work of the hypnotherapists is that cathartic therapy is best initiated immediately after an emotionally upsetting experience, when the events still have sufficient intensity and recency to overcome habitual resistance to emotional discharge. Using this as a starting point, less recent memories and concerns, as well as the emotions associated with them, may be more readily uncovered. Thus, life experiences with enough affective intensity to breach patterns of emotional suppression open the way to further and deeper probing of past experiences and feelings. Not only do traumatic events loosen defenses, they also restimulate old upsets; memories of significant early events may therefore be easier to uncover after times of crisis. Swift psychotherapeutic intervention at crisis points is especially appropriate with cathartic therapy.

And finally, the clinical reports on the effects of hypnotherapy lead us to conclude that it has some validity. The symptoms treated, particularly in the case of the war neuroses, are so clear-cut and dramatic that the crucial criterion of improvement, so often a questionable matter in the evaluation of psychotherapy, is quite straightforward. One can more readily accept a clinician's report that a hysterical paralysis has been removed than that a long-standing characterological problem invading many areas of a patient's functioning has been corrected. The former symptom change is readily observed; the latter is extraordinarily difficult to measure.

It is important to note, however, that the cases described above involved acute symptoms, most of which were not longstanding, and all of which had emerged in circumstances of enormous stress. Thus, these patients had no time to develop rigid defensive patterns, aside from those containing the immediate feelings or to add chronic personality problems to the symptoms aroused by the trauma.

CHAPTER 5

Catharsis in Group Treatment

To understand the role of catharsis in group treatment it is necessary to understand the unique therapeutic potential of the group. Instead of relating to one person, the therapist, a group therapy patient must react to a number of people. The therapeutic use of the interaction with several people is the definitive mechanism of change.

Groups are more complex and amorphous and also offer a more naturalistic situation than individual therapy. When catharsis occurs in individual therapy, it is generally a reaction to events that occur outside of therapy, and through it the patient typically ventilates his stored-up feelings. The same thing may happen in groups when a member cries while telling the group of some painful event. However, even when the focus is on events that occurred outside the group, the context is different. Instead of ventilating feelings in the presence of a single person, the therapist, the group member learns to accept and discharge his feelings in front of a number of people, many of whom may be like his everyday associates.

In individual therapy, patients typically regard the therapist as a safe confidant. He is seen as a person who is present to serve the needs of the patient, and whose experience with a variety of people has made him an accepting supportive listener. The entire audience consists of one, friendly person. It is not so with groups. The situation is more threatening for most members and their titre of anxiety is proportionately higher. In this context, venting emotions is generally both more frightening and more powerful. A group member may learn that his feelings are acceptable not only to the therapist, but also to the whole group. He may learn that others in the group have had comparable experiences, and that they maintain similar reservoirs of suppressed feelings. Through identifying with other members, guilt over revealing certain emotional responses can be lessened. Groups also foster a certain amount of social pressure and provide modeling, which can facilitate catharsis, particularly if the leader so directs.

Despite certain advantages of sharing private feelings with a group of persons, such an approach does not utilize the full potential of interaction with others. (Group approaches devoted largely to intense catharsis that assign a pre-eminent role to individual catharsis are discussed in Chapter 7.) Instead, the interpersonal transactions that occur within the group session offer the richest material for therapeutic gain. In addition to ventilating feelings generated by outside experiences, group members can learn to recognize and express feelings aroused by what goes on within group sessions. This opportunity to express feelings directly takes place in a protected atmosphere under the guidance of a professional leader trained to facilitate such re-educative transactions. Groups provide more of a chance to learn to remove inhibitions against experiencing and expressing emotions immediately as they occur than does individual therapy. Furthermore catharsis of pent-up feelings from the past that takes place in a group setting may also make it easier to risk expressing emotion aroused by present reactions to others in the group.

We will here consider the role of catharsis in three major types of approaches: group psychotherapy, psychodrama and encounter groups.

Group Psychotherapy

The origin of group therapy lies in mass religious movements and early Greek drama, and its history also includes previous therapeutic settings such as Mesmer's group hypnotic sessions. In its present form, however, group therapy is largely a twentieth-century American phenomenon.

Among the first to develop the therapeutic potential of groups in the early part of the century were Joseph Hershey

Pratt and J. L. Moreno. Pratt was an internist in Boston who developed a group approach for working with advanced tuberculosis patients (1). Aware that his patients' psychological reactions to their infirmity could have a significant influence on their prognosis, Pratt treated not just the disease, but the whole person. He began by holding weekly meetings with a class of twenty-five patients in his consulting room. In these meetings patients shared medical progress reports with each other, but perhaps more importantly they shared their feelings of hope and despair. Pratt encouraged the patients to talk and interact as a means of combating their feelings of depression and isolation. That is, he was using the group mechanisms of cohesiveness and mutual support. Occasionally, he would have a star patient testify about his progress and optimism. Pratt felt that this approach was an effective means of promoting enthusiasm for the medical regime, and also helped regenerate hope in despondent patients.

J. L. Moreno, a Viennese psychiatrist, was another leading figure in the early history of group treatment. Indeed, Zerka Moreno (2) has pointed out that he coined the term "group psychotherapy." However, Moreno is primarily associated with psychodrama and his work will be discussed below.

Following Pratt, two American psychiatrists, L. Cody Marsh and Edward Lazell, used the group framework for the treatment of hospitalized mental patients, largely for didactic forums as an adjunct to their therapy (3). In weekly meetings, these two psychiatrists taught their patients about psychiatric disorders, trying both to reduce their anxieties and to foster socialization and mutual support. Encouraged by favorable reports on these early uses of group treatment for therapy, several psychiatrists began to explore the uses of groups for psychotherapy in the twenties and thirties.

Trigant Burrow, whose writings are as philosophical as they are clinical (4), combined an interest in social forces with an analyst's conviction of the importance of unconscious forces. In what he called the "group method of analysis," Burrow used the group rather than the couch as his vehicle for analytic treatment. Writing in the *Psychoanalytic Review*, Burrow described the group as a social microcosm where consensual validation and peer group pressure were invaluable mechanisms of change.

Louis Wender and Paul Schilder after him also used analytic concepts in group psychotherapy (5). Both believed that the therapy group recreates the family situation and as such is an excellent stimulus to transference. Samuel Slavson, who specialized in work with children and adolescents, stressed the importance of catharsis in his approach to group treatment (6). In his "activity group therapy," Slavson encouraged his young patients to work out their conflicts and inhibitions in a controlled play setting. Although he used analytic principles, his method was action-oriented rather than verbal. The groups were composed of seven or eight children of approximately the same age, and Slavson tried to balance the groups in order to maximize learning. Thus, he might put a withdrawn child in the same group as an aggressive child. The group room was outfitted with equipment for crafts, hobbies, and games that were used to stimulate the children's play and fantasy.

Slavson emphasized the value of maintaining a permissive atmosphere in his groups. He invested a good deal of energy in making them seem safe and predictable in order to help overcome the children's anxiety and defensiveness. Although he maintained that the leader should play an inactive, nondirective role, he stressed the importance of the leader in fostering security and acceptance. He wrote (7), "Since catharsis reveals the innermost feelings and attitudes of which the patient may be both afraid and ashamed, it can occur only in a positive transference relation."

Slavson's observations are valid for cathartic therapy with adults as well as children. Emotional discharge is directly related to the amount of pain a person feels, and inversely related to his defensiveness. Therefore, an essential requisite for catharsis is that the patient feel safe and comfortable in the therapy setting, since otherwise he is liable to consciously resist the arousal and expression of feelings. Indeed, lack of a feeling of safety and security is probably one of the basic reasons for emotional suppression. Slavson's encouragement of action rather than language as a vehicle of expression in his groups is reasonable for children, since they are of course less verbally oriented than adults. However, it seems that verbal expression should be de-emphasized to achieve catharsis, even with adults. The verbiage of an adult often inhibits the experience and expression of emotion. Therefore, to promote catharsis in adults it may be wise to explore the use of preverbal forms of experience, such as nonverbal action and visual imagery. Slavson was, however, convinced that words should be the vehicle for catharsis in adolescent and adult groups, and he emphasized the cognitive aspect of uncovering and sharing verbal reports of feelings associated with undisclosed experiences and topics felt to be taboo.

Slavson also pointed out the importance of the individual's private past experiences, and explicitly emphasized the value of regression (7). "The value of catharsis lies in the fact that it induces regression to stages in emotional development where arrest or fixation occurred." Certainly, part of the value of catharsis does involve therapeutic regression. Crying and shouting are childlike forms of expression. Furthermore, some of the elements of the group setting may facilitate this regression by increasing the chances for restimulation of memories. Also, identification with others in the group who experience emotional arousal and discharge may enhance the likelihood of catharsis by lessening the guilt feelings often associated with emotional expression. However, we believe that regression and cathartic ventilation of personal experiences are probably more appropriate for individual than for group therapy. It is easier to regress in the presence of one parentlike figure than in the presence of several peers. Furthermore, the value of the group lies in its being a social microcosm in the here-and-now, rather than a vehicle for sharing private and past thoughts and feelings. Thus, learning to remove repressions against emotional expression stimulated by present interactions in the group may be more helpful, especially for children and adolescents, than the discharge of pent-up feelings.

Slavson described the gain to be derived from emotional release in the immediate context of the group. Patients who learn to express angry feelings in the group also learn that even vivid expression of hostile feelings need not be devastating. Indeed, one of the most important opportunities a group offers is the chance to learn to express anger in a constructive manner. Because of the fear associated with the expression of a "negative" emotion such as anger, it is often suppressed until it reaches such proportions that the person explodes in a rage. But with the support and control of the group therapist, members can learn to voice their hostile feelings before they reach unmanageable proportions. Timid and withdrawn group members may gain the most from this opportunity.

However, the expression of extremely intense or unrestrained hostility may be unwise. The violent discharge of anger, characteristic of television and movie portrayals of groups, is probably counter-therapeutic. People are afraid of anger because they think it can be hurtful and destructive. To witness violent outbursts of hostility directed from one group member to another only serves to confirm this fear and thus to reinforce suppression. A distinction must be made here between the discharge of pent-up anger toward someone outside the group and the violent expression of hostility toward another group member. Group members may retain their security in the face of even the most vehement display of anger if the enraged person is merely letting off steam generated by an experience outside the group; however, anger becomes threatening and destructive when one group member acrimoniously attacks another. Fortunately, such dramatic blowups can be forestalled by the group therapist who helps his patients to express angry feelings toward one another, before the feelings build up to dramatic proportions.

Although intermember hostility should not be allowed to become destructive, the more typical problem is the need to overcome resistance against expressing emotion. To overcome the patients' fears of regression, Slavson said, they must feel assured of the acceptance and tolerance of the therapist and other group members. In an atmosphere of trust, the patient may come to feel free to act out or speak out. The value of acting out in a therapeutic setting is particularly important in work with children, and needs to be stimulated and encouraged by the therapist. Catharsis helps break through repressions based on unconscious guilt-producing and anxiety-inducing feelings, thoughts, and strivings.

World War II brought rapid expansion of and advances in group psychotherapy. The primary reason for this was of course that it was more feasible to treat the large number of psychiatric casualties in groups than to try to treat each individually. The barbarous slaughter of war also stimulated an interest in the phenomena of group dynamics, in order to understand and perhaps check social forces of destruction. Furthermore, in order to cope with the demands of war, soldiers and civilians alike were forced to work in groups for their survival. This also focused attention on the group as an object for study as well as treatment. Coping with the sheer number of cases made group treatment necessary. Group therapy therefore flourished in many treatment facilities during the war, among them the center at Northfield in Britain (8). Here were gathered a host of leaders in the group therapy field: Anthony, Bierer, Bion, Bridger, Foulkes, Main, and Rickman. The Northfield center served as a training ground for group theorists and practitioners.

By the close of the war virtually every orientation to individual therapy had its adherents who applied their methods in groups. Recent years have seen a continued acceleration of this trend with an ever increasing cascade of new approaches. Conventional approaches have often been overshadowed by the novelty and promise of quick change of the latest approach. Unfortunately, the proliferation of novel approaches to group treatment has not been matched by empirical evaluation of their effectiveness.

Although there is absolutely no rigorous empirical evidence for the value of catharsis in groups, there is, however, no lack of theoretical and subjective statements about its curative potential. In 1936, Wender (9) wrote of the importance of emotional release ("derepression") of stored up feelings in group therapy. A later review of group psychotherapy literature (10), based on 300 articles, categorizes the effective dynamics in group therapy into nine classes of mechanisms. One of these classes is "Ventilation," which consists of such items as catharsis, release of emotional tension, and ventilation. Catharsis was the single most frequently mentioned curative factor in the 300 studies.

In a more recent work on group psychotherapy, Yalom (11) lists catharsis as one of ten curative factors. He and his colleagues obtained curative factor Q-sort data from 20 subjects considered to be successful group therapy patients. Of 60 items presented, five related to catharsis. These items and their rank order are: Getting things off my chest *(31 tie)*. Expressing negative and/or positive feelings toward the group leader *(18 tie)*. Learning how to express my feelings *(4)*. Being able to say what was bothering me instead of holding it in *(2)*. Furthermore, the single item ranked as most helpful was Discovering and accepting previously unknown or unacceptable parts of myself. Although this item was categorized under insight, it is certainly related to the process of catharsis. Of 12 categories of curative factors, catharsis ranked second. Yalom says of catharsis, "This low prestige but irrepressible curative factor appears to operate in virtually every form of psychological healing endeavour." However, Yalom considers catharsis to be part of the curative process in group therapy, not curative in itself, and says that it is important because it leads to the affective sharing of experience and then acceptance by others. It is the acceptance by other group members of avoided or unknown aspects of experience that Yalom considers therapeutic, not simply the ventilation of pent-up feelings.

Another report on the efficacy of catharsis in group psychotherapy, done by Berzon and co-workers (12), was also based on the subjective report of group members. After each of 15 sessions, eighteen members of two outpatient groups described the most personally helpful incident. These 279 statements were then sorted into nine categories of curative factors. Two of these categories related to catharsis, one directly, the other vicariously experienced: "venting emotions," and "witnessing the expression of emotionality in others." The therapeutic impact of witnessing emotional discharge in others presumably is due to modeling and any catharsis in the observer would then depend upon the perceived characteristics of the model, attention on the part of the observer, the degree of positive reinforcement the model received, and the opportunity for the observer to respond similarly at a later time.

One other uncontrolled study also points to catharsis as an important therapeutic element in group psychotherapy (13). In the context of a college course on the techniques of psychotherapy, 12 sessions were devoted to "group counseling." Following these sessions members made verbal statements and written reports on what they found most helpful. The most frequently mentioned factors were an increase in emotional awareness, acceptance, and expression. "The experience has helped me throw off a little of the restrictiveness in my emotional life and has allowed greater interplay of my personality with others, especially in the more intimate situations where restrictions and pressures exert a serious block."

The impact of these findings is naturally attenuated by their lack of investigative rigor. The most serious flaw in this study is that the author neither identifies the therapist's bias toward or against the use of catharsis, nor indicates what kind of techniques were used. If the group members were exposed to a therapist who favored the use of cathartic techniques, then their report of finding that the most helpful procedure has to be suspect.

Psychodrama

In psychodrama, patients act out their conflicts, rather than discuss them. Action then becomes a vehicle to stimulate emotional arousal and discharge (14, 15, 16, 17, 18, 19). Furthermore, the psychodramatists' use of auxiliary egos, alter egos, role-playing, and role reversals greatly intensifies the emotional impact of the recreation of affect-laden experiences.

The techniques of psychodrama evolved out of Moreno's work in the *Stegreiftheater* (Theater of Spontaneity) in Vienna during the early 1920s (20). At a time when psychoanalysts were moving away from the intensely vivid re-evocation of affect, Moreno began to re-emphasize it. To do so, he chose theater as a vehicle, except that he used psychodrama to promote catharsis in the actors rather than in the audience. In effect, psychodrama combined the insights of classical theater, the Freudian ideas published in *Studies in Hysteria*, and some added elements of group involvement and discharge through action.

Moreno had been directing experimental theater when he discovered that a play could have a therapeutic impact on actors and audience alike. In his first major work, *Psychodrama, Volume I* (21), Moreno described an incident that helped to shape his transformation of theater into therapy. When one member of the company confided to Moreno that he and his wife had been arguing at home, Moreno invited the couple to act out their domestic quarrel before an audience. The two acted out a series of scenes from their childhoods, their marriage, and their hopes and dreams for the future, profoundly affecting both the audience and the couple themselves. "After every performance," Moreno writes, "some spectators would come up to me, asking why the Barbara-George scenes touched them so much more deeply than the others (audience therapy). Some months later, Barbara and George sat alone within the theatre. They had found themselves in each other again, or better, they had found themselves, in each other for the first time. I analyzed the development of their psychodrama, session after session, and told them the story of their cure."

Moreno's theories are complex and abstruse, but his method is simple, direct, and powerful. A psychodramatic performance involves participants, who enact a scene from one of their lives, using a variety of techniques to heighten emotions and clarify conflicts; and observers who, though they may not be directly involved, often profit from the experience. Catharsis, as Moreno tells us, is a fundamental aspect of psychodrama: "It is an effective combination of individual with group catharsis, of participation with action catharsis." And again, "One of the important achievements of psychodramatic therapy is the development of the idea of catharsis." The immediacy of psychodrama also promotes spontaneity, empathy for others, and an opportunity for testing various modes of behaving. It is, in short, an opportunity for learning through experiencing, since catharsis and spontaneity are intimately related; for, when feelings are checked, so is the capacity for freedom of action and behavior. An emotionally rigid person who fears affective expression replaces spontaneity with inaction and rigidity. In psychodrama, through ventilation of suppressed feelings, a patient may become able to behave in an unencumbered, spontaneous manner.

Moreno indicates that four kinds of catharsis are involved in psychodrama: somatic, mental, individual, and group. By somatic catharsis, he means not only the bodily discharge of affect in tears, laughter, and shouts, but also the rekindling of physical expressivity through action. This latter aspect of somatic catharsis is not really a cathartic ventilation. Rather, it is a matter of exercise and practice—which may become feasible after cathartic discharge. Mental catharsis is Moreno's phrase for the rediscovery and expression of faded memories of past experiences. In short, it is what Freud and Breuer meant by catharsis, and what we have called cognitive catharsis.

Psychodrama can be individual- or group-oriented. The major actor, patient, or protagonist is the center of action, and the play can mainly benefit him. Group interaction is always involved, however, as others participate in the drama with the protagonist. In a recent article, Moreno (20) maintains that psychodrama can be conducted as individual therapy, with one patient and one director; or as group therapy, with several patients serving different roles and as auxiliary egos. However conducted, it is, we believe, primarily an individual-centered approach, with the members of the group interacting not on the basis of a genuine relationship, but rather to help each other, singly, to better understand private experiences. Moreno, on the other hand, says (21) that every role is a fusion of private and collective elements, and that only minor portions are private and personal. However, though several persons may be treated at once in psychodrama, the technique falls short of being a truly group-centered approach because it does focus on private and external life experiences. Psychodrama is less a microcosm of group life than a therapeutic imitation of life.

Even though the action in psychodrama imitates events outside rather than within the group, the action takes place in the present and in a group setting. Feelings, whether stimulated by past or present events, are always live. The psychodramatist refrains from speaking in the past tense because doing so would dilute the emotional impact of the performance. The patient must truly be an actor rather than a narrator or story-teller. Furthermore, although the aim is to recapitulate past (or future) events, precise reproduction is neither possible nor desirable. The goal is to begin with a real situation but to modify it into a therapeutic facsimile. The director takes therapeutic license in order to modify other characters and to help the protagonist act out unexpressed aspects of the situation. The protagonist may be encouraged to say and do what he previously couldn't or didn't want to express. This very often means revealing and ventilating suppressed emotions. Thus, psychodrama is often cathartic. But however desirable emotional discharge may be, it should not be aimed for at the cost of spontaneity. Usually, the protagonist is encouraged to maximize all his expressions—actions, words, and feelings, and even delusions, hallucinations, thoughts, and fantasies. Constant pressure to emote may end up countertherapeutic, however; telling a patient to be expressive is an injunction which paradoxically may curb his spontaneity and lead to a contrived show of emotion. Freedom to experience and express feelings is more to be desired in any form of treatment than a rigid directive to produce feelings.

Zerka Moreno (22) also states that catharsis is fundamental to psychodrama, and that the catharsis achieved in psychodrama is more than the drain off of feelings from traumatic wounds. It involves, she says, action and interaction that will help free the actors' spontaneity and creativity. Thus the therapeutic goal is not only insight, not only catharsis, but also creative spontaneity, involvement with others, and learning by experiencing—both a mastery of the past and a rehearsal for the future.

In this action-oriented therapy there are five essential components: the group; the patient or protagonist; the psychodramatist or director; his therapeutic aides or auxiliary egos; and a system of therapeutic techniques. Use of the group involves the expansion of the patient-therapist situation to a more typical social one and hence the results may be more generalizable to ordinary life situations. Typically, what happens is that the group comes in, takes seats, and begins discussing various topics and problems. This discussion serves both as an icebreaker and a means of bringing individual members' problems to the surface. After this initial interaction or warm-up, the group may begin to focus on a problem of common concern; or the director may encourage an individual patient to come forward with a situation that he wishes to work on. Once a problem area is selected, action is begun.

In the warm-up period the psychodramatist may focus on group interaction and communication, or on individual dynamics, depending upon his particular bent. The group-oriented therapist will concentrate on mobilizing group involvement, and will help select one member to serve as the session's center of involvement. This "star" patient then serves as a focal point for communication within the entire group, who identify and interact with him. A director who is more individually oriented will use the warm-up largely as an opportunity to relax the group and select a protagonist and a therapeutic problem. Often the director may simply ask, "Who has a problem to work on today?" Once the protagonist has delineated his problem, the director explains the techniques to be utilized in bringing the problem to life.

The role of the director-therapist fluctuates during the course of each session in response to the demands of the situation. He may alternately be passive, directive, or provocative. In addition to his professional training as a therapist and familiarity with the techniques of psychodrama, the director should himself have a flair for the dramatic. With a touch of the muse and a gift for showmanship, a director may be able to assume various difficult roles or evoke strong reactions in others. For example, when a woman patient had difficulty re-experiencing frustration and anger toward a blanket, representing her demanding infant, the director curled up on the floor and started to whine, cry, and finally scream. The young mother was pushed right back into the exasperation she felt at home. Although the director may become an actor, his chief function is to provide structure by introducing new situations and techniques to enhance the therapeutic effect of the dramatization. In this respect the psychodramatist is like an encounter group leader, and must be able to use techniques that stimulate action at impasses without relying too much on gimmicks that will interfere with spontaneity. He must be able to stimulate the dramatization of painful, anxiety-provoking, or even bizarre scenes, and at the same time be open enough to tolerate his own anxiety while protecting others from too intense anxiety. The director must be perceptive enough to diagnose momentary changes in the situation, and quick enough to respond to alterations as they develop. If individual therapy is like driving an automobile, psychodrama is like driving a racing car. The distance travelled may be the same, but the speed is greater.

The psychodramatist is at his best when he most fully uses the unique dramatic and emotional potential of his method. He must aim toward the generation of catharsis and spontaneity. This is not to say that cognitive gains do not accrue. Indeed, interpretations may be made. However, to maximize the benefit of this dramatic method, interpretations should be made through action—that is, rather than simply stating his interpretation, the director directs that a scene be played in a particular way.

Auxiliary egos provide therapeutic assistance to the director. They help reproduce dramas from the protagonist's life. In addition to re-creation, they act to intensify the emotional impact of the scenes. Thus the protagonist works out his conflicts through dynamic interaction with other persons. But because the auxiliary egos bring their own personalities and reactions to bear, the protagonist must deal with conflicting and conflictual emotions as they occur, not with a relatively passive therapist, but with other characters who react spontaneously. By virtue of numbers alone these additional therapeutic agents provide increased points of interaction for the patient. From an analytic point of view, they provide extra prototypes of family figures, thereby increasing the number of transference possibilities. Alternately, these auxiliary egos can be seen as providing restimulation of various suppressed emotional reactions. From a social learning vantage point, they offer the chance to try out new responses. Psychodrama thus provides opportunities for resocialization as part of a learning process.

Numerous production techniques may be used to structure sessions and to probe beneath surface responses. Among these technical ploys some have become relatively standard (23): role reversal, the double, soliloquy, and the mirror.

Role reversal is a procedure in which actors switch roles. For example, a wife protagonist may play the role of her husband. Taking another's role can improve sensitivity, compassion, and empathy for the other person, and can also give the protagonist the opportunity to see his own actions from a different perspective. In this sense, it provides distance enough to allow a fresh look at ego-syntonic responses. Role reversal may also promote catharsis by enabling the protagonist to identify with the feelings of others. Often emotionally well-defended persons are more easily able to cry over the misfortunes of others than over their own; that is, crying for others is considered a sign of sensitivity, while crying for oneself is self-indulgent. Role reversal may also stimulate spontaneity in rigid and inhibited patients. The person who has learned not to be spontaneous as himself may become extremely spontaneous in the role of his father, wife, or his pet cat. Expressiveness is enhanced as this play-acted spontaneity increases.

The soliloquy provides the protagonist an opportunity to express hidden thoughts and action tendencies without the necessity of interacting with others. Even dramatized significant others may be anxiety-provoking enough to paralyze certain responses. If suppression stems from the presence of family members, then the soliloquy may offer even more distance than role-playing from restimulated anxiety.

Even profoundly inhibited patients can profit by seeing themselves portrayed in relevant situations by auxiliary egos in the mirror procedure. Though the portrayal may not truly be a mirror image, it is likely to include key aspects of other people's perceptions, and to give form and substance to ill-perceived thoughts and feelings. This may provide the silent protagonist with a tremendous sense of being understood, which can go a long way toward overcoming inertia born of fear of responding. In addition to these procedures, the psychodramatist may use videotape playback, future projection, and dream enactment, as well as such standard therapeutic techniques like reassurance, reflection, and interpretation.

Catharsis is unquestionably a central though not exclusive healing mechanism in psychodrama. Re-enactment of key life situations with the addition of emotive techniques regularly triggers intense emotional discharge. This catharsis may occur not only in the protagonist, but also in spectators, auxiliary egos, and even the director (16). It is also necessary to be concerned with what follows cathartic discharge. In individual therapy, the clarified understanding that is thought to follow abreaction may occur automatically (24), or may be facilitated through interpretation. Actions and passions don't magically disappear following discharge; instead they fall into perspective, so that old experiences assume new meaning, and are seen more realistically. Once catharsis opens the possibility for profound and enduring modifications, psychodrama is able to provide the occasion for testing them out.

Encounter Groups

The entire field of group treatment has been shaken and changed by the encounter group movement. Begun as a practical means of studying small group dynamics, T-groups have spawned a proliferation of new approaches which in turn have captured the imagination of the public. The rate of growth of this populist movement has been so phenomenal as to far outstrip our understanding or control of it.

In view of the fact that such groups are typically designed for persons who are not patients, it is not surprising to discover that this movement originated outside the domain of professional mental health care. In 1946, the executive director of the State of Connecticut's Interracial Commission asked a team of social psychologists and educators led by Kurt Lewin to help implement a Fair Employment Practices Act (25). Lewin's charge was to train schoolteachers, businessmen, and labor leaders to deal effectively with interracial tensions, and to help change public attitudes in the direction of compliance with the new act. Three small discussion groups were set up, of ten members each, led by Leland Bradford, Kenneth Benne, and Ronald Lippitt. These discussion groups focused on solving practical problems faced by members in their own communities. In addition to analysis and discussion, role-playing was employed to articulate problems and test solutions.

Observers kept a record of the process of the group meetings, and these observations were shared with the workshop staff during evening planning sessions.

Some of the group participants asked permission to attend these evening sessions, and Lewin permitted them to do so. Soon all of the participants and workshop staff were involved in analysis and interpretation of small group dynamics and the members' behavior, and thus, serendipitously, a powerful technique for human relations training came into being. Instead of sitting back and passively absorbing what they were told, members were confronted with a very active and personal learning experience. They found the opportunity to gain direct feedback on how groups worked and on their own behavior and its effects on others both useful and profitable—so much so that the staff planned a similar three-week workshop to be held the following summer in Bethel, Maine.

This second workshop consisted of small discussion groups in the mornings and large group meetings in the evenings. The small discussion groups were called basic skill-training groups, a name later shortened to T-Groups. These small group sessions were led by a "trainer" and focused on discussions of substantive issues and problems that members encountered in their home communities. In addition, these meetings had an observer who provided immediate feedback to the participants concerning their in-group behavior. This feature became the essential characteristic of T-groups. The immediate feedback was thought to provide group members with useful information for understanding themselves in the context of the functioning of a group. This basic T-group formation has given rise to a wide variety of offshoots. The initial focus on cognitive applications to back-home problems and group dynamics has shifted to include techniques of feedback, confrontation, openness, self-disclosure, the challenging of personal values and beliefs, here-and-now processes, and individual dynamics. Along with these changes in emphasis, new names have been introduced—awareness groups, growth groups, human relations training groups, sensitivity groups, and encounter groups, which is the one most widely used.

Encounter groups feature a wide variety of styles, techniques, and goals. Our interest here is only to examine the role that emotional expression and discharge plays in these groups.

Despite a multitude of variations, encounter groups share a core of common features. Most involve an intensive high-contact group experience; they are generally small enough (6 to 20 participants) to permit a great deal of face-to-face interaction; and they focus on the behavior of members as it unfolds within the group. A premium is placed on openness, honesty, interpersonal confrontation, and self-disclosure. These procedures almost guarantee strong emotional expression. In fact, the central theme of encounter groups may be expressivity, which includes self-disclosure and interpersonal confrontation, as well as emotional expression, ventilation, and discharge.

The great difficulty people in our culture have in experiencing and expressing intense emotions helps explain why they are so popular. Freud uncovered man's irrational and emotional forces and developed a therapy to understand and control these forces. The encounter group movement focuses on liberating and granting expression to these forces. Encounter group participants are led from the abstract to the concrete, from the mind to the body, and from the intellect to the emotions. Affective experiencing lies at the heart of the movement.

Like cathartic psychotherapy, hypnotherapy, drug-induced abreactions, and emotive religious rituals, encounter groups function to liberate emotionality by disrupting everyday defenses to emotional responding. In encounter groups this disruption of everyday, socially-reinforced patterns of interaction is achieved through concentration on the immediate group process and emphasis on personal relations and personal remarks. The resultant subjective experience is infused with intense emotional experiencing.

Most of the conditions and procedures of encounter groups are designed to strip away defenses. The shock of the initial encounter with a group of strangers, the minimization of outside roles and status, the ambiguity and lack of structure, and the separation from usual surroundings all act to breach defenses. A powerful set is also created in members, most of whom have previously heard or read that encounter groups generate a highly expressive atmosphere. In addition to the set and setting, various techniques enhance the expectancy that something impactful is going to happen. Under such conditions, affective arousal is bound to occur. Attempts to reconstitute defenses or to escape from the emotional atmosphere of the group by discussing outside problems are sharply curtailed. Furthermore, affectively charged interactions cannot be sidestepped or ignored, since the norms of encounter groups pressure the participants to say the unspeakable and to feel the emotions that in ordinary life are suppressed. Feedback is used to highlight transactions, to intensify emotions, and to bring to completion interactional gestalts.

The emotional expressivity that plays so central a role in encounter groups includes but is not limited to catharsis. Different groups vary in their relative emphasis on group and individual dynamics. Those with greater emphasis on individuals permit and encourage more discharge of pent-up emotions. Those that stress group processes foster catharsis of an individual's feelings less than they do direct expression of feelings toward other members of the group. In general, encounter groups encourage their members to learn how to express emotions as they are stimulated, rather than to unburden old angers and hurts. In these groups, members are simultaneously faced with the task of forming new relationships and pressure to understand what they are doing. Here, too, emotional expression is basic, and it is precisely this aspect of relating which, though underplayed in everyday transactions, is highlighted in the encounter movement. At its best the encounter group methodology integrates emotional expression with an intellectual understanding of the value of that expression. Ideally this produces not only an impactful experience, but also insight that can be transferred to life outside the group. Although there is as yet little evidence that such learning does take place, some encounter group participants argue that groups provide a moving experience which is desirable for itself and has no need to be justified by evidence of lasting change. By fostering strong emotional expression they create a unique experience which is a relief from emptiness and boredom. For many, the group experience may be an end in itself, independent of its effectiveness in solving personal problems or changing behavior. The trouble is that such groups are generally advertised as the vehicles for change. It is this claim, explicit or implicit, that legitimizes, no, necessitates careful evaluation of the effects of encounter group experiences. The theorist must explain how intense interactions with other people, direct feedback, and emotional expression have an effect on participants and modify their behavior. The researcher must document both that such changes occur and that other, unwanted, effects do not.

The vacuum left by lack of objective evaluation has been filled by subjective opinion, generated more often by visceral reaction than by thoughtful consideration. Some extol the human potential movement as the definitive cure for modern man's alienation; others see in it a dangerous forum and license for quackery that leads to irresponsible and primitive expression of impulse. Carl Rogers (26), for instance, has described encounter groups as "an avenue to fulfillment" and a life remedy. Bruce Maliver (27), on the other hand, points to suicides and psychoses precipitated by such experiences, and describes the group culture as fostering profound emotional fascism.

So far, however, only a handful of controlled evaluations have been performed. After reviewing the effects of human relations training, Gibb (28) concluded that "changes do occur in sensitivity, feeling management, directionality of motivation, attitudes toward self, attitudes toward others, and interdependence. Because these effects are closely related to hoped-for therapeutic outcomes, the evidence is strong that intensive group-training experiences have therapeutic effects. It is yet to be demonstrated whether the magnitude of the effects is sufficient to justify an increased use of intensive group training, or whether the effects are therapeutically significant in comparison with the effects of more conventional methods of therapy." And in a recent review, Smith (29) discusses 100 controlled studies of encounter groups that involved at least 20 hours of training. Of these, 100 studies, 78 showed change in one or more measures of outcome. Furthermore, of the 31 studies which included follow-up observation, 21 showed continued improvement.

There has been one major study of encounter groups that does shed some light on the impact of emotional arousal and ventilation on outcome, published by Lieberman, Yalom, and Miles (30), who made a comparative evaluation of the effects of seventeen different encounter groups. Included were: Gestalt, T-Group, Psychodrama, Synanon, Psychoanalytic, Transactional Analysis, Esalen Eclectic, Rogerian Marathon, Eclectic Marathon, personal groups, and tape-led groups. The groups were conducted in conjunction with an academic course at

Stanford University and all participants were volunteers. This study is particularly valuable, because it examines specific aspects of the leaders' behavior, as well as other group conditions, including norms, members' behavior, and the techniques employed. These process variables were in turn related to measures of outcome. Outcome was assessed by questionnaires and ratings. The questionnaires included the Personal Description Questionnaire, designed to measure tolerance of others; The Rosenberg scales, used to assess self-ideal discrepancy and personal constructs; The Members of This Group, a sociometric device; Personal Anticipations, to sample values relevant to encounter group norms; a Life-Space Questionnaire, to assess life goals; the Personal Dilemma Questionnaire, to assess interpersonal problem-solving approaches; the FIRO-B, designed to measure preferred interpersonal style; and finally, a Friendship Questionnaire, to assess quantity and quality of friendships outside of the group. An index of Encounter Group Attitudes was employed to evaluate how members perceived the groups they were in, on such dimensions as dangerous/safe and relevant/irrelevant. Open-ended questionnaires were also administered on which members were asked to evaluate the personal significance of their group experience. In addition to these self-report measures, participants were also rated by leaders, other members, and friends. Approximately half of the participants were interviewed a few months after termination.

These data were extensive enough to provide a broad sampling of opinion concerning the benefit each person derived from the group. They do not however, constitute a rigorous or objective evaluation of behavior change. Although people typically join encounter groups to "have an experience" rather than to change some specific behavior, assessing opinions as to the impact of the groups remain less convincing that some more direct evaluation of such changes as might occur. Nevertheless, the Lieberman, Yalom and Miles data are still quite valuable even though their conclusions should be viewed as tentative.

Sixty percent of all participants felt they had benefited from their approximately 30 hours of group experience. Six months later, this figure dropped to 50 percent. Group leaders judged 90 percent of the participants to have changed positively, and 33 percent as having made substantial gains. Friends and relatives of participants saw change in 75 percent of the group members of their social network. Questionnaire data suggested that values and attitudes changed more than behavior. Taken as a whole these results suggest an over-all modest positive impact of the groups.

To provide more specific information, 15 of the 174 persons who completed the group experience were selected as High Learners. These were the people who apparently benefited most from their encounter. These highly successful participants rated the most important impact of their group experience as: emotional closeness, emotional catharsis, cognitive gain, and open communication, in that order. Thus, emotional openness and catharsis were seen as key ingredients of successful encounter group experiences. These ingredients were also reflected in the descriptions, by participants and observers, of what occurred during group sessions. These descriptions revealed that intense emotional expression such as crying, shouting in anger, and pleading for help was highly approved in most groups. In fact, expressing feelings was judged to be the third most important factor after feedback and learning that one's feelings were similar to others' over all groups. Furthermore, most of the successful leaders were characterized as releasers of emotion. Over-all, leaders were seen to have spent 29 percent of their time in evocative behavior. Clearly then, encounter groups are characterized by a great deal of emotional expression.

Factor analysis of observers' ratings revealed four basic leadership functions: emotional stimulation; caring (or support); meaning attribution (or interpretation); and executive functions (or structuring). Group leaders differed markedly in terms of how much emphasis they placed on these four types of behavior. Interestingly, differences in leadership style and technique were seen to be unrelated to theoretical orientation. In short, leaders' behavior is apparently related to personal style more than to school labels. Based on the various measures of outcome, the most effective leadership style was seen as being moderately high on emotional stimulation, high on caring, moderately high on executive functions, and included the use of meaning-attribution.

In addition to assessing positive change, data were collected on psychological casualties. To detect casualties, participants were interviewed if they were identified by any of the following criteria: requested psychiatric aid during the course of the group; dropped out from the group; were evaluated by peers as having been hurt; dropped in self-esteem (as measured by the Rosenberg self-esteem measure); rated their experience as being destructive; were rated by leaders as having had a negative experience; or were reported by observers as having suffered as a consequence of the group. Of the 104 participants who fell into one of these categories, 16 were considered by the interviewers to have become psychologically distressed, as a result of the groups. The authors noted that group leaders were not particularly sensitive in picking out casualties. In fact, only two of the 16 casualties were identified as such by their leaders. Some casualties might have been identified by pregroup screening, since these persons had unrealistic expectations of instant psychotherapy or of forming lasting friendships. Others probably would not have been so identified. These members apparently suffered as a result of aggressive and intrusive behavior by other group members, rejection by the leader or group, input overload, or pressure on unstable defenses.

Lieberman, Yalom, and Miles conclude by stating that, consistent with encounter group lore, emotional expressivity is an important component of encounter groups, but so is cognitive functioning. They end by saying "Instead of 'Let it all hang out,' let more of it hang out than usual, if it feels right in the group, and you give some thought to what it means."

Encounter groups certainly seem to be effective in generating strong emotional experiences. Leaders promote, model, and elicit emotional expression. Many exercises are designed to overcome defenses and generate expressivity. When members seem blocked, the leader may introduce some procedure to promote the flow of emotional interactions. Reducing inhibitions and breaking down barriers to feelings seem to require more activity on the therapists' part. Thus, more active and directive leaders may generate more emotional expression. Typical means of encouraging the expression of aggression include pushing, wrestling, and slapping. Affection is often expressed by having members hug, massage each other, or hold hands. It is apparent that defenses against emotional expression and discharge are more difficult to maintain when the interaction shifts from verbal to nonverbal.

The paradox of many of these exercises is that they are

games introduced to facilitate the expression of "real" feelings in "authentic" encounters. Such techniques may get around resistance, but great care must be taken lest they become artificial, since ersatz trust, affection, and hostility cannot substitute for the real thing. "Tell him how you feel," conveys a message that feelings are being avoided, and a directive to express them. Ideally, the encounter group member will be encouraged to risk more expression of his feelings, and be able to realize that he can do so without catastrophe.

Single occasions, or weekends of intense contact and emotional eruption may be very powerful, but they probably need follow-up to produce lasting change. An encounter group experience may begin to liberate a person's emotional responses, but to provide real change role testing and modification in daily life is necessary. For this, the sustained experience of group psychotherapy is probably more effective.

Two types of emotional responding occur in groups: arousal and expression (both cognitive and somatic) of feelings generated in the here-and-now interaction between group members; and cathartic ventilation and discharge of private, personal feelings generated by historical experiences outside the group. The vivid expression of anger towards another group member who is hypercriticial is an example of the former; while crying about the loss of a loved one exemplifies the latter mechanism. In our judgement, experiencing and expressing emotional responses in the immediate context of a session is a powerful and effective procedure in group treatment. Cathartic ventilation and discharge, on the other hand, while powerful and probably therapeutic for individuals does not maximize the potential of groups for fostering learning to improve interpersonal interaction.

CHAPTER 6

Bereavement

*T*he death of someone dear evokes many of life's most profound feelings, and catharsis plays a vital role in helping to deal with these powerful emotions. Unfortunately, although mental health professionals have long recognized the need for catharsis in bereavement, this awareness has not been widely shared by the general public.

Death is a fact of every person's experience. It confronts us not only as the terminal point of our own lives, but also through the loss of those we love. In recent years existential philosophers have urged us to face the fact of our inevitable demise as a prerequisite to living fully and authentically. Martin Heidegger portrays man as the being who lives facing his own death, and Sartre sees nothingness lying coiled like a serpent at the heart of human experience. For these men, life is grounded on the consciousness of death and annihilation. Likewise, Hemingway's heroes see life with a special clarity because they have beheld death at close range. Although this philosophical encounter with the idea of death may have profound implications for enriching life, it rarely matches the intense emotional impact of experiencing the death of someone you love.

Bereavement has been the subject of considerable psychoanalytic attention, as well as some experimental study, both of which have had impact on the practice of psychotherapy.

In "Mourning and Melancholia," Freud (1) explores the relationship between mourning and depression or melancholia. A period of mourning, during which the bereaved grieves, is required for successful adjustment to the death of a loved person. In Freud's terms, grief work is necessary to free the libido from the lost object. One ignores death or denies grief at the risk of psychological equilibrium. Those who do not confront the pain directly pay for it in inner conflict, and are often unable to relate to the suffering of others in a helpful manner. Grief is commonly viewed as a spontaneous and relatively uncontrolled expression of personal emotions; however, counterforces attempt to control grief and often successfully suppress it. Grief is a complex emotion, and may include elements of anger and pleasure, as well as sadness.

When a loved person (or object) is lost, mourning ensues. Mourning becomes depression when the grief work is suppressed. Depression is characterized by dejection and loss of self-esteem, and may possibly culminate in psychosis and the delusional expectation of punishment. When a loved one dies, reality demands that libido be withdrawn from the lost object and eventually reinvested elsewhere. This aim arouses opposition which takes the form of attempts at denial. Even in the ideal case, reality cannot be obeyed at once; in the pathological instance, it is never fully accepted. Mourning requires a cathartic process of reviewing memories of the lost one. If this process is subverted, particularly if the bereaved cannot accept his ambivalence toward the lost person, depression may result. Reproach is shifted from the lost one onto the bereaved's own ego, resulting in painful recrimination. Thus, when catharsis is blocked and ambivalent feelings are present, depression is the probable result (1, 2, 3).

In her paper, "Absence of Grief," Helene Deutsch (2) wrote that the death of a beloved person must produce a catharsis of feelings or a pathological reaction will ensue. Blockage is due to the interaction between the strength of the ego and the intensity of affect. That is, grief is resisted when the pain is too intense, or when the bereaved lacks the resources to undertake mourning.

Of course, possibilities other than expression or suppression of grief exist. The operation of other defense mechanisms may result in some discharge of tears. For example, the "Wolf Man" showed no reaction to the death of his sister, but burst into tears at Pushkin's grave (3). Here grief was postponed and displaced. Omitted grief always finds substitute expression. Sometimes it is in depressive bouts of weeping, sometimes in hysterical symptoms, and sometimes it is displaced to extreme empathy for the grief of others. Deutsch cites such an example (2).

> She found vicarious emotional expression through identification, especially with the sad experiences of others. The patient was capable of suffering a severe depression because something unpleasant happened to someone else. She reacted with the most intensive sorrow and sympathy, particularly in cases of illness and death affecting her circle of friends. In this form of experience we could trace the displacement of her own rejected affects.

Although it provides some relief, this substitute form of discharge will not resolve the grief. The painful affect and inability to form new attachments persists until mourning for the real loss is carried to completion.

Studies of adrenal cortical function in depressed patients corroborate the clinical theory that depression is a pathological avoidance of the experience of the exquisite pain of loss. When plasma or urinary samples of corticosteroids are analyzed to monitor changes in pituitary-adrenal activity, the changes provide a gross estimate of biological stress and are correlated with the subjective experience of arousal and distress (4, 5, 6).

Mason (4), notes that when patients are most severely psychotic and withdrawn, corticosteroid levels (and affective distress) are low. This is consistent with Freud's view. Furthermore, the manic state is also associated with lower than average corticosteroid levels. This too is consonant with the clinical interpretation of mania as resulting from defensive denial of painful experience.

In some of the most carefully controlled studies in this field, Sachar and his co-workers have studied the adrenal cortical response to psychotherapy of depressed patients (7, 8, 9). This work was designed specifically to test Freud's idea that one type of depressive reaction is precipitated by a loss, which causes emotional distress followed by a pathological syndrome during which the painful loss is no longer experienced emotionally. Psychotherapeutic intervention in such cases is often designed to facilitate confrontation of the loss, a difficult and painful process.

Sachar monitored the corticosteroid responses of six hospitalized depressed patients during: (1) the initial phase of depressive equilibrium; (2) brief psychotherapy involving confrontation of the loss; and (3) following recovery (9). In five of the six cases corticosteroid levels rose significantly during the period of confrontation. Each of these five patients improved rapidly and was discharged from the hospital. The one patient whose corticosteroid level did not rise during confrontation did not improve, and was subsequently treated with electroconvulsive shock. These findings are consistent with Freud's distinction between mourning (confrontation of the loss) and melancholia (depressive equilibrium).

Although Freud related only depression to the suppression of grieving, others have observed that alternative pathological consequences may result, including psychophysiological reactions, anxiety states, hysteria, obsessional tension states (10), and catatonic stupors (11).

Melanie Klein (12) relates pathological mourning to manic-depressive states. The excited, hyperactive behavior of the manic is seen as a desperate attempt to block the tears normal to grieving. This control is thought by Klein to lead to a state described as psychic constipation. She points out that crying brings relief because it discharges tension and because it involves a symbolic unburdening. Thus, she underscores the point made by many others that it is crucial for an adaptive resolution of bereavement to fully experience mourning with its attendant sorrow and despair. This much of Klein's research does little more than substantiate Freud's thesis. However, she goes on to explore the developmental antecedents of adult bereavement, work that does shed light on the development of the adult's disposition to respond to losses.

Klein sees the mourning of the adult as restimulating the early childhood experience of losing the position of dependence on the mother. This move toward independence indeed involves a loss for the child, although it is seldom thought of in such terms. This epoch is referred to as the "depressive position," and if the child's grief is incompletely expressed it is thought to be revived whenever a loss is experienced in later life. The child's experience of losing his special position of dependence is thus a prototypic experience for learning to grieve effectively to resolve life's inevitable losses (13).

Among the analysts, Bowlby (14, 15) is chiefly responsible for recognizing the importance of mourning in early childhood. He observes that inadequate mourning in the early years of life frequently takes a course unfavorable to future personality development. To prevent this eventuality, Bowlby stresses the necessity for "grief work" involving weeping and the expression of anger. The process of mourning, he points out, follows a predictable sequence in adults, children, and even lower animals. It begins with craving, angry attempts to recover the lost object and appeals for help, followed by a period of apathy and disorganization that eventually allows the individual to relate and again find satisfaction in new objects.

Bowlby thus describes mourning as involving protest, despair, and detachment, and occuring even with prolonged separation from the mother. In the protest phase, the child cries loudly, and shakes and throws himself about seeking to regain his mother. These responses may have originated in instinctual behavior designed to solicit help, and their biological utility as a means of recovering the lost object has also been observed by both Darwin and Lorenz (16). If these behaviors prove unsuccessful, the child, filled with grief, enters the phase of despair. During this period, the mourner's longing for reunion does not diminish, but as hope fades he experiences unutterable misery. If the grief work is completed, he can detach himself from the one he lost and re-attach his affections elsewhere.

These observations suggest that pathological variants of mourning, including clinical depression, result from defensive processes that interfere with affective expression. It is likely that incapacity for mourning is often based on an inability to tolerate the position of weakness and supplication that it entails. Also common is the unwillingness to accept and express the anger that naturally attends the frustration associated with loss.

Although grief and mourning have been written about extensively by other analysts, Lindemann is virtually alone in the firsthand study of acute grief (17). On Saturday evening, November 28, 1942, a disastrous fire raged through the Cocoanut Grove night club in Boston where 1,000 people were packed into a building that had a capacity for 600. The tragedy, which left 491 persons dead and many more badly injured (18), provided Lindemann with a rare opportunity to observe the mechanisms of grief by which the bereaved coped with their losses (19).

In addition to his study of the bereaved survivors of the Boston fire, Lindemann also interviewed others who suffered loss: neurotic patients who lost relatives during treatment; relatives of patients who died in the hospital; and relatives of members of the armed forces. He concluded that acute grief is a definite syndrome, which may appear immediately after a loss, or be delayed. (Lindemann's view of grief as an illness is supported by George Engel (20).)

Lindemann observed a fairly consistent pattern of normal grieving, including somatic distress, feeling weak and exhausted, a slight sense of unreality, increased emotional distance from people, intense preoccupation with thoughts and images of the deceased, and feelings of guilt. One young woman, for example, was guiltily preoccupied with the fact that her husband died following a quarrel; one young man was obsessed with self-blame because during the fire he fainted too soon to save his wife from death. Those suffering acute grief wished not to be bothered, and were often irritable, even hostile. They were aimlessly restless, but lacked initiative and zest. Many seemed to assume traits of the deceased. As Freud observed, this identification may be a way of denying the loss.

Lindemann observed that the duration of the grief reaction depended upon the success with which the person did the grief work, undergoing a catharsis that enabled him to loosen ties to the deceased and readjust to the environment. Lindemann supports the contention that suppressing emotion may delay the grief reaction or even lead to psychiatric pathology. "One of the big obstacles to this work seems to be the fact that many patients try to avoid the intense distress connected with the grief experience and to avoid the expression of emotion necessary for it." He notes that men especially struggle to avoid expressing grief.

When the grieving process is blocked or incomplete, various types of morbid reactions may arise. A delayed grief reaction may occur when bereavement is suffered at a time when the patient is confronted with an important task that he does not wish to have interrupted. Delay prevents a thorough working-through process, and may in turn leave the bereaved susceptible to restimulation. Lindemann finds that a manic defense, whereby the patient is intensely overactive and struggles to avoid perceiving the loss, is common.

Many bereaved persons in Lindemann's sample who did not grieve successfully took on the symptoms of the deceased. Frequent resentment of their loss was found in the bereaved, some of whom displayed intense hostility toward their own doctors, or the doctor who cared for the deceased. This hostility is seen as a defense against depressive feelings and a projection of resentment toward the deceased. Others were characterized by a wooden, robot-like defense against hostility, since overt hatred would violate their standards. One patient said that if he were to have any feelings at all, he would be angry at everybody.

In a small fraction of cases, Lindemann observed agitated depression in those who were unable to mourn; some members of this group were dangerously suicidal. This seemed related not only to the mourning process, but also to the nature of their prior adjustment and their relationship to the deceased. Obsessive and depressive persons were most likely to develop agitated depression (17, 21), with unexpressed hostility toward the deceased increasing the possibility of such symptoms.

Lindemann's studies led him naturally into consideration of therapeutic intervention in the management of grief reactions. The process of working through a loss involves actively thinking of the deceased, and of the painful side of the loss, and the patient must be encouraged to deal with his grief directly and to accept the pain of bereavement. In addition to accepting grief, Lindemann also urged catharsis. If the bereaved is to reach an adaptive resolution, "He will have to express his sorrow and sense of loss." This also includes verbalizing hostility or feelings of guilt.

Others writing on the management of bereavement recommend strategies similar to Lindemann's. In a recent survey (22) of 133 professional consultants (medical, psychiatric and religious), 91 percent urged that expression of feelings and tears be encouraged. Almost half felt that attempts to forget painful memories should never be encouraged. George Engel (20) advises hospital staff members of their responsibility to aid the bereaved in the management of their grief. He urges granting requests to view and take leave of the deceased, to emphasize the reality of death, and to promote a catharsis of feelings. Anguished outcries are not a sign of morbidity, Engel observes, but a necessary part of the restitutive process. Of the ways in which a nurse can aid the bereaved, he says, "Most important is encouraging the bereaved person to cry." And the importance of funeral rites that emphasize the reality of death and provide a socially acceptable context for catharsis of grief has been repeatedly stressed.

Catharsis of feelings is advocated not only for the management of acute grief reactions but also as a means of working through old and often repressed losses in psychotherapy (24, 25, 26, 27, 23, 28, 29, 13). Grayson sees a trend away from recognizing the value of catharsis in the resolution of grief. He decries this trend and stresses that catharsis is both important and necessary: "Deeply rooted in culture and tradition, catharsis and abreaction have been utilized through the centuries as a means of working through grief, thereby making this emotional separation." Grayson's work is particularly interesting, because he extends the use of mourning to include symbolic losses and frustrated hopes, as well as lost persons. While we have known since Freud that persons mourn abstract losses, Grayson's cathartic therapeutic approach to grief takes in not only bereavement, but also frustrated hopes, ambitions, and fantasies. Grayson often finds that patients feel sadness over lost adolescent opportunities to gratify sexual or aggressive urges. His approach is to help the patient mourn the missed experience by facing the loss in a direct way. This process, he notes, is often a lengthy one. Much denial has to be overcome, and many memories have to be reviewed.

The techniques of drug-assisted abreaction developed in the treatment of traumatic neuroses have also been used in the treatment of grief reactions. Barnacle (24) has found that if an individual has difficulty expressing himself or cannot release suppressed emotion, abreaction via sodium pentathol may be helpful. He cites the case of a woman who exhibited symptoms of restlessness, pressured speech, frigidity, and a morbid preoccupation with the stillbirth of her child. She was, however, unable to confront this loss or her sadness directly. She appeared unable to express any emotion. Under sodium pentathol, "She relived with great emotion and in detail the past griefs of her life. She felt enormously relieved at the termination of this treatment, and it was necessary to see her on only a few subsequent occasions."

Some critics, on the other hand, argue that catharsis is a superficial approach, leading only to palliative relief without insight (29, 31). Brammer and Shostrom have said, "There is little evidence available to us which might indicate that periodic, emotionally cathartic sessions have much psychotherapeutic value other than the temporary supportive effect of draining off excess tension." Another common criticism is that catharsis may lead to psychotic decompensation (10). Both these criticisms will be considered in more detail in Chapter 9. In this context, however, it should be pointed out that there is no substantial evidence for either charge. In fact, cathartic mourning of losses may strengthen, rather than weaken, the ego (25). Furthermore, those who advocate catharsis in the resolution of grief are aware that it may be necessary to apply other techniques as well. For example, when treating psychotic agitated depressive patients, or when the risk of suicide is high, electroconvulsive shock may be used instead of, or in addition to, catharsis (24). Also, emotionally charged mourning may be used to facilitate the development of insight (25, 13).

Catharsis has been used recently in family therapy as well as individual therapy to work through losses. Paul, who has done extensive work on the role of mourning in conjoint family therapy (23, 30), has introduced the concept of "unresolved mourning" to account for significant difficulties within families. He observes "Our abbreviated mourning ceremonials, often carefully hidden from children, neither impart empathetic understanding nor provide catharsis for this experience." His clinical observations suggest that the lack of ability to face and cope with loss is often transmitted by the family. In a clinical study of 50 families with schizophrenic members and 25 families with neurotic members, maladaptive responses to object loss were widespread. These involved affective denial in which losses were never worked through, and morbid grief was easily stimulated (30). In another study (10), it was estimated that 9 percent of the total of psychiatric patients were disturbed as a consequence of morbid grief. Paul believes that the key to treating such cases is to mobilize affect. He does so by bringing the family together and facilitating the expression of feelings and reactions to losses, especially in the identified patient. He inquires not only about current losses, but about more remote ones as well. In this treatment, which he calls "operational mourning," Paul repeatedly reviews the details of a loss, while encouraging catharsis of feelings. Others in the family are encouraged to respond empathetically to the mourner. This not only facilitates cathartic review of the loss, but also sets a norm of giving acceptance and support when affect is expressed within the family.

Other family therapists have found catharsis of grief to be a useful technique on occasion, even though it is not central to their approach. For example, Guerin and Fogarty (26) cite the case of a family whose members had stoically tried to accept without grief the untimely death of the grandfather. "His death left a large empty space in the family. The boy and his mother frequently thought of him. But mother wouldn't talk about it, 'because it's morbid.' The son wouldn't talk about his thoughts and feelings, 'because it would upset mother'." The consequence of this affective suppression was that the son was unable to concentrate and had difficulty sleeping. Nevertheless, he kept up a "brave soldier" front. When the therapist recognized this suppression, the issue of the grandfather's death was brought up in a family session, and the family members were not allowed to sweep it under the rug. Both the mother and son ventilated their grief, with a subsequent lifting of the son's depression and an improvement of his school performance.

Unfortunately, despite the wealth of clinical data on the importance of catharsis in mourning, there is often an insufficient recognition of its value in the culture and tradition of urban secularized societies. Too often such a culture does not provide an opportunity to complete grief in a socially acceptable context. In primitive societies whole communities gathered and conducted rites and ceremonies of death, and some societies still do encourage free expression of grief, including wailing, throwing oneself on the ground, and weeping over the corpse. However, societies like ours which rely heavily on rationalism have abolished most of these customs.

Most people have had their first personal encounter with the fact of death by the age of ten. This first experience may be the death of grandparents, of other family members, or even of a beloved pet. And yet, death generally remains taboo as a topic of conversation. In a recent survey conducted by the editors of *Psychology Today*, fully one-third of 30,000 respondents did not recall ever discussing the topic of death within the family. Another third remember it as being spoken of with discomfort

(32). The implication of these findings is that the reality of death is denied or at least not dealt with openly in the majority of American families. This denial of death both helps people avoid admitting their own mortality, and also is part of a general tendency in this society to deny any powerful emotional experience. The denial is unquestionably made easier by the fact that our elderly are frequently removed to nursing homes or retirement villages, and death typically occurs in hospitals. Many people have never actually witnessed the death of another human being, which of course makes it easier to distort the reality of the event. Just as withdrawal from social reality may contribute to the formation of delusional thinking, so also may the failure to experience the impact of death foster distorted notions about it.

In a fascinating study of death and mourning in contemporary Britain, sociologist Geoffrey Gorer (33) concludes that the majority of British people are without guidance about how to deal with death and bereavement. He found that this circumstance, certainly not unique to the British, has many determinants. Mourning in response to grief is not adequately recognized as natural and healthy, and the prolonged suffering resulting from its denial is not well perceived. The repressed stance of many toward death and mourning is like the prudery associated with sex a century ago. Several factors combine to reinforce denial of death. Giving way to grief is often stigmatized, probably because many people become anxious and embarrassed when exposed to emotional display. Thus, friends may try to distract the bereaved from his pain, both because of the erroneous assumption that a bereaved person should not give vent to his feelings, and because they themselves want to avoid contact with grief.

Gorer found denial to be characteristic of half the various styles of mourning. One form of denial is that supported by religious belief (in fact, religion may have originated as a cosmology to deny the fact of death). The modern sects of Spiritualism and Christian Science dogmatically deny the existence of death, for example. According to Christian Science doctrine, death is part of an erroneous belief that life is matter. Both notions are vehemently denied. Death is described as an illusion, like the horizon—an imaginary line that is never crossed. The loss of a loved one is compared to the flight of a bird that does not cease to exist when it flies out of view into the clouds. Despite these poetic metaphors, the denial of death is meant to be taken quite literally: "If our departed friends could speak to us, they would assure us that they are now, just as we are, enjoying life, peace, harmony, and blessedness, and that there is therefore no need for grief and sorrow." This may be a moving and meaningful way to structure the abstract nature of life; however, beliefs like this which entail denial of the pain of bereavement cheat the bereaved of the opportunity to grieve.

Some accept the reality of death, but deny or attempt to hide their grief. People with this attitude typically believe that giving way to grief is morbid and unhealthy. Instead, they sublimate their energy into "carrying on" and "keeping busy." Characteristically, they rationalize by saying they are acting in accord with what the deceased would have wished. Such people often believe that they are sparing those around them the pain of bereavement. One woman in Gorer's survey denied grief at the death of her adopting mother, saying, "There is nothing you can do about it." But the interviewer noted that "Tears came into this woman's eyes nearly every time she mentioned her Nana, who had died twelve months earlier." The failure to accept and experience grief seems to have prolonged the woman's suffering, and Gorer comments on others who similarly denied their grief; "I had the feeling that, by denying expression to their grief, they had reduced their lives to triviality, even though their purposeful busy-ness warded off any overt symptom of depression." Others in this survey who avoided mourning were described as despairing, sitting alone in the dark, speaking with toneless voices and halting words. In every case, at least twelve months had passed since their bereavement, and the description suggests reactive depression.

Another form of denial of death involves a symbolic attempt to preserve the dead. This often takes the form of preserving the house and every object in it precisely as it was when the deceased was alive, as did Queen Victoria, who preserved every object as Prince Albert had left it. She even had his clothes laid out every day and his shaving gear brought to his room.

Similar behavior was also observed by Marris (34), who interviewed a sample of 72 widows. One fourth of these women acted as though their husbands were still alive and their behavior, thoughts and feelings still revolved around their lost mates. As one woman said, "'I used to put the kettle on and make tea for him. Or when I'd come home and find him not there, I'd think he had just gone out'." A number of other widows talked to their husband's photograph, imagined that he answered and advised them, clung to all his possessions, and returned to places they had frequented together.

People who respond to bereavement in this manner "never get over their loss." They proclaim their affection for the memory of the deceased as evidence of their dutiful and loving nature. In fact, this pattern suggests a failure to accept the reality of the loss, to work through the grief, and subsequently to readjust to another kind of life.

Other people, although fully accepting the reality of death, deprive themselves of the social occasion for mourning because they dislike the ritual and the expense associated with funerals. Some responses to the *Psychology Today* Death Questionnaire (32) reflect this point of view. "The most sickening aspect of death is the socially created ritual surrounding it." "I strongly endorse immediate cremation. Funerals are the heights of hypocrisy. I believe it is cruel to put one's survivors through such a ritual." Many people can sympathize with this viewpoint. Plush funeral parlors, costly ceremonies, and hypocritical eulogies can be offensive. However, the problem is not necessarily with funeral ceremonies per se; certainly it is possible to have funerals that honor the dead without making corpses into lewd objects of the mortician's craft, and without denying the psychological needs of the bereaved. Rites that feature evasion and concealment of death can be changed without doing away with all funerals.

Grief is apparently most successfully worked through in intense, time-limited mourning, during which the mourners withdraw from normal routine and allow themselves intense weeping. One example of a religious tradition that supports this kind of grieving is the Orthodox Jewish mourning procedure. Here prescribed customs are dictated to guide the bereaved through a period of grieving. Jewish rites play a vital role in the healing work of grief (35). Shock and grief are structured by definite and solemn procedures. The funeral is conducted as a rite of separation, and neither painful memories nor anguish is expected to be suppressed. The bad dream is real.

At the funeral ceremony, the deceased's virtues are extolled by a rabbi and by a lay friend. The loss is not denied, but openly confronted. All those close to the deceased, even children, are encouraged to attend. Thus, the ritual is a community affair and the bereaved receive support and understanding. *Kaddish,* a special prayer for the dead, is recited and then repeated by the bereaved when he attends religious services (as often as twice daily) for the next eleven months. Kaddish is recited thereafter on the anniversary of the death.

The seven days after the death are devoted to intense mourning. This period is called *shiveh,* the Hebrew word for seven. During the seven days of *shiveh,* friends and well-wishers visit the bereaved to offer support and condolence. Instead of distracting the bereaved, visitors are encouraged to speak of the deceased, thus helping to facilitate the mourning process. Following *shiveh* comes a thirty-day period in which normal activities are resumed but places of entertainment are avoided and special prayers are recited. Although this may appear to be an overly elaborate and lengthy process, it is consistent with clinical evidence that successful mourning takes a year or more.

All respondents in the Gorer survey who had gone through a period of intense, overt mourning found it therapeutic. They felt that it was important that they could not hide or cover up their grief. Crying, they said, helped them to recover. Thus, the ability to weep freely is taken as a sign that mourning is being successfully resolved. This interpretation is strongly supported from both the clinical literature and social custom.

CHAPTER 7

Recent Emotive Approaches
to Psychotherapy

The last few years have seen the rise of a proliferation of approaches to psychotherapy in which emotional catharsis is the focal point. These avant garde procedures have elicited much interest, from both the under-critical public and the overcritical professionals. Although proponents of these various approaches take pains to differentiate among themselves, their similarities far outnumber their differences. They use jargon where ordinary language terms are available to increase their own cohesion and to separate themselves; but whether it is called "discharge," "primaling," "biophysical expression," "implosion," or "release," sobbing and tears still amount to crying. Consequently, there has been little synthesis between these emotive therapies and even less careful evaluation of their effectiveness.

Objective evaluation of these cathartic therapies has been hindered by their advocates' tendency toward schoolish mystification. Janov (1), for example, claims his approach is totally unique and denies its obvious precedents in early psychoanalytic theory and practice. His extravagant claims of effectiveness are supported by only very unsatisfactory evidence. And Harvey Jackins' Re-Evaluation Counseling uses nonprofessional helpers, who may indeed be highly effective change agents, but whose work cannot be verified because of their antiprofessionalism and mistrust of research. Thoughtful appraisal of extant cathartic therapies depends upon a demystification of the underlying theories and empirical study of their outcomes. Demystifying them means translating specialized jargon into ordinary language, and describing the actual treatment processes. Though diverse in orientation and practice these therapists do have some things in common: they are convinced of the therapeutic value of catharsis; they believe that repressed dysphoric affects, such as anger or grief, are pathogenic until discharged by emotive expression; and they all preach that feeling more is the key to feeling better.

The theories that guide this group of therapists emphasize in varying degrees either past or current instances of emotional blockage. Primal therapy and Gestalt therapy represent the extremes on this continuum. Both approaches share the view that emotional disordering results from a failure to fully experience and express feelings. In Primal therapy the important experiences are thought to have occurred in early childhood, and current problems are believed to be but a reflection of unresolved events from the past. Scant attention is paid to existing life circumstances; instead, efforts are concentrated on helping the patient relive and abreact childhood traumas so that he can be freed of their residual influence. Gestalt therapy, on the other hand, focuses on the immediate present. Here catharsis is thought to be a byproduct of efforts to help patients to achieve spontaneity and openness in the here-and-now. Feelings are dealt with as they occur, with no attempt to uncover buried events. The point we wish to make here is that theories about what is therapeutic are relevant to the extent that they guide what the therapist actually does. It may be that somatic emotional expression is therapeutic regardless of whether the emphasis is on historical or recent experiences; but if his theory emphasizes one to the exclusion of the other, the therapist may deny the importance of and help to suppress certain aspects of his patients' experience. To be most useful, theory should serve only as a guide, and therapists should remain flexible enough to work with whatever material their clients produce, without insisting that it fit the straightjacket of their belief in what "really counts."

It is ironic that some cathartic therapists, while ostensibly working to unblock barriers to emotional expression, erect their own by insisting that their patients produce only certain emotions or that only emotions related to a certain time frame are worth dealing with. If emotional discharge is therapeutic, therapists should be open to the acceptance of any and all expressions of feeling, without maintaining a relentless pressure to relive past events. As we shall see, this openness is not always present, even in those who profess to encourage free and honest affective expression.

Wilhelm Reich: The Union of Psyche and Soma

It was Wilhelm Reich, a contemporary of Freud's who made the transition from concern with talking about feelings (cognitive catharsis) to physical discharge of emotions (somatic emotional catharsis). As early as 1927, he became interested in going beyond what he called "a merely intellectual understanding" of feelings to an effort to release affect in his patients (2). This led him to consider those factors that interfere with the discharge of affect. These resistances, he felt, were often basic personality attributes, slowly but deeply ingrained patterns that impede the experience of affect. His treatment evolved from a purely psychological analysis of what he called *character armor* to a combined physical and psychological attack on what he called *muscular armor*.

Reich eventually became concerned primarily with the treatment of physical blocks against the expression of emotion. Furthermore, his approach was embedded in a highly idiosyncratic set of theories about the nature of man and of the physical universe; however, we are more concerned with Reich's therapeutic procedures here than with the cosmology he used to explain his results.

Reich began as a relatively orthodox student of psychoanalysis, who made original contributions to the task of analyzing resistance. Freud himself moved from considering resistances hindrances to analysis to be dealt with by breaking through them (for instance, by touching patients on the forehead while suggesting that they recover lost memories) to recognition that resistances required analysis in order to remove them. Reich came to feel that resistances were basic character traits, and that the analysis of character resistances amounted to the analysis of character. Thus Reich drew a distinction between neurotic symptoms, which he saw as ego-alien, and the neurotic character traits he described as ego-syntonic. He began to devote the bulk of his therapeutic energies to the analysis of character resistances, which he believed were the key to understanding how people block off the experience of affect.

Anxiety, he pointed out, is bound by character armor, which protects the person from painful affective stimuli—either from within or without. Analytic therapy represents a danger to this neurotic equilibrium, and so in therapy the character armor manifests itself as resistance. As he became increasingly concerned with analyzing character armor, Reich began to concentrate more on how his patients were saying things and less on what they were saying. This made him realize that patterns of resistance involve somatic control. That is, posture, or tone, or pacing can be used to control affect as well as to avoid certain topics. In his early work Reich counseled against trying to force the patient to give up his character armor. Instead he urged exploring its meaning, in the same way that Freud explored the meaning of symptoms; thus the character armor, like the symptoms, becomes ego-alien, and patterns of defensive behavior are interpreted as a method of analyzing character rather than overcoming resistance in order to understand unconscious material.

About 1935 Reich shifted his emphasis to the somatic realm, and moved to an advocacy position dedicated to liberating his patients from emotional and sexual repression, both internal and external. Reich's concern with the conflict between internal demands and social institutions was highly controversial. So was his stress on sexuality which surpassed even Freud's. In its fully developed form (3), Reich's character analysis consisted of: (1) loosening character armor; (2) breaking down character armor (destruction of neurotic equilibrium); (3) breaking through deeply repressed and strongly affect-charged material; (4) working through liberated material without resistance; (5) reactivation of infantile genital anxiety and of genitality; and (6) appearance of orgasm anxiety and establishment of orgastic potency. The establishment of healthy orgastic sexuality became for Reich the criterion of healthy adult functioning.

The theoretical link between character analysis and what came to be called "vegotherapy" and "orgone therapy" was Reich's notion that chronic muscular rigidity develops to ward off, first, anxiety and, later, affect in general. Thus character armor becomes muscular armor; and Reich's therapy became even more concerned with chronic muscular rigidity. There are at least three major strategies in orgone therapy: muscular massage; encouraging a direct expression of somatic emotional discharge; and analysis that involves the development of insight via confrontation, clarification, interpretation, and working through. A less explicit tactic, but nevertheless pervasive, is conveying certain attitudes about the naturalness of sexuality and the wrongness of its suppression. In an autobiographical account of his orgone therapy, Orson Bean (4) says that the most powerful impact the therapy had on him was to confirm and enhance his belief in the goodness of sexuality.

After Reich observed that neurotics have muscular armoring, he tried to dissolve it directly, and found as a result, that he could help patients release their pent-up emotions more effectively. Reich believed that neurotics have a great deal of bound-up energy, derived both from suppressed affect and frustrated sexuality. According to his theory, energy is accumulated and stored for use in emergencies, such as battle or exhausting work, and to drain it, sexual release is advocated (2, 3, 5). If sexual release is not achieved, a person may become rigidly armored and neurotic, with a surfeit of blocked energy. Thus, armoring is partly a consequence of repressed sexuality, and partly a consequence of defense against emotional expression. Unlike other cathartic therapists, Reich recognized that pleasurable as well as unpleasurable feelings may be repressed. In fact, the neurotic often forgoes the experience of pleasure to avoid the possibility of pain.

Elsworth Baker, a student of Reich's and a practicing orgone therapist, described it as follows (5): "To relieve the situation it is necessary to reverse the armoring process by a dissolution of the armor, releasing and draining off the repressed emotions layer by layer, from latest to earliest blocking, until unitary function is restored and natural sexuality is reached." Here we find in Reich an appreciation of the complexity of the process of therapy, often absent from other theories reviewed in this chapter. Defenses, he recognized, are labyrinthine and require complex strategies for dissolution rather than simple breeching through gimmickry.

The orgone therapist releases emotions and dissolves muscular armor by physical as well as psychological means. In the initial interview a relatively brief history is taken. The therapist ascertains what the patient's presenting complaint is, how he functioned in the past, and how he is currently functioning. Regardless of whether or not the patient mentions it, inquiry is routinely made into the history of his sexual functioning. The prospective patient is evaluated for psychological pain and a sincere desire to change. No other requirements are mentioned.

Reich was willing to treat psychotics, and in fact his own personal experiences seem to have given him a powerful empathic understanding and valuing of schizophrenia. He said, "The schizoid character has a far better contact with the insight into the functions of nature and society than *homo normalis.*" Although schizophrenics are not excluded, great care is advocated in treating them. Reich warned that the schizophrenic patient's emotional release should not get out of control. They are amenable to treatment involving catharsis of deep layers of emotion, but the potential for harm exists if the therapist does not provide necessary control. In his description of orgone therapy with a schizophrenic woman, Reich describes a careful process of bringing out her emotions, one at a time, "Accordingly, I encouraged her crying which blocked the rage, and after some tearful release of sorrow I let her develop her rage by encouraging her to hit the couch."

An important variable among therapists is their ability to allow controlled expression of powerful emotions and their comfort in the face of these feelings. The therapist cannot be helpful if he encourages more emotional expression that he himself can be comfortable with, since his own fear of the patient's feelings will surely be conveyed to the patient. In this situation, where reassurance is necessary, discomfort with expressed affect is countertherapeutic. Reich, himself, seemed comfortable with an extreme range and intensity of feelings. In one of his case descriptions, he tells of having allowed a schizophrenic woman to act on her impulse to choke him. Reich felt this was cathartic, and the patient described it as "releasing steam."

Baker does say that not all patients are amenable to Reichian therapy. Those who lack the ability to resynthesize their defenses after they have been breached in therapy should be excluded. Thus, despite the dramatic nature of orgone therapy and the fact that deep emotional ventilation with psychotics is sometimes undertaken, there is a healthy respect for the complexities of treatment. "One must approach human life and human problems with caution," Baker says. And, "On the other hand, once a patient has been selected as a suitable candidate for therapy, considerable daring and risk are necessary."

Physical examinations with laboratory workups are a routine part of the initial evaluation. To facilitate overcoming defenses against feelings, patients are treated on the couch. Furthermore, they are generally clad either in underclothes or a bathing suit. This is done not only to help overcome defensiveness, but also so that the therapist can directly observe and manipulate the patient's muscles. Early in treatment, the orgone therapist endeavors to establish a rational, working alliance with his patient. The therapist explains that defensiveness and chronic muscular rigidity have resulted in buried feelings that need release. Passivity is discouraged, and the patient is warned that therapy involves difficult, often painful work.

Reich conceived of the body as being divided vertically into seven segments, each of which has unique muscle groups and characteristic armoring. Orgone therapy attempts to break down the armoring, segment by segment. The segments are: the ocular, oral, cervical, thoracic, diaphragmatic, abdominal, and pelvic.

The first segment to be de-armored is the ocular. Typically this is done by having the patient open his eyes wide as in fright and forcing an emotional expression. He may be asked to roll his eyes about and concentrate on the feelings that are stimulated. As with each succeeding segment, deep muscle massage and exercise is used to loosen armoring and to stimulate repressed emotions. Reich stressed the value of nonverbal work, because language is often used as a defense to block affective expression. Verbal language is, therefore, reduced to a minimum in orgone therapy. An interesting consequence of this, not mentioned by Reich, is that since fewer interpretations are made, the ones offered may be more salient.

The second bodily segment is attacked after the first one seems to show no or few signs of chronic muscular rigidity and fixity. To free up the oral segment, the patient may be asked to change his voice pattern or move his mouth and jaw vigorously. Sometimes the patient is asked to simulate crying to bring about a release of tension. This, by the way, is a technique that often stimulates actual tears and sobbing (5, 6). As he proceeds, the orgone therapist persistently attempts to facilitate emotional expression along with his massaging. Reich's position is that working on the muscular armor directly tends to lead to catharsis, but does not cause it. As he puts it, " . . . one cannot reactivate any emotional functions by mechanical means."

The cervical segment is difficult to reach directly. Loosening it is accomplished by eliciting a gag reflex, and by having the patient shout and scream. In discussing his orgone therapy, Orson Bean (4) describes his amazement and annoyance when his therapist suddenly forced him to gag. However, this tactic provoked a great deal of catharsis in the wake of hidden memories and re-evoked painful emotions. Bean felt that elicitation and re-evaluation of these memories were an important component of his treatment, though Reich himself held that memories are not important and that only the somatic component of catharsis is important. Reich recognized that traumatic memories of mistreatment, frustration, and disappointment appear in the course of dissolving muscular armor; however, he wrote (2), "The eliciting of memories is not important in orgone therapy; they help little without the corresponding emotion. The emotion in the expressive movement is ample for an understanding of the misery suffered by the patient, and finally the memories come up by themselves if one works correctly."

Reducing the muscular armor of the thoracic layer requires that the patient breathe deeply while the therapist exerts a countering pressure on his chest. In this manner the muscles of respiration are vigorously exercised. The resultant strain often stimulates memories and feelings of anger or sadness. These two emotional reactions often occur in conjunction with each other, and, unfortunately, one may neutralize the other. Baker recommends that aggressive feelings be released first, which in turn enables the tears to flow like an unblocked stream. "The most important emotion to elicit is rage (hate) and until this is released he cannot allow the softer feelings of longing and love to emerge." Reich also felt that anger must preceed sadness. Therapy cannot proceed, he said, without releasing the rage.

Diaphragmatic tenseness is reduced by gagging and by full respiration. Reich drew an analogy between the person and a bladder. When the person's armor is rigid, the body is tense, like a compressed bladder—filled with anxiety. The person, like the bladder, requires movement and change. If the patient is incapable of achieving this motility, assistance is required. Thus, the therapist may provoke movement or may massage muscle groups. Always, though, Reich stressed the unity of psychological and somatic functioning. Either sphere may be the target, but both will inevitably be affected. "The difference lies merely in the efficacy of the various methods; a memory will not produce affect outbreaks like the dissolution of, say, a diaphragmatic block."

De-armoring the abdominal layer is said to be simple if the higher segments have been freed. The final segment is the pelvic. Its liberation involves contracting and relaxing the pelvis, which tends to elicit anxiety and rage.

Orgone therapists speak of their method as being "biophysical," not psychological. In their writings the somatic components of treatment are consistently stressed, and this unique aspect of orgone therapy has attracted much notoriety. It is also true, though, that Reich as well as contemporary orgonamists did and do continue to use many principles of psychoanalytic therapy, thus acknowledging that cathartic release may only be a means of reducing rigidity and tension. Furthermore, the cognitive restructuring that must follow requires the guidance of a skillful therapist. Interpretations are as basic as massages.

To some extent the orgone therapist conveys his values— for instance, sexuality should be liberated—and world view to his patients. Baker asserts that the demand for sexual abstinence in adolescence is responsible for many conflicts, both for adolescents and adults. This abstinence is said to stem from basic societal mores that teach that the framework for sex is marriage, an institution not encouraged for adolescents. Baker also observes that the usual solution to the conflict entails suppression of sexual energy. He comments that "suppression always leads to psychic and somatic disturbances, but it helps him [the patient] avoid the conflict with society and with his own developed morals."

Other interpretations are closer to standard analytic practice, and involve pointing out and offering explanations for various resistances, and commenting on the patient-therapist relationship. Orgone therapy even includes the interpretation of dreams. The psychological components of orgone theory are designed to complement the somatic in the discharge of affect. Sometimes emotions are released most effectively by psychological means, such as reflection or interpretation, rather than direct manipulation of muscles. Baker maintains that if enough were known, and if the therapist were sufficiently perceptive, therapy would be entirely psychological.

In Reich's writing, he speaks of "word language" as opposed to "body language." In his later work, body language seems to gain primacy. Reich began by saying that consistent dissolving of character resistances would provide an avenue of approach to resolving conflicts, but this process came to be more and more physical rather than verbal. Finally, his criterion of success was "orgastic potency." That is, to break out of neurosis, it is necessary to abandon bodily inhibitory mechanisms and achieve orgastic discharge of dammed up energy. Affects break through after the patient yields his psychic defenses. This in turn requires the disruption of muscular armor. For as Reich put it, "As I have shown elsewhere, a traumatic infantile experience can have a present-day effect only if it is anchored in a rigid armor." The orgone therapist thus concentrates on muscular armor, breathing, and tension. Reich vehemently denied that this is a simple, mechanical process. He said, "We do not 'manipulate' mechanically; we induce emotions in the patients by letting them initiate willfully this or that emotional expression." This technique, he claims, leads to a slow but thorough overcoming of emotional blocks.

Orgone therapy is tailored to fit specific problems, and thus is more sophisticated and complex than the work of latter day emotivists like Arthur Janov. Suiting therapy to the patient is based on a rather standard analytic interpretation of various diagnostic categories. For example, in treating a masochist, Baker asserts that the strategy should be to turn the masochism into the sadism from whence it came, allowing the patient to express and discharge his hostile feelings directly. Depressed patients are encouraged to discharge tears, and also the rage thought to be at the bottom of the manifest depression. Baker consistently interprets the behavior of a patient who relies on intellectualization, as a defensive style. "If he is permitted to talk he will successfully evade his problems. He needs a great deal of character analysis—particularly of the defensive function of his intellect—and he must learn to face and tolerate his anxiety and guilt." Therapists are advised first to reassure an anxious patient, and then to encourage him to express his anxiety directly, by looking frightened and screaming. Later, aggressive hitting and raging are encouraged. On the other hand, aggressive patients are made to stop their aggression, which is described as a cover for anxiety. "A servile patient needs to be provoked into the anger his attitude is covering up; confronting him with that servility is effective." Although these formulations seem somewhat pat, Baker is aware that patients often merely go through the motions of expressing emotion. Therefore it is incumbent upon the therapist to work sensitively with each individual patient in order to achieve a real catharsis of feelings. This involves a consistent effort to overcome resistance and repression. As repressions are dissolved, buried emotions are expressed, beginning with the most superficial and proceeding to the deepest layers.

Reich had a great deal to say about the conflict between natural human demands and social institutions. While it is useful to separate his therapy from his ontological speculation, it is interesting to note that he believed that therapy was only one approach to achieving psychological wellbeing. In the long run, the hope of prevention lies in educating parents to permit and encourage emotional freedom in their children. Thus, Reich taught his patients and students that the real enemy was "the emotional plague," which is why man is born free, but is everywhere in chains. This plauge is related to genital frustration and the suppression of affect.

Reich's major contribution is that he recognized the concrete physical embodiment of "psychological" defenses and developed procedures for diminishing them. (It is of course only for convenience that we draw the artificial distinction between the "mental" and "physical" realms.) He brought a renewed respect for the life of the body into psychotherapy, without abandoning reason as a therapeutic tool. Unlike some contemporary emotivists, Reich's transition from an intellectual, analytic approach to a cathartic one was not simply reactive. Instead of substituting emotional expression for insight and understanding, Reich combined them in his therapy.

Although Reich himself sought to blend reason and emotion, mind and body, his influence has led to a reactive shift away from rationality in psychotherapy. The humanistic myth that surrender to feelings and passive acceptance of bodily impulses leads to happy and productive living has spawned in Reich's wake, therapies devoted to purging, not liberating emotions. Reich consistently emphasized the value of catharsis lay in freeing people to express and be guided by their feelings; he did not regard catharsis as an end in itself, or believe that emotions are an unnecessary evil to be discharged and expunged.

Reich recognized that cathartic discharge, together with renewed awareness and acceptance of feelings, was an incomplete goal for psychotherapy. If catharsis within therapy were sufficient to produce lasting change, then temporary breaching of defenses would be all that would be necessary. But with no lasting reduction in defensive armament, the post-cathartic patient may simply begin a new cycle of repression. Reich therefore labored, not so much to produce catharsis, as to reduce the defensiveness that prevents it. Furthermore, he helped his patients to learn about their armoring, so that defenses could be less readily reconstituted after therapy. Catharsis combined with insight into the nature of defenses helps patients to counteract repression long after therapy is over.

Reich ultimately came to believe that to change persons, society must be changed. Liberated people, he suggested, could not thrive in a repressive society. Unfortunately, he advanced these views in terms of a rather bizarre metaphysics. Cathartic therapists following Reich have generally avoided the metaphysics, but tended to cluster in communities. It seems to us that psychotherapy and social reform are separable. However, withdrawal and cloistering seem to follow from a failure to develop coping skills in addition to achieving catharsis and emotional openness. While therapists often emphasize either catharsis or coping, a combination of the two seems a more appropriate solution.

Reich's influence can be recognized in a wide variety of current approaches to psychotherapy, and especially in the renewed attention to physical means of treatment. Whereas traditional therapeutic practice, since Freud, stressed mind over body, Reich opened the way to a combination of somatic and psychic therapies for psychological distress. Nowhere is Reich's influence more directly manifested than in Alexander Lowen's work.

Alexander Lowen: Body as Character

Lowen's approach, which bears the cumbersome title of Bioenergetic Analysis and Therapy (7, 8), offers nothing original theoretically but does contain some interesting extensions of Reich's therapeutic technique. Lowen's understanding and treatment of man is as a mind-body unit. More than merely a nice conceptual extension, this viewpoint has very practical consequences. Lowen analyzes not only the psychological life of his patients, but also their physical nature, including body structure and movement. He points out that changes in muscles and posture are not just the result of repression of feelings, but are the mechanisms of repression itself. Thus, the distinction between two forms of energy, physical and psychic, is rejected. Lowen speaks of only one type of "fundamental energy in the human body"—bioenergy.

Lowen's rejection of any mind-body dualism has enabled him to concretize some of the structural aspects of Freudian theory. For example, he considers the musculature as the mechanism by which the superego exercises control. It is "unconscious" merely because the process goes on without awareness. As Lowen puts it (7), "But the muscles which are subject to the inhibitions of the superego are chronically tense, chronically contracted, and removed from perception, so that the individual is unaware that this part of his muscular system is nonfunctioning in certain ways." If impulses are restrained by muscular contraction, it follows that a great deal can be learned about what is being restrained by studying the tense musculature. Furthermore, chronically tense muscles often lead to structural and postural alterations that are easily seen.

Thus, in Bioenergetics, inadequacies of posture and movement are analyzed and related to deficiencies in personality development: the person with a ramrod-straight back and military bearing is apt to be personally inflexible and rigid. The idea that study of a person's carriage may provide some clues to his character is not unreasonable; however, Lowen advances many formulas that seem too pat and oversimplified. "Retracted shoulders represent repressed anger, a holding back of the impulse to strike; raised shoulders are related to fear; square shoulders express the manly attitude of shouldering one's responsibilities; bowed shoulders convey the sense of burden, the weight of a heavy load." Only when such formulations are used as hypotheses to be confirmed or disconfirmed will violence not be done to individuality.

According to Lowen, physical movement is inexorably related to character. As a child learns how to behave, he also learns muscular control and coordination. Many responses become automatic and characterological, so that character is molded by and reflected in muscular activity. However, Lowen probably overstates the case when he says that character is functionally identical with muscular armor.

Lowen identifies the etiology of neuroses with trauma and deprivation. These in turn result in the repression of emotions and impulses. This is, of course, one of Freud's earliest ideas, antedating the conflict theory of neurosis. Feelings, Lowen believes, are part of man's irrational nature: they are denied or repressed at great cost. Suppression of grief or anger, for example, may leave a person subject to depressions and violent rages. When feelings become encapsulated by muscular contraction, psychopathology may result. Children learn to suppress their feelings from parents who in turn learned it from their own parents. "The intolerance some mothers show towards a baby's crying reveals the degree to which they have suppressed their own feelings."

One of the basic aims of Bioenergetic therapy is the abreaction and releasing of traumatic experiences of infancy. Lowen gives central importance to catharsis. "The emotional significance of muscle tension is not adequately understood. The increased emotional conflicts of childhood are structured in the body by chronic muscular tensions that enslave the individual by limiting his motility and capacity for feeling. These tensions, which grip the body—mold it, split it, and distort— must be eliminated before one can achieve inner freedom."

In one case study (7), Lowen uses catharsis to relieve blocked emotion resulting from a single traumatic incident. The patient is a woman who complains that she is unable to develop an attachment to a man. Despite meeting many, she could never establish an intimate and lasting relationship. Her history revealed that some years prior to coming for therapy she had witnessed her husband's death. At that time, "She did not utter a sound but turned and walked away. At no time did she release the feeling in tears. She separated from their mutual friends and soon after enlisted for service with the armed forces. As she lay on the couch during the second session I could sense from her breathing a catch in her throat. Palpitation revealed a powerful spasm of the throat musculature. A quick pressure on these muscles produced a scream of fright which was followed by deep crying. The traumatic incident flashed into her mind. During several succeeding sessions I produced the screams and the crying. Each time she relived the horrifying experience. Then it was over. I continued therapy for a while longer and shortly afterward she fell in love with a man and they were married." As this quote demonstrates, Lowen believes that depression can be prevented by venting anger or tears. If disappointments can be relieved by crying, the person is able to work them through effectively. This is the natural infantile reaction to frustration, and Lowen believes that in adult life as well emotional discharge is an effective means of releasing certain tensions. "A feeling of loss," he says, "calls for tears."

Bioenergetic therapy generally lasts many months, and follows a regular pattern. First, a very thorough history is taken by which the therapist tries to record a complete developmental sketch. The therapist also makes a careful physical study of his patient, including body structure and specific tensions or blocks. The most striking feature of the therapy is the extensive use of physical means to reduce defenses and achieve catharsis. However, depth analysis along characterological lines is also carried on at the same time.

One of the early tasks in therapy is to help the patient become aware of specific areas of physical tension. The majority of people, Lowen finds, are unaware of most of the tensions in their bodies, except perhaps for headaches or lower back pain. He helps patients experience their chronic stiffness and limited motility by subjecting various muscle groups to some stress. For example, he may have a patient try to arch his back. The experience of being able to do so only to a limited extent and with considerable pain may make him realize that these muscles have been chronically contracted so long that they have partially lost their elasticity. Because he believes that the capacity for emotional expression is proportionate to the degree of muscular coordination, Lowen devotes a great deal of attention to developing a full repertoire of expressive movements. Following Reich, he places heavy emphasis on full and deep respiration. Breathing is deepened by various exercises—Lowen prefers to call them "positions"—designed to reduce diaphragmatic blocks. He uses some passive positions, such as having the patient arch his back over a chair and attempt to breathe deeply. This is usually followed by a number of active, expressive movements. Here again, Lowen tends to run through a standard procedure. For example, he routinely has patients strike the couch as a means of releasing anger. He also has patients lie back on the couch and kick it with their feet. When the patient can let himself go, the striking or kicking leads to emotional catharsis. The patient may feel "carried away," surrender his usual controls and freely vent his feelings and impulses.

> Every patient has something to be angry about, otherwise he would not be in therapy. It can be shown that he was always afraid to express his anger. It can be pointed out to him that a healthy person is capable of identifying with a feeling of anger sufficiently to permit him to execute the movements of hitting or kicking in a coordinated and integrated manner. When the patient realizes that his incoordination reflects his inability to express feeling, he accepts the physical procedures outlined earlier as necessary to his improvement.

Any therapist who has worked for the catharsis of painful feelings has probably encountered conscious resistance by patients who say that it is painful to experience such feelings and who do not want to suffer. Lowen deals with this by explaining that the pain of experiencing emotions is like a frost-bitten finger, which hurts only when it begins to thaw out. He also explains the fact that the release of unhappy feelings is usually followed by tearful feelings of desire and affection, by saying that when the frozen exterior is thawed, longing for contact and warmth erupts in crying. Lowen stresses the therapeutic value of discharging the sadness over merely recognizing it. "It is one thing to be able to recognize that one is sad; it is another to be able to cry."

Stanley Keleman: Bioenergetic Workshops

Neo-Reichian therapy is also conducted by Stanley Keleman in the milieu of California's growth centers. His approach (9) consists almost entirely of physical work aimed at releasing feelings and chronic muscular contractions. Keleman encourages his clients to hit, kick, scream, and yield to their impulses. In short, he teaches people to give up control in order to increase energy and open themselves to sensate experience. Keleman describes his work as "re-eroticizing" the body. He believes, in common with other humanistic psychologists, that forces of "self-actualization" are somehow contained within each of us and need only some assistance to become evident. This faith in mysterious "inner" forces is implied when Keleman says, "Every deep contraction prevents surrendering to the spontaneous, the mysterious, the undirected movements, perceptions and expressions of our authentic selves."

Keleman conducts large workshops in which one individual at a time is invited to come up to the front and work on his problems. Participants are required to wear bathing suits so that their muscles are in plain view. Keleman sizes his subjects up physically and psychologically, and recommends appropriate physical activity to mobilize energy. This may involve lying down, deep breathing, or kicking and beating. All are designed to increase awareness of physical underdevelopment and restraint in the hope of eventually eliminating the need for psychophysiological compensation and adjustment. Keleman feels that it is vitally important to discharge emotions as well, and the transcripts of proceedings at some of his workshops show that he makes a fair number of interpretations, many of which seem to lead to emotional catharsis. For example: "I see the tightness in your neck and the tightness in your buttocks (you are squeezing there) as being your expression of 'I won't reach out,' or 'I'm not going to speak up'." When these interpretations are accurate—felt to have meaning by the patient—they often lead to the discharge of feelings.

Lowen's and Keleman's approach—learning to strip away defenses through body action—has a simplistic appeal; and for those patients who are groping to find reasons for their emptiness, learning to shift attention from the intellect to the body may be very helpful. However, losing the mind in order to find the body is a technique that is probably most useful for obsessive personalities and middle-class neurotics. Unfortunately, no attempt is made to screen appropriate candidates for body therapy, or to limit attention to particular types of problems. What may be useful for a college professor, long out of touch with his physical being, may not be useful for an impulsive, hedonistic adolescent. Secondly, the assumption that *all* emotional conflicts involve a distortion of body movement is unsupported and overgeneralized. Reich's genius enabled him to see that many habitual psychic constrictions were translated into chronic muscular rigidity; his followers emphasize this aspect of his work without paying due attention to the complex nature of psychological conflict. Conflict ingrained over many years cannot simply be dissolved by loosening the body and loosing its feelings. This loosening process may indeed stimulate latent conflictual impulses, and perhaps enable people to work on more appropriate solutions. However, the reasons for the original restraint, which are embedded in day-to-day living, don't suddenly disappear. The de-armored patient must develop new strategies to protect himself from pain, and relearn coping strategies. To the extent that bioenergetic therapists lose sight of this, they may be doing their clients a disservice by leaving them relatively defenseless.

Rolfing and the Alexander Technique

A number of current practitoners address their therapeutic energies solely to the physical body. Most notable among these are adherents of "Rolfing" (10, 11) and the Alexander technique (12). Although direct descendents of Reich, these physical therapies have at least a spiritual inheritance from Alfred Adler, who noted that personality may develop to compensate for physical deficits and weaknesses. These physical therapies are designed to ameliorate basic physical disharmonies in order to eliminate the need for compensatory strivings.

In *Body and Mature Behavior*, Moshé Feldenkrais (13) wrote that the somatic element is vastly more important in producing personality change than is generally realized. Since neurotic behavior is part and parcel of structural and postural damage, the cure must be applied to body as well as mind. "In short, a recurrent emotional state always appears together with the attitude of body and the vegetative state with which it was conditioned earlier. . . . I contend that all successful analysis, whatever technique is employed, is invariably accompanied, and probably preceded, by an alteration of posture and a change of muscular habit both in body and face." He argues that even Freud's use of the couch worked by eliminating the effects of gravity. This relaxes habitual tension in antigravity muscles, which is a first step to the unlearning of anxiety. Feldenkrais prescribes exercises to help restore healthful posture. For someone whose deferential attitude has led to a chronically slumped spine and bent head, he suggests lying on the floor (thus freeing the antigravity muscles in the neck), gently lifting the head and bending the knees. This apparently eases the spine back into a more healthful configuration.

This approach was developed much further by F. M. Alexander (12). The Alexander technique involves no vigorous exercises or deep breathing, but rather changes body alignment by an increasing awareness of posture, the use of suggestion, and gentle repositioning of limbs. Alexander was an Australian would-be actor whose voice failed. He developed a method of physical re-education to deal with his problem, and eventually moved to London where he developed a flourishing practice. His method is designed to teach graceful freedom in mind and body, and works primarily by helping people inhibit learned patterns of muscular tension and postural restraint. That is, the emphasis is on preventing misdirected activity. The same philosophy applied to the emotions suggests that constraints against the expression of feeling should be lifted. However, Alexander did not draw this conclusion, and in fact warns against allowing great freedom of emotional expression.

Another offshoot from Reich's orgone therapy which focuses almost exclusively on somatic therapy is Ida Rolf's Structural Integration (10, 11). Rolf is a biochemist and physiologist, who believes that body structure is the incarnation of personality, and that tense muscles are the physical equivalent of psychological defense mechanisms. Muscles tensed to suppress feelings gradually become functionally impaired and painful. If the suppression is not longstanding, a combination of psychological support and physical pressure on the tense muscles may relieve the block and release the feelings; however, at an advanced stage of chronic tension the muscles cannot thus be relaxed, since the elasticity of muscle tissue becomes impaired. This is analogous to repression, which unlike suppression cannot be wilfully abandoned.

Once chronic tension has reached an advanced state, Structural Integration, or Rolfing, attempts to produce fascial reorganization through deep massage (the fascial envelope is the thin layer of tissue over muscles, and is what loses elasticity). Dr. Rolf proceeds in a regular sequence to manipulate and massage, with her knuckles, the fascia in all of the body's major muscle groups. Deep emotional discharge typically accompanies Rolfing, as the physical manipulation stimulates old painful memories. Dr. Rolf herself recognizes the importance of this cathartic component of her work, but is apparently content to simply allow it to happen, without directly concentrating on it. Other practitioners, such as William Schutz (11) explicitly recommend integrating the emotional discharge with the physical side of the experience.

A purely physical and mechanical procedure like Rolfing is clearly not a form of psychotherapy. We discuss it here because it does reflect the fact that proponents of catharsis share with physical therapists an implicit faith in the wisdom of the body, and believe that freedom of movement, joined to liberation of emotions and impulses, will help people to lead satisfying and productive lives. However, even though therapy that emphasizes man's physical being is a useful antidote to cerebralism, it remains incomplete as therapy because it neglects to consider the impact of continuing challenges in family, vocations, and community. This therapy mistakenly assumes that if the body and its emotions can be liberated, the difficulties that caused the problems in the first place will somehow automatically be resolved.

People become more open, physically and emotionally, following somatic therapy, and so they have to learn to renegotiate the tensions and conflicts of normal living in this new and unfamiliar state. Unfortunately, with controls released, this renegotiation is not always an improvement. Some impulses, better restrained, may lead to trouble and pain, bringing increased suffering followed by a re-establishment of rigid defenses. These renewed conflicts require therapeutic planning and guidance. Therefore, somatic treatments should be considered as part of a program of therapeutic hygiene, so that whatever desirable effects may be achieved through physical awareness and expression can be nurtured as the newly opened person learns to cope with conflict in his more vulnerable state.

Gestalt Therapy

Gestalt therapy has become one of the most popular recent approaches to psychotherapy, as reflected not only in the number of therapists who identify themselves with this approach, but also by the wide circulation among the general public of popularized accounts of Gestalt therapy. Largely the creation of one man, Frederick S. Perls, Gestalt therapy has been in the vanguard of the humanistic psychology movement. Perls himself had a background of medical training and instruction in psychoanalysis. He received analytic supervision from Wilhelm Reich, and later. through his work with Kurt Goldstein, became influenced by the ideas of Gestalt psychology and adopted its emphasis on phenomenology and immediate perceptive experience.

A second principle Perls took from Gestalt psychology is the model of "organismic" self-regulation (14). Needs and feelings, he wrote, disappear once they have been satisfied or discharged. This process is like the completion of a "gestalt," or achieving a sense of closure. Yawning and sighing are examples of discharge by organismic self-regulation. When the process is blocked, anxiety is produced. Therefore, to dissipate anxiety, a cathartic process of need-satisfaction or emotional discharge is encouraged. As early as 1947, Perls recognized that restoration of balanced self-regulation is often not a simple process, because powerful resistances may have to be overcome. Eventually he developed an extensive set of potent therapeutic techniques to facilitate this return to spontaneous discharge. Like Reich, Perls concentrated on reducing resistance to recapture spontaneity. In his earliest major work, *Ego, Hunger and Agression* (15) he outlined a theory of culture as potentially devitalizing; it is noteworthy that every major therapeutic approach in which catharsis is preeminent contains a similar notion.

Perls started with the observation that socially-required self-control is often achieved only at the cost of repression and devitalization of the personality. In the extreme case, neurosis is produced. The therapeutic correction of this imbalance is described as a regression to a state of unblocked biological health. However, the avoidance of feeling and desire which is basic to neurosis impairs the liberation of natural functioning. Having begun with these premises, Perls went on to emphasize procedures for undoing resistances and avoidances. "If one wants to draw water from a tap, one would not dream of squeezing the water out of the pipe; one would simply loosen the resistance, the tap, which holds the water back."

Although catharsis does play a key role in Gestalt therapy, the essence of the approach is an attempt to heighten awareness of immediate personal experience (16). This focus is in obvious contrast both to Freud's emphasis on the past, and Adler's concern with the future. Less obviously, it also differs from approaches that concentrate on the "here-and-now" in the Rankian tradition. Perls' emphasis on the present does not refer to the patient's current life situation or even merely to the therapy relationship. Rather the attempt is made to help the patient experience what is happening (what he is doing), instant by instant. In Gestalt therapy, reporting the experience of the moment holds a place as central as does free association in psychoanalysis (17). Perls summarized (18) the importance of "experiencing the now" in this formula: "Now = experience = awareness = reality." Thus, Gestalt therapy aims at helping people become aware of their immediate experience and encouraging them to take responsibility for their behavior. Many of the techniques employed are designed to keep the patient in constant contact with what he is doing. He is instructed to act fully and completely, and to become entirely aware of his behavior, even his unconscious movements (19):

> A constricted, overinhibited man is tapping his finger on the table while a woman in the group talks on and on. Asked if he has anything to comment about what the woman is saying, he denies much concern with it but continues the tapping. He is asked then to intensify the tapping, to tap louder and more vigorously, and to continue, until he feels more fully what he is doing. His anger mounts quickly and in a minute or so he is pounding on the table and expressing vehemently his disagreement with the woman. He declares that she is "just like my wife," but in addition to the historical perspective, he has had an experiential glimpse of his excessive control of his strong assertive feelings and the possibility of more immediate and hence less violent expression of them.

Although the Gestalt therapists are more directly concerned with facilitating awareness of immediate experience than with emotional expression, the two are inexorably intertwined. Patterns of resisting and of avoiding experiencing the moment lead to emotional isolation and alienation. When awareness of experience is blocked, so are feelings. This repression leaves a person with little energy and a great deal of what the Gestaltists call "unfinished business."

Unfinished business—incomplete experience and unchanneled excitement—is a consequence of blocked awareness. Need cycles are not completed; tension is aroused but not reduced; feeling mounts but is not discharged. The flow of behavior is clogged with unexpressed action; vitality and flexibility suffer in the ensuing constriction and frustration.

As therapy proceeds and the patient becomes aware of his immediate experience, feelings will be aroused, but generally they are repressed quickly and automatically as defenses come into play to interrupt awareness of affect. Open expression of needs and emotions is habitually repressed, and this process involves a muscular holding back of impulses to discharge emotions. This conception of repression as largely a motor phenomenon is consistent with Reich's position.

As Naranjo has pointed out, the technique of focusing on immediate experiences in a therapeutic session tends to elicit particularly significant feelings. If there is no major external emotional stimulus, the feelings that emerge are likely to reflect characterological concerns. Thus if a patient feels embarrassment, he may become aware that he is ashamed of himself. An obsessive person may begin to brood over what is going to happen, and either fear or hostility may come into focus. As the patient becomes aware of his sensations and emotions, the Gestalt therapist helps him to work them through. "Unfinished business" is finished. Feelings emerge spontaneously when the defensive, phony, layer is broken through, and suddenly freed, pent-up (imploded) feelings will explode. Perls' model of personality has four layers, the phony layer, the phobic impasse, the implosive, and finally the explosive layer. When the explosive layer is unblocked, the emotion is transformed into movement, or discharge.

The implosion (emotional paralysis) becomes explosion. The

death layer comes to life, and this explosion is the link-up with the authentic person who is *capable of* experiencing and expressing his emotions. There are four basic kinds of explosions from the death layer. There is the explosion of genuine grief if we work through a loss or death that has not been assimilated. There is the explosion into orgasm in sexually blocked people. There is the explosion into anger, and also the explosion into joy, laughter, joi de vivre. These explosions connect with the authentic personality, with the true self.

Note that Perls refers to the constriction of joyful emotions as well as more painful ones. This fits with his notion that feelings are a valued aspect of experience, not just something to be expelled. Usually, however, we are conditioned to suppress emotional discharge. For example, sadness is generally characterized by a dejected posture, drawn mouth, and empty facial expression. If, as part of holding back, the patient tries to smile and destroy the pattern associated with sadness, he thus interferes with both awareness and discharge of the emotion. The result is that all sorts of feelings and impulses are restrained by chronic muscular contraction. The therapeutic goal is to unblock the need-fulfillment pattern, which is defined as helping emerging figures (as in figure-ground) to find expression (20).

> If the patient seems ready to cry, for example, if there is an emerging activity the therapist can see "on the surface," if he notices squeezing and contractions in the face and perhaps a glistening of the eyes, he knows that the figure of crying is emerging. Suppose, however, that the impulse is being held back by the patient. The therapist works to unblock the impulse so that it can organize the field.

This unblocking involves teaching the patient how he prevents himself from crying. Thus, much of the process initiated through enhanced awareness of feelings is completed through awareness of defenses.

Another clinical example of catharsis in Gestalt therapy highlights the notion of blocked emotions as unfinished situations. Here is a woman who suffered from headaches after a girl friend insulted her (15):

She says that after the friend's insult she felt like crying, but did not shed a single tear. This looks as if crying were converted into headache. But just as I cannot conceive how repressed libido can change into a headache, so I cannot accept such a conversion of crying. Every conjuring trick has a rational explanation. Identified with dignity and pride, she was incapable of identifying herself with the biological need of finding relief in crying, so she contracted her eye and throat muscles to stop the flow of tears. Intense muscular contraction leads to pain; the squeezing of head muscles results in headache . . . her headache is the signal of an unfinished situation; she is unable to finish, get rid of her resentment, because she has a tremendous reluctance to let herself go.

The ultimate goal is not to expel and be rid of feelings, but to undo repressions and to become aware of and responsive to the actions that feelings prompt us to. Catharsis focuses attention on and liberates suppressed feelings, thus freeing the patient to respond with well-modulated affect in the present. In addition, as the following quotation from Polster (21) demonstrates, enhanced perceptive and cognitive awareness are apt to follow catharsis.

"Now I remember that horrible night that my first husband had a heart attack." Another lengthy pause followed where she appeared under great tension and absorption. Then she said in a hushed tone that she was aware again of the pain, the anxiety, and the whole experience of that night. At this point, she gave in to deep, heartfelt crying, which lasted about one minute. When she finished she looked up and said, "I guess I still miss him." Now the vagueness was gone and I could experience the reality and the wholeness of her relationship with her husband. The clear transformation from superficiality to depth was apparently brought on by the buildup in sensation through self-awareness and concentration, letting her own sensations lead the way rather than her ideas or explanations.

As Fagan (22) puts it, "One of the major contributions of Gestalt therapy is the power of its techniques, which makes possible the very rapid reaching of deep emotional levels."

Catharsis thus plays a central role in Gestalt therapy.

However, Gestalt therapists warn that uncovering deep layers of emotion places special responsibilities on the therapist. For one thing it is important to recognize the emergence of feelings, and without shrinking, to help catalyze their expression. Shepherd (28), for example, writes, "Since Gestalt techniques facilitate access to and release of intense affect, a therapist using this approach must neither be afraid nor inept in allowing the patient to follow through and finish the experience of grief, rage, fear or joy." Fagan, on the other hand, cautions that since one of the major contributions of Gestalt therapy is the potency of its techniques which makes possible the very rapid reaching of deep layers of emotion, there is a danger of overusing technique at the expense of genuineness and humanness. Furthermore, there is also the danger of opening a patient to the experience of long-buried feelings and then not being properly supportive of him during a period when he is exquisitely vulnerable.

In addition to its potential danger, catharsis is thought to have limited usefulness, as Perls himself has pointed out. He says that emotions are not merely to be discharged and gotten rid of, according to what he calls Freud's "excremental theory" of emotions. Emotions, he says, are part of our natural expression, part of relating to the world. It is important to discharge the energy of emotions blocked from expression, but following this it is critical to learn to deal effectively with affect outside of therapy, in "the real world." That is, catharsis may be a valuable prescription for psychotherapy, but it is not a prescription for good living. Abreaction of murderous rage in a psychotherapeutic situation of minimal constraint may have immense value; but the free expression of hostile feelings toward an important person in the environment may lead to disaster. In fact, the desire to turn emoting into a way of life, in a culture that does not permit such freedom, is the motive force behind the establishment of special communities among those who share a common belief that feelings should always be expressed.

In describing a happy balance between suppression of and complete openness with feelings, Perls uses the metaphor of a castle. If a person is too resistant to expressing feelings, he is like a castle with a locked door and a misplaced key. On the other hand, if he has too little restraint on the expression of feelings, he is like a castle with gaps and breaks in the walls. In brief, Perls treats emotions as gestalts that can be complete or incomplete. In the healthy person aroused affect becomes part of the "figure" or need state, is discharged, and eventually is replaced by others. In the maladjusted, this process is interrupted, and emotions recede from figure into ground. The result is confusion, indecision, and stultified behavior.

Perls cites (15) sadness as an example of an incomplete emotion. "Sadness, for instance, can last for hours and days if it does not gather enough momentum for discharge in an outburst of crying which will restore the organismic equilibrium." "Suppression of crying is harmful as it prevents the organism from adjusting itself to loss or frustration." "The unpleasant character of negative emotions entails the wish to avoid the emotions themselves which, however, cannot change back into their pleasant opposites if we do not allow—by discharge—their change from over-tension to bearable tension, and further on to the organismic zero-point." Ideally, then, after blocked emotions are discharged in psychotherapy, the adaptive person will discharge emotions in small quantities before they again build up and bind energy.

Perls' is the least simple of the evocative therapies. In place of a singular focus on expressiveness, Gestalt therapy includes catharsis along with awareness and responsibility. Indeed, it is awareness rather than discharge that is its primary focus. Renewed awareness of momentary experience leads not only to catharsis of old hurts, but also to fresh and surprising perspectives and enhanced perception. Perls' accomplishment is that he both makes this recognition explicit, and offers a program of therapy to deal with the post-cathartic experience.

Emotional discharge, carried to its logical extreme, leads to inaction, just as does emotional paralysis. If feelings are nothing but something to be gotten rid of, an employer angered by an employee's lateness might save his feelings for therapy, rather than try to correct the situation. In Gestalt therapy, such helplessness would be considered unacceptable. Not only must the patient become aware of and express feelings, but ultimately he must take responsibility and learn to be guided by them. Personal growth may be something more than merely social adjustment, but surely it is not less than dealing effectively with the environment.

Gestalt therapy shares with the body therapies an emphasis on awareness, sensitivity, and expressiveness. Both aim at facilitating grace and vitality. The body therapists try to liberate energy and flexibility by physical re-education; similarly, Gestalt therapists hope to achieve excitement and change by focusing on the intensity of cognitive, emotional, and visceral experience. Where they differ is in the extent to which they deal with the dual process nature of conflicts. Conflicts involve both impulses and counterforces. Body therapists and emotivists tend to oversimplify by suggesting that liberation of impulses resolves conflicts. But liberated feelings and impulses will again be blocked and submerged if nothing is done to resolve counterforces. Needs neither disappear nor automatically lead to gratification following awareness. Likewise, though discharge may help eliminate residual effects of suppressed feelings, further suppression will follow unless the conditions that led to blockage are altered. Conflict that results in blocked feelings and impulses is like an argument between two people. First one person expresses a point of view, then the other disagrees. If the disagreement becomes acrimonious, both people, fatigued and despairing, may withdraw into silence. Nothing is settled; communication has simply been broken off. Solution of this impasse requires more than encouraging one of the people to express himself. Instead, both need to be heard from, and some resolution or compromise achieved. In the same way, the resolution of an emotional conflict requires more than awareness and expression of feelings. Both impulses and counterforces must be evoked, so that a new or compromise solution can be found. Perls' recognition of this dual aspect of conflict resolution distinguishes his work from that of the purely emotive theorists.

In addition to recognizing that feelings are part of needs which require action as much as ventilation, Perls was also aware that not all impulses can be gratified. Experience and catharsis of blocked feelings play an essential, but only partial role in conflict resolution. Awareness and full contact with feelings lead inevitably to discharge; what follows, however, can either be conflict resolution or re-entrenchment. Gestalt therapists do not leave this to chance; instead they use the therapy to help work through conflicts following cathartic ventilation.

Harvey Jackins' Re-Evaluation Counseling

One recent approach to psychotherapy, Harvey Jackins' Re-Evaluation Counseling (6, 24), relies almost exclusively on catharsis to produce therapeutic change. Jackins has not had formal training in the behavioral sciences. A former labor union organizer, he developed his approach in 1950 while trying to help a friend's friend cope with a psychological crisis. Jackins' efforts to reason with this troubled person were complicated by the fact that each time they sat down together the man started crying. Eventually Jackins decided that crying might be as helpful as talking. As he listened and gave support, a recurrent storm of bottled up emotion gushed out. After each such outburst, the man was able to think more rationally and constructively. Jackins has remained without professional or academic involvement; not surprisingly, his theory is simplistic and the techniques of his Re-Evaluation Counseling are quite pragmatic.

The experience of helping a severely troubled person convinced Jackins that a professional, therapist-patient relationship may not be necessary to resolve painful psychological problems. He thereupon established groups of lay Re-Evaluation counselors. This self-help approach is called co-counseling, because participants take turns helping and being helped. After hearing an introductory lecture on the theory behind Re-Evaluation Counseling, interested persons may apply to learn the techniques of co-counseling through an eight-week series of didactic and experiential classes. Teachers accept as students only those persons who seem to have sufficient personal resources to enable them to perform the role of helpful listeners as well as receivers of help. Those judged not suitable for the co-counseling model are referred elsewhere for therapy—what Jackins calls "one-way counseling."

Jackins has insisted that a fairly strict set of procedures be followed by teachers of co-counseling classes. This insures a high degree of consistency among the various Re-Evaluation Counseling communities, and tends to limit the likelihood that teachers will impose their own idiosyncratic ideas and techniques on their students.

In the introductory classes, students learn the techniques and philosophy of Re-Evaluation Counseling, and are encouraged to meet regularly for co-counseling sessions with other members of the initiated community. Advanced classes for more experienced co-counselors are also conducted, and some of the participants may go on to become teachers. A fairly extensive network of co-counselors has thus been established, opening a variety of channels for self-help. Jackins himself, who is a forceful speaker and a gifted clinician, travels widely, giving lectures and conducting workshops.

Somers' evaluation (25) of the theoretical framework of Re-Evaluation Counseling places it squarely in the mainstream of humanistic psychology by virtue of its holistic approach; its value-based orientation; the democratization of the therapeutic relationship and its authenticity; and the emphasis on positive, creative, loving, and cooperating human forces as opposed to an illness model. Jackins begins with the assumption that lovingness, zest, and rational intelligence are basic to man's nature. If allowed to develop in an ideal environment, each of us would be characterized by vastly greater quantities of these three basic qualities than most now possess. These assumptions are more than abstract theorizing; they are imbued in the Re-Evaluation therapist, who in turn communicates this attitude to his clients.

Briefly stated, it is Jackins' notion that these core qualities become eroded by the repression of emotions. As he develops, a child experiences various distressing events which evoke noxious affect. The unsocialized child deals with this noxious affect with spontaneous emotional catharsis, which Jackins calls "discharge." Unhappily, with socialization, discharge, this natural process of recovery, becomes blocked, for in our culture, the direct expression and discharge of feelings is usually taboo. From an early age, we hear, "Big boys don't cry," "Don't feel bad," "Don't be angry, "You didn't really want that, anyway," and so on. In short, we are taught not to discharge feelings. This pattern of emotional suppression is so ingrained that we respond to it almost reflexively. If someone cries in our presence, we grow anxious and typically offer comfort by urging him to stop. "Don't cry. It'll be all right." According to Jackins this happens because discharge is mistakenly identified with the pain that stimulates it. However, discharge is not the hurt. Tears are not grief. They are the means of expressing and recovering from emotional pain. But as Somers says,

Through our developing years we are conditioned to the view that heavy discharge, especially crying and trembling, are "wrong," painful, and even a sign of decompensation. Sobbing and trembling only lead to decompensation when they are aborted and the distress continues to mount in the person, leading to self-defeating control and coping mechanisms. The acquired social meaning of crying can be so embarrassing, humiliating, "unmasculine," etc. that the crying may be perceived as painful.

A malignant process is thus maintained in which "chronic patterns" (compare Reich's "character armor") develop to ward off feelings, because experiencing feelings without the opportunity to discharge them is frustrating. Jackins believes that undischarged feelings tie up a certain amount of rational energy, and that the effect is cumulative. In psychoanalytical terms, the ego maintains repressions at the cost of creative responsiveness in the present. The more repressed emotion a person has, the more he is likely to react nonrationally to future situations. Furthermore, the invidious nature of these un-discharged feelings is such that they are easily restimulated by like experiences. A woman with unexpressed feelings of anger toward her domineering mother will not only have less rational energy, but she will also tend to overreact to domineering peo-ple encountered in her adult life, responding to them not so much as new individuals than as reminders of her mother's domination. The depth of her reaction will depend on the ex-tent of her residual feelings of anger toward her mother. Therefore, whenever a patient describes a strong emotional reaction to some current situation, Jackins suggests following up by asking what previous experiences it reminds her of.

Jackins proposes that we must get in touch with and dis-charge repressed feelings from the past and learn to do the same in the future. In counseling, discharge is thought to free up the core qualities of lovingness, zestfulness, and rationality. After discharge, the client is said to be able to achieve insight ("re-evaluation") into his problems due to his increased flexi-ble energy. When sufficient emotional discharge takes place the client is freed from the stultified feelings and behavior left by the distress experiences, and the basic qualities of rationality, zest, and lovingness are then liberated. "The in-crease in rationality makes it possible to create the most effective solution for those conditions and people in one's life that continue to oppress and distress" (25).

Paradoxically, discharge is promoted by two seemingly antithetical maneuvers. First, the counselor gives "free attention." This simply means listening with undivided and undistracted attention while the client tells his story. Interpretation and analysis are eschewed in favor of just listening and "being with" the client. When questions are asked, they are meant to indicate interest and bring out vivid detail about what is being said, rather than aimed at explaining why things happened as they did. However, the counselor must also be alert to the client's defensive maneuvers ("control patterns"), and defeat the client's attempts to shield himself from truly experiencing his feelings. The client's task is not just to talk, but to reveal and discharge emotional pain. Doing so involves refocusing the client who attempts to avoid painful emotions, going over material until no further discharge is forthcoming, or even putting the client off balance by asking him not to smoke, or to change the rate or tone of his speech.

Jackins stresses the importance of the client's being aware of the reassuring presence of his concerned listener, the counselor, in order for discharge to occur. For if the client is totally enmeshed in the distressful material (typically an event from the past), he may merely relive the experience and, just as he was unable to discharge originally, still not be able to discharge. Thus a balance of attention must be maintained between awareness of the painful incident and awareness of the safety and support of the therapeutic relationship. With most clients the challenge is to increase their awareness of the distressing experiences. In fact, considerable ingenuity may be required of the counselor who must try various ploys such as role-playing, paradoxical expressions, or physical movements to make the emotional experience vivid once again. However, some clients, including psychotics or persons who have recently experienced severe distress, require considerable help to draw sufficient attention to the safety of the present. When this balance of attention is achieved, but discharge does not occur, then a control pattern must be operating. The simplicity of this theory clarifies the therapeutic task.

Different individuals require varying amounts of attention paid either to their distressful experiences or the safety of the present; in order to discharge, the same person may have varying needs with different experiences. For time-bound hurts, such as a minor embarrassment, focus on the experience itself may be sufficient to produce discharge. There are painful feelings so chronic that they seem almost part of the personality, however; feelings of worthlessness, loneliness, or anxiety that are constantly present save for infrequent moments of distraction. Jackins calls these characterological painful feelings, chronic patterns. In order to achieve discharge, the person mired down by such a chronic pattern must have his attention momentarily drawn away from it. Following this, the re-experience of the pain is felt sharply, rather than accepted as part of a state of equilibrium. A bereaved person may be so preoccupied with his loss, for instance, that the grieving necessary to work through mourning is never completed. Such a person may be obsessed with sad thoughts about his lost love, and even talk freely about her, but without catharsis. A shift of attention away from the sadness may be achieved by asking for happy memories of the lost one: how did they meet? what was their happiest time together? when did they first fall in love? By remembering his happiness, the bereaved person will be temporarily distracted from his chronic pain, and afterwards he is likely to become so painfully aware of the loss that he may sob and cry, perhaps for the first time.

Jackins believes that catharsis reduces tension and helps people to cope with traumatic experiences. A stronger claim is that cathartic discharge alone can alter basic character structure by changing chronic patterns. Jackins stops just short of making this strong claim. While he focuses on discharge and urges co-counselors to concentrate only on facilitating this aspect of counseling, he believes that discharge potentiates new insights and a rational re-evaluation of patterns of living.

In some measure, Jackins' emphasis on discharge may be a heuristic device to insure that co-counselors don't become directive advice-givers. The simplicity of his theory and technique makes it possible for him to teach members of the lay public to be helpful. He explicitly warns against efforts to structure or interfere with clients' re-evaluation, although he also maintains that such re-evaluation is critical to character change. Chronic patterns, which Jackins regards as basic aspects of personality, are enormously difficult to change. He points out that "Permissive counseling will not suffice to undo a chronic pattern, though it is usually quite sufficient for a latent one." Chronic patterns arise because of a history of unevaluated distress experiences. In resolving such patterns insightful re-evaluation is as essential as catharsis. Jackins differs from other theorists in his faith that such re-evaluation will follow cathartic discharge spontaneously, with no assistance from the counselor. Discharge is said to be the outward manifestation of a profound healing process which includes freshly clarified perception—thinking about and finally understanding experience in a new, more rational light.

Separating catharsis from attempts to achieve insight may be a productive tactic, whether one believes that insight spontaneously follows catharsis or requires working through in the therapeutic relationship. It seems unlikely that one can experience catharsis and cognitive restructuring at the same time; consequently, it seems wise to suspend attempts to understand experience until a full measure of catharsis has been achieved. Following intense discharge, with enhanced rationality, reconceptualization can occur; however, once deep layers of emotion have been ventilated, a trained therapist or experienced co-counselor can be quite helpful in facilitating new understanding. The danger to which Jackins speaks is that the helper may impose his own values and solutions on the client.

Is complete recovery possible? Jackins says yes, at least theoretically. Such a utopian standard may lead to two different outcomes. Buoyed by hope, some people may continue struggling toward ever greater health and happiness; or, others, striving for perfect adjustment, may never be content despite relatively high levels of functioning. In either case, Re-Evaluation Counseling will continue to be part of co-counselors' lives, and in this respect it is as much a social movement as a method of psychotherapy.

Although derived from a very different framework, Re-Evaluation Counseling is consistent with the basic philosophy of the community mental health model, in the sense that it is one way to utilize nonprofessionals for widespread early intervention. There is no reason that psychological helping need be the exclusive domain of mental health professionals and this voluntary association of peers for co-counseling does provide many flexible opportunities to aid in emotional growth. Furthermore, when co-counselors take turns helping and being helped, they profit from the "helper therapy" principle (26)— that is, the act of helping may itself be therapeutic because it builds a sense of worth and competency. Re-Evaluation Counseling is an example of valuable preventive self-help groups. Whether emotional catharsis is an effective vehicle for peer counseling, however, is a matter that requires further study.

Janov's Primal Therapy

The latest—and most sensational—form of cathartic treatment is Janov's primal therapy. Despite his own extravagant claims (1, 27) of a revolutionary new procedure with miraculous cures, Janov's theory and approach are clearly Freudian. Janov was a practicing analyst who moved from a focus on insight to stressing that the roots of neurosis lie in childhood trauma and repression, and that the cure is catharsis.

Janov's position is compellingly simple. The sole cause of psychopathology is blocked painful emotion, and the single cure is to re-experience these painful emotions. A growing child is so helpless that his parents must provide certain necessities if he is to grow to be a happy and healthy adult. These requirements include affection and stimulation as well as food and shelter. When these needs are frustrated, the child experiences traumatic distress, what Janov calls "primal pain." This pain is escaped by repressing awareness of the needs, and substituting symbolic gratification. Thus a child whose parents rarely demonstrate love for him except for praising his accomplishments may become an adult driven to achieve. However, since the satisfaction sought is symbolic, the real needs are never recognized or gratified and thus a self-perpetuating neurosis is established. Janov says that suppressed needs create neurotic tension (anxiety). The avoidance of anxiety then becomes one of the major motivating forces in the neurotic's life. All the symptoms of neurosis are ways of draining the tension resultant from repressed pain. But since they don't eliminate the primal pain, a vicious circle is maintained. Primal pains and their neurotic sequelae are permanent, until and unless the person becomes aware of and fully experiences them. This is extremely unlikely outside of therapy, because the primal experiences lie deeply buried in memory. Childhood sufferings and frustrations are often unconscious because some occurred prior to the development of consciousness (or pre-language according to Sullivan); and because parents pass on the suppression of emotions that they themselves learned at an early age.

Although he speaks mostly of neurosis, Janov also applies his theory to psychoses as well as to other patterns of maladptive living such as alcoholism, homosexuality, schizophrenia, and drug addiction. Of the heroin addict, Janov says: "Heroin is pressed into service when the neurosis cannot suppress Pain. . . . Some neurotics can feel better with the use of marijuana but marijuana is far too mild for the Pain of the heroin addict. It may be that the heroin user started with marijuana but graduated to stronger drugs when marijuana couldn't do the job. . . . In any case, it isn't marijuana which leads to the use of heroin; it is Pain." Undaunted by the complexity that makes paranoia difficult to explain, Janov offers more of the same. "Though the content of the paranoia will differ with each individual, the process is the same—to protect the person against intolerable Pain." Of course Janov is correct, in the trivial sense in which all behavior can be described as motivated by the wish to maximize pleasure and minimize pain. The same explanation applies so widely to human behavior that it offers us no insight into pathological behavior. However, Janov does not mean this very general formulation. Rather, he states clearly that all of these forms of pathology result from frustrated needs and consequent repressed emotion. Janov's treatment consists of thawing out the frozen childhood pain, using regression and catharsis.

In the initial session, Janov inquires about the problem for which therapy has been sought. As the telling proceeds, Janov is alert for the emergence of affect as well as memories of childhood. Whenever recollections of the past evoke feelings, Janov urges the patient to attempt to re-experience them. As he becomes more engrossed in the emotion, the patient is told to cry out to his parents; to tell them of the terror and anger and frustration of childhood. Various props, including teddy bears, cribs, baby bottles, punching bags, and life-size photos of the parents are used to assist the processes of memory (10). Even a birth simulator, constructed of rubber inner tubes, is used to expel patients from a rubber womb.

The crux of Janov's treatment process is the "primal." The primal occurs when the patient intensely re-imagines childhood experiences involving agonizing pain. The patient cries out in childlike language, "Mommy! Daddy!" and experiences catharsis of his pent-up frustration by screaming in anguish. This "primal scream" is *the* curative mechanism in Janov's system. Primal experiences are exquisitely painful moments. The patient may writhe in agony as he experiences his long-forgotten pain from early childhood.

In contrast with Jackins, who promotes catharsis by making the client feel safe and understood and by manipulating his defenses, Janov's approach is a frontal assault on the defenses. Even before therapy begins, a new patient is instructed to isolate himself in a hotel room with no distractions, and to remain awake for twenty-four hours before his first session. Janov explains (1), "The isolation and sleeplessness are important techniques which often bring patients close to a Primal. The aim of isolation is to deprive the patient of all his usual outlets for tension, while the sleeplessness tends to weaken his remaining defenses; he has fewer resources to fight off his feelings." In therapy, tension-reducing behaviors, such as assuming a humble or polite tone, or foot tapping, finger drumming, or smoking are not allowed. The therapist constantly batters the patient's defenses and insists that emotions be experienced, not discussed.

Some patients may be ready for this onslaught—capable of experiencing and integrating their emerging feelings, and of growing through the process. Others, however, may be debilitated. There are no studies of Janov's procedures, so we cannot know if any or many of his patients become suicidally depressed. However, data that show a relatively high number of psychological casualties resulting from encounter groups suggest that primal therapy may very well also produce some walking wounded. Primal patients do have the advantage over encounter group members of being intensively involved in therapy for an extended period of time, rather than being thrust prematurely back to their home environments relatively defenseless; indeed, Janov does encourage his patients to drop out of their normal routines and devote full time to therapy. Not working for six months may make regression a safer prospect, but even this may have complications, since some people require a certain amount of structure. For these patients, an extended period of withdrawal and regression may be very damaging.

Just as Jackins speaks of a process of re-evaluation which follows discharge, so Janov says that the primal patient not only re-experiences his early childhood pain, he also reconceptualizes it. The essential difference between both of these approaches and other forms of interview psychotherapy is their heavy emphasis on the debilitating effects of suppressed affect. Once the affect is discharged, the patient is said to understand his own life better and to be more capable of reorganizing it.

After about three weeks of intensive individual therapy, primal patients join groups. As many as 40 or 50 patients participate in these groups during each meeting, along with several therapists. Janov is so convinced that patients require only to feel and discharge their emotional pain to be cured, that he undervalues the importance of the patient-therapist relationship. In fact, both for individual and group sessions, different therapists are used interchangeably (28). Janov thus ignores the fact that the therapeutic relationship between the patient and therapist is an important determinant of success, and may be particularly important in cathartic therapy where a patient must feel very secure in order to risk regression and giving up defenses. There is also a risk that, once having ventilated deep layers of emotion, a patient may feel violated unless he has great trust and confidence in the person with whom he was working.

After cathartic work in individual therapy, Janov believes that his patients are capable of continuing the process of uncovering buried feelings without much further help. No doubt the presence of a room full of other people in various stages of emotional catharsis acts as a powerful triggering stimulus. In addition, Primal patients are shown melodramatic movies—*The Yearling,* for instance, or *La Strada*—and go to costume parties where they are encouraged to act out their fantasies. After several months of this kind of weekly group work, the patient completes his therapy with a final week of intensive individual therapy.

Janov describes the healthy personality as defense-free: "I see a normal as a totally defenseless person, someone without an unreal self." Defenses are viewed as the enemy that must be driven back and then totally annihilated. Therapy so conceived involves no more than uprooting defenses as quickly as possible so that the patient can feel his pain and be cured.

Part of the defining characteristics of many forms of psychopathology, particularly the neuroses, is the rigid inhibition of feelings and impulses. Somatic-emotional discharge of these feelings may be an effective means of uncovering the impulses and actions associated with them, and for this to occur, some relaxation of defenses is required. Once uncovered, impulses need to be selectively channelled into appropriate forms of gratification. Janov fails to see this as a problem, because he assumes that once emotions are discharged, the needs and impulses for which they are dispositions automatically disappear. In fact, however, instead of being at peace, the undefended person will probably be at the mercy of his impulses. Without restraint, certain impulses are likely to lead (again) to severe frustration—the same sequence that originally caused both action and affect to be repressed. For this reason diminished and flexible defenses that permit appropriate gratification of needs seems to be more desirable than defenselessness.

Much of the positive evidence for the effectiveness of primal therapy is testimonial; on the other side of the ledger, some of Janov's patients report his approach as an intolerable emotional brainwashing. Neither judgment is an impartial evaluation. Janov himself has presented (27) some empirical support for primal therapy. On the basis of some questionable physiological measures of outcome, he finds a significant decrease in residual tension following primal therapy—for instance a decrease in frequency and amplitude of cortical EEG which he claims reflects a decrease in neurotic defensiveness, although EEG experts regard this imputed association as totally unfounded. Furthermore, Janov fails to offer the kind of data, such as the stimulus conditions under which the recordings were made, that would allow these findings to be scrutinized. His other physiological finds in post-primal therapy patients include a drop in rectal temperature and a decrease in pulse rate though no change in blood pressure. With stunningly unsophisticated logic, he attempts to equate the drop in rectal temperature with therapeutic improvement by saying, "When temperature is excessive, the adult may become momentarily psychotic and hallucinate. Lower temperatures, therefore, may be indicative of lessened neurosis." Additionally, he reports that post-primal therapy patients engage less in what he considers to be neurotically compulsive activities, such as sex, religion, smoking, drinking, and political activism. That is, his model of psychological health is passive noninvolvement with life.

Many clinicians practice cathartic approaches similar to Janov's. Some also call what they do Primal Therapy; others, like James Smith with Primal Feeling Therapy, and Werner Karle and Joseph Hart with Feeling Therapy, slightly vary the name and the practice. Karle and Hart stress constructive behavioral solutions to their patients (or "proaction" and "counteraction" as they call it), although they use catharsis; Smith focuses exclusively on catharsis. Smith believes that emotional ventilation is therapeutic through partial extinction and stimulus differentiation of adult from early childhood experiences. He is also less directive and active than others in the tradition of primal therapy, and uses silent visualization more than role-playing and verbalization.

A detached view of Primal therapy is difficult to achieve, partly because of Janov's own behavior. His refusal to acknowledge the contributions of his predecessors is parochial, and his claim for the originality of Primal therapy entirely ignores both folk wisdom and the history of psychotherapy. Janov's theory of personality development is merely a restatement of Freud's traumatic theory of neurosis. Furthermore, though Primal therapy does include some novel and imaginative techniques, the idea that defenses must be dismantled to uncover repressed material was pioneered by Freud and refined by Reich, and long before Janov, Fritz Perls had developed techniques to achieve deep emotional release.

Janov's theory of psychopathological development is intuitively appealing because it suggests that basic needs are physiological, not psychological. This Reichian notion helps to highlight the vulnerability of the infant. The reductionist logic also draws attention away from the psychological trials and tributions of adolescence and adulthood. It is a little like assuming that since the Mississippi River originates with melted snow, when the river becomes polluted, the snow must be dirty. That may be one place to look, but there are others, downstream, as well.

When his basic needs are thwarted, the argument goes, the child feels pain. This profound hurt causes him to deny expression of the needs to avoid further frustration and pain. The denial becomes internalized as both pain and need are repressed. Subsequently the child develops a facade or false self. This false self helps avoid much pain, but at the cost of never gratifying key desires. (This, of course, is a simplified synthesis of Freud, Reich, Winnicott, and Laing.) The shift from a real to an unreal self may involve one major trauma ("primal scene"), or a series of minor ones. Actual needs are then sequestered with painful memories, and distorted derivatives become the goals of the self-defeating neurotic. Janov's theory of psychopathology thus hinges on the pivotal concept of repressed pain from unmet needs and buried hurts.

Unfortunately, primal theory and practice are not flexible; instead, the therapist tends to orchestrate the feelings of patients to conform to theory. Catharsis of recent experiences is seen at best as a prelude to the "real" repressions, and this relentless pursuit of ever earlier primal scenes leads patients into symbolically acting out events too early to remember. Having been told that "birth primals" are the ultimate cathartic event, primal patients often engage in convulsive thrashing, wailing, and screaming, reactions that seem less the spontaneous release of feeling than desperate attempts to do what the theory says is necessary.

Janov claims that primal patients do more than remember and ventilate—they literally relive repressed core experiences, feeling the same feelings, but expressing them for the first time. This claim rests on the naive assumption that emotions are stored in pure form for a substantial number of years, an assumption he shares with other cathartic therapists. However, it seems more likely that the emotions expressed during primal scenes represent adult frustrations, or the affective component of the adult's thoughts about the sadness of the child.

Janov is easy to criticize, yet he has a great many satisfied customers. The main reason is that he put together a program that effectively enables Primal therapy patients to have a profoundly cathartic experience. Primal patients are prepared for therapy by first being taught about Janov's theory, so that they know what to expect. For the most part, they are prepared for and willing to accept a basically emotive approach, and this information offers a rationale for what may be a difficult and at times uncomfortable procedure, and this helps establish accurate expectancies, and prepares patients to accept a cathartic experience.

Secondly, Janov is very effective in dealing with the defensiveness aroused as he helps his patient to achieve somatic-emotional discharge. As Primal therapy begins, patients are deprived of many of their usual outlets for tension. Then, as therapy proceeds efficient means of uncovering buried material are brought into play. Patients are told to speak freely (free associate), and encouraged to explore painful memories. Deep breathing and other neo-Reichian techniques are used to help release feelings. Effective use of role-playing adds immediacy to the process. Patients are directed to objectify their feelings by addressing them to absent persons. Saying, "Daddy, I miss you!" has far greater emotional impact than saying, "I miss my father."

In sum, Janov seems to have developed an efficient procedure for helping people achieve access to and to express feelings. They are helped to couple feelings with memories and perceptions in a manner that generates a great deal of ventilation. Whether this emotive discharge is a sufficient antidote for unhappiness by itself is as yet unclear.

Casriel—New Identity Therapy

Daniel Casriel has developed a form of cathartic therapy which bears striking similarity to the work of both Jackins and Janov. The hallmark of Casriel's groups, which he calls New Identity therapy, is screaming. Like Janov, Casriel uses screaming as a tool to help patients express long-buried emotions. As he puts it (29), "Screams can release emotions repressed since childhood, and the freedom of release can affect significant positive changes in personality." Screaming is merely the most sensational form of expression in these groups, which focus on discharging feelings rather than talking about them. Casriel recognizes the similarity of his approach to that of Janov in the use of screaming, and points out that Janov seems to have arrived independently at a technique very like his own. Janov begins treatment by seeing a patient for an intensive series of individual sessions, and later places the patient in a group. Casriel, on the other hand, works almost exclusively with groups. Like Jackins, Casriel uses lay persons with experience in groups as group leaders. In addition to a belief in the curative power of emotional discharge, he also shares with Jackins the notion that the group leader should not be emotionally distant from the other members of the group.

Casriel believes that most of his patients have in common experiences of childhood deprivation and estrangement from their feelings. This, he believes, is the root cause of most psychopathology. Although he agrees that certain disorders, such as schizophrenia, begin with an organic deficit, this does not affect his focus on emotions because he no longer accepts psychotics as patients. Like Janov, Casriel subscribes to the early Freudian traumatic theory of neurosis. Thus he speaks of personalities being damaged in infancy by deprivation of their physical and emotional needs. Furthermore, he says that in our culture the tendency to suppress emotional reactions is ubiquitous. As a consequence, most people suffer from "anaesthetization of their basic emotions." Consistent with this conception of psychopathology, Casriel has developed a series of techniques to break rapidly through defenses and bring patients in touch with their repressed feelings.

Casriel trained in psychoanalysis and spent ten years as a practicing analyst. He dates the beginning of his evolution into cathartic therapy from his first contacts with Synanon, a therapeutic community for the rehabilitation of drug addicts, in which encounter techniques play a central role. Regular group sessions are held that focus on two treatment strategies. First, feelings are released to drain off emotional pressure that might otherwise build and lead to attempts to escape it through return to drugs. Second, members are confronted directly and sometimes brutally with others' perceptions of them. Since self-deception is regarded as a particular danger to addicts, these encounter groups often include frontal attacks when they are deemed necessary to prevent a member from evading the truth about his behavior.

Casriel was so impressed with the Synanon approach that he began to run groups based on its encounter style in which patients were angrily confronted with their defensive behavior and challenged to give up their destructive symptoms. When he became psychiatric director of Daytop Village, a therapeutic drug rehabilitation community modeled on Synanon, he used the groups there to test new styles and techniques. He began to use advanced patients as catalysts, and trained them to lead groups under his supervision. He also tried out Bach and Stoller's marathon technique at Daytop, a significant step in his gradual change from encounter to catharsis as the major therapeutic element in his groups. Marathon groups, may last from approximately 24 hours to an entire weekend, so that fatigue becomes one of the factors that helps to wear away defenses and facilitate emotional breakthroughs.

As a result of the marathon sessions he held at Daytop Village, Casriel became impressed with the value of emotional catharsis. "This tremendous abreaction of historical feelings has proved to be extremely therapeutic in helping the person become aware of current feelings, attitudes and behavior." Gradually, he began to view catharsis as having therapeutic value beyond merely facilitating insight. "We saw that deep feelings required expression just for themselves. Group members were encouraged to scream out their anger or fear or pain 'full measure,' at the top of their lungs."

Casriel has continued to use other mechanisms besides catharsis. He relies on group pressure to bring about change in specific problem behaviors. When a new patient joins one of Casriel's groups, he is told to stop his symptomatic behavior. If the patient protests that he cannot stop, he is instructed to act "as if" he did not have the symptoms, and to return and report to the group about how he feels. Furthermore, group members do not allow each other to tell long self-pitying tales as alibis for not giving up their symptoms. It is interesting to find this appeal to patients' responsibility by assault used in combination with catharsis, because it reflects an opposite metapsychology. Belief in the curative power of catharsis generally rests on appeals to inner forces over which individuals have little direct control. When catharsis is used in therapy, explanatory concepts revolve around notions of an inner space thought to be a repository for affects, the unconscious, and forces of repression. In this framework, individuals are relieved of responsibility for symptoms which are said to result from "repressed affects." Contrarily, the use of group pressure to force a person into taking responsibility for and then abandoning his symptoms implies that behavior can be changed without reference to inner forces over which a person has no control, and is consistent with a behavioral or social psychiatric framework. Casriel has therefore apparently managed to integrate techniques based on social forces with those based on inner forces, at least according to his own descriptions of the workings of his groups.

In addition to providing group pressure for behavior change, Casriel also believes that the group format is particularly relevant in our culture because so many people are alienated and isolated. Groups can provide a safe structure to help people learn to become more open and intimate with each other. As Casriel puts it, "Emotionally oriented groups stand in contradiction to the inhibitive culture in which we live. They provide a safe and trusting atmosphere in which you can express any emotion openly to others. Groups can promote a bondedness that becomes the basis for learning to trust."

As we have already said, Casriel does not treat psychotics, and he also warns that his groups may not be appropriate for all nonpsychotic patients. Some people do not have the personal resources to withstand a series of emotionally charged encounters, interspersed with returns to their daily isolation. Casriel thus differs from Janov and Jackins about who should be included in cathartic therapy. His position seems appropriate in light of the fact that he works with outpatients and that most of his group leaders are not professionally trained mental health workers. All the leaders are former patients, trained to lead groups by Casriel. These leaders do not assume a detached, emotionally distant role in the groups, but rather are actively involved in the group process. Casriel believes that their nonprofessional status enables the leaders to be more open emotionally, and to act like peers. He does not say why having leaders perceived as peers is an advantage, but it seems reasonable to assume that it means the leaders are free to engage in expressing emotions themselves, and may thus serve as models of emotional openness. The leaders are supervised by Casriel; in addition, he conducts a group for the leaders devoted partly to training, and partly to continuing work on the leaders' own problems.

A new patient at the Casriel Institute begins with three group sessions per week, and after a few weeks is asked to take part in a marathon session. Casriel's marathon sessions used to last approximately thirty hours, taking place over a weekend. Since screaming has been found to hasten the breaching of defenses marathon sessions are now only approximately sixteen hours long. Casriel requires that patients who undergo a marathon session, with its potential for probing deep layers of emotion, commit themselves to weekly follow-up sessions of two to three hours each for 12 weeks. The two-hour groups are made up of eight to twelve people, and the three-hour groups may have as many as eighteen participants.

A typical group session starts out with a group go round in which each member in turn describes some of the events that have occurred in the previous week. This emotional icebreaker lasts about fifteen minutes. Following this the leader invites a volunteer to begin working on some problem area. Other group members respond by listening, alternately encouraging the person to get deeper into his feelings, and making encounter style, challenging interpretations. When a woman describes her difficulties with her boyfriend, other members may sense that she is avoiding her feelings and say to her, "You're angry because he won't marry you." If this interpretation seems accurate, the woman may be encouraged to shout, "I'm ANGRY!" As she shouts, other members may try to push her further and further into the experience of anger. However, unlike Re-Evaluation Counseling groups, where members are encouraged to be supportive of the person on "the hot seat," members of Casriel's groups may confront each other with the accusation that they are avoiding their true feelings. The atmosphere is extremely provocative, with pressure intended to force members to go beyond their defensive behavior. Group members who resist being swept up in their feelings may be told to alter something in their posture or voice that seems to be restraining them. For example, while expressing angry feelings, a member may be told to put his hands on his hips while he shouts out invectives. Sometimes a particular phrase may be suggested to help the person experience his feelings. Simple, pithy phrases seem to stimulate the most affect. Thus a patient may be asked to say, "I'm angry," "I hurt," "I need your love, daddy." If using the phrase seems to come close but not quite lead to emotive discharge, a different phrase or a different emphasis may be suggested. Sometimes, merely repeating a phrase over and over does the trick. Sometimes repeating an emotionally provocative phrase may seem silly, so that the person begins doing it with an "as if" quality. Often, however, after a few repetitions, deep feelings are experienced and expressed. As a person begins to experience his deep feelings words usually change to sounds—shrieks of fear, yells of anger, or wails and whimpers of pain.

Casriel has found that some exercises can facilitate emotional discharge. When a person is experiencing fear, Casriel suggests that he slouch down, tilt his head back, shut his eyes, and scream in fear, using whatever words seem to fit. If the person really gets into the fear, the words generally become just a scream, which he is encouraged to repeat over and over until the feeling is exhausted. Mats are placed on the floor and members are encouraged to lie on the mats and yell, while striking and kicking the mat. This experience obviously has a strong regressive quality, as Casriel observes:

> I have often held people as they were screaming on the mats and have heard and felt in them an almost total regression through one feeling to another—and back to the helpless, piping cries of infancy. It is a wordless, feeling reliving of their emotional history.

Reading such descriptions may make the reader feel embarrassed discomfort or supercilious disdain. Imagine a patient jumping up and down, shouting "I hate you!," or another crying out "Love me!," while others embrace him. We are so experienced in being "too sophisticated" to bare our naked emotions in public that we may feel scorn or pity for others who do so. When reading of a group member rising and saying "I need love.," the reader may feel embarrassed "for him." In fact, the embarrassment may be due to the fact that a powerful cultural more is being violated. Although print can convey only the verbal content and physical activity, there are many factors that make these scenes real and acceptable when they are actually seen. Some of these factors are anxiety, awareness of one's own emotional needs, and a special atmosphere that demands the acceptance of feelings. Casriel describes a climate of emotional closeness, including a good deal of hugging and touching to express affection. When one woman was crying about her mother, Casriel instructed her to say, "Mommy, I need you." This phrase apparently touched the woman, for after repeating it a couple of times she sobbed uncontrollably. When her tears subsided, members of the group gathered around her and embraced her.

After the group leader has worked for a while with one or two members, the group is broken into small groups of threes and fours for about forty minutes. This allows individual members to work out any feelings that may have been stimulated by earlier activity in the whole group. Often the particular content dealt with by one member has sufficient universality to help other members get in touch with similar experiences from their own lives; working in a concentrated way with one or two people in the large group is therefore an excellent catalyst for stimulating buried feelings in all the group members. After working in subgroups, the whole group reconvenes. At this time the leader checks on whether any members have failed to get into their feelings. If so, the leader takes some time to work with them. At this point, the focus of the group's attention alone is a powerful stimulus for catharsis. Thus group members who were unable to discharge any feelings earlier are often able to do so when the whole group concentrates on them. Casriel closes each group with a group scream.

Casriel believes that his major therapeutic achievements result from the discharge of historic feelings, after which insights and new perceptions flow smoothly and help consolidate gains. Casriel believes that following initial experiences of openness to feelings, shells of emotional suppression will again form over from habit, and must be broken through periodically. When a patient has continued difficulty in allowing his feelings to emerge, Casriel may provide a few individual sessions. He regularly rotates members through different groups to overcome projection and transference that may make it difficult for them to get into feelings with a particular group. Sometimes he experiments with teenaged groups or couples groups, but in general he believes that heterogenous groups are most successful.

All of the elements in Casriel's New Identity therapy are also used by other therapists: confrontation by the encounter group movement, pressure for behavioral change by Synanon, the emotive techniques by neo-Reichians. In general, this kind of ecclecticism tends to be counterproductive. A patient may profit from either psychoanalysis or Gestalt therapy, and he may also gain from having first one, then the other form of treatment. It is not even inconceivable that he could benefit by being in treatment with both a Gestaltist and an analyst at the same time. However, when fundamentally different techniques are combined by the same therapist the result is apt to be inconsistent, diluted, and confusing.

Furthermore, as we have already said, somatic-emotional catharsis is best achieved in an atmosphere where patients feel safe enough to relax their defenses. The use of vigorous confrontation and attacking of defenses in Casriel's groups make them less than ideal as situations where patients are asked to unmask painful emotions. To do so in an atmosphere where angry confrontation is acceptable, means taking a risk of having deep feelings exposed to ridicule and attack. It seems likely that Casriel's patients attack and confront each other until catharsis begins, but then become supportive. People are not naturally cruel—especially when they are all in the same boat—and are able to sense when others need support. Furthermore, if untrained and insensitive group members do attack one who is exposed and vulnerable, hopefully the group leader will intervene.

In Casriel's groups, moreover, instead of being encouraged and facilitated, catharsis is demanded. In fact, it may be the only sure way for a patient to escape criticism and rebuke. Demanding catharsis, many evoke in these circumstances a dramatized imitation of spontaneous emotional expression. The screaming in these groups seems to be, like the writhing and moaning of Primal therapy patients, forced compliance with group pressure, rather than spontaneous. Not only are dramatic emotional displays demanded, rather than encouraged, standard exercises are used to generate feelings. When gimmicks are used in a routine and predictable manner, they increase the chance that feelings are being wrung from group members in a manipulative fashion.

Summary

All of the authors considered in this chapter share a firm conviction in the therapeutic value of catharsis for treating essentially characterological problems. Virtually all of them believe that repressed affects such as anger are accumulated and stored, thereby creating the "psychic abcesses" that account for a variety of pathological behaviors. Associated with this position is the thesis that cure is not possible until these pockets are drained. This point of view goes back to Freud through Reich. With the exception of Perls' Gestalt therapy, cathartic approaches add little to Reich's formulations; instead, they tend to stress various aspects of his work. Each shares Reich's view that psychopathology develops when defenses erected to ward off painful feelings result in blunting feelings as well as awareness.

Underlying these therapies is the supposition that man is by nature inherently good, and that if he is provided with an environment that does not interfere with his own natural development—that does not impose repressions upon him—his development will be satisfactory. They are also based on faith that, despite years of maladjusted behavior, man's psychological difficulties can be corrected if he but releases the disabling affect that has been stored. Perls is the exception, here. He views emotional release as only part of the therapeutic process, which allows the patient to begin to find new and more effective ways of functioning in the here and now. The Gestalt therapist endeavors to help patients become aware, not only of their feelings, but also of their thoughts and actions and their responsibility for the totality of their behavior.

In general, theories that regard man's behavioral problems solely as the result of unexpressed affect are not easily applied to long-lasting behavioral problems. In such cases, it becomes theoretically necessary to assume that feelings aroused very early in life but not fully expressed persist somewhere in the psyche; that they accumulate as they link up with new stimulation; and that they remain pathogenic unless discharged. Freud wrestled with the problem of how to explain the persistence of intense affect over extraordinarily long periods of time, and concluded that this can occur only in special cases as a function of the personality involved and possibly the circumstances under which the feeling was aroused. Modern cathartic theorists seem to have made no effort to develop any better explanation. Considering the wide variety and the quantity of affect that is provoked in any individual in the space of a relatively short time, much less over a period of several years, it is difficult to imagine how it can accumulate, even in one who is not severely repressed, without leaving us all behaviorally helpless. It does seem likely to us that even though specific affects may go unexpressed, they eventually find indirect partial expression, or else fade out to some degree. On the other hand, unexpressed affect very likely prompts development of certain behaviors, certain ways of interpreting stimuli, and certain outlooks on life designed to protect against events that might provoke unexpressible affect. One result of such defensive maneuvers could be an image of oneself and of the world which is either very limiting or at odds with reality. This would have profound effects on behavior, and it is conceivable that the defensive behaviors engaged in to protect against particular affects may make one even more vulnerable to further affective provocation in the future. Thus, certainly with respect to long-standing behavioral problems, it seems reasonable that while affect plays a significant role in the development of disorder, the role is hardly exclusive, and the cure will require more than its release. Among other things, the patient ought to be helped to alter a way of life that makes him particularly vulnerable to being hurt. There are other arguments, too, against an exclusively affective theory. For if emotional repression is the root cause of all forms of pathological behavior, how then can we account for the great diversity of behavioral disorders? Furthermore, it is becoming increasingly apparent that certain disorders, most notably schizophrenia, involve some kind of biological predisposition.

Critics of the wide ranging use of catharsis in therapy often point to what they consider to be the danger of sweeping away defenses and promoting loss of control. The policy of encouraging regression and loss of control which characterizes most cathartic therapies troubles many professionals and terrifies many patients. Patients, sensing the turbulence of many of their own internal forces, feel threatened by the madness which they fear might result from a loss of control. The cathartic therapist, on the other hand, holds that the experience of relinquishing control and the opportunity to learn that the self, underlying the defenses, is worthwhile and solid is an enormously reassuring experience. Having such an experience may confirm a patient's earlier faith in himself or it may be a dramatic revelation having a conversion quality to it. In either case the emotive therapist would see the experience as being a constructive, strengthening one.

Emotive psychotherapists do express some diversity of opinion concerning the wisdom of encouraging the relinquishment of defenses. Casriel takes the most conservative position, and stresses that patients should have "ego strength." At the other end of the continuum, Jackins believes that the breaching of defenses can be done safely with all patients. Although most of his clientele are not psychotic, he has worked with severely psychotic patients whom he regards simply as people with more stored up pain than most, and who need emotional discharge more than most. With such "heavily distressed persons," however, Jackins tends to make a greater effort to draw attention to the present situation than to the past distressful experiences. In some respects, Jackins' position is similar to Ronald Laing's. Laing holds that the schizophrenic must give up control (the "false self system") and experience his psychosis in order to grow into a healthier, more integrated person.

As he has said (30), "Indeed, what is called psychosis is sometimes simply the sudden removal of the veil of the false self, which has been serving to maintain an outer behavioral abnormality that may, long ago, have failed to be any reflection of the state of affairs of the secret self."

Patients who are encouraged to discharge their emotions are like people whose swimming instructors toss them into the pool either to sink or to learn to do the adaptive thing. It is very likely that some of them will indeed swim. Others may well sink; still others, if they survive, are through with learning to swim. Some patients exposed to heavy doses of catharsis can cope with it; others go under, or withdraw. With certain patients, psychotics included, under certain circumstances, catharsis can be beneficial; for other patients, including some who do not seem seriously disturbed, relinquishing defenses can be quite detrimental. Clinicians must therefore decide for themselves when to attempt a cathartic approach. The theoretical underpinning for using catharsis with long-standing characterological disorders is extraordinarily thin. Even proponents of the cathartic approaches have reservations about the safety of using them in connection with certain types of patients. This means that apparently serious harm may occur in certain cases, and, in fact, the anecdotal evidence is that such harm does from time to time befall patients. Thus, it is not sufficient to pursue these approaches on the basis of personal conviction and enthusiasm alone; and we do urgently need more research in this area. It is also important that we test the effectiveness of the cathartic therapies—both detailed tests of their effects, and the specificity of such effects for particular individuals. Before catharsis can be accepted as the effective therapeutic tool for serious characterological disorders that its proponents claim it is, we must have scientific studies that prove its safety and its clinical value.

CHAPTER 8

The Empirical Evaluation
of Catharsis

Rather than accept historical accounts and clinical testimonials about catharsis as received knowledge, the sophisticated reader will await more convincing evidence. For clinicians, this often means basing judgments upon one's own clinical experience. Unfortunately, the usual pitfalls of therapist bias may be magnified in evaluating catharsis. Because of their training and experience few clinicians will ever generate the sort of intensely cathartic sessions claimed to be effective by the advocates of specific cathartic therapies. Thus, their own experience with catharsis may be limited to rather brief episodes, often associated with environmental events of sufficient impact to overcome their patients' defenses against emotional discharge. On the other hand, those with training and experience in any of the cathartic approaches may accept it as an article of faith that catharsis heals. Catharsis is an immediate and dramatic manifestation of movement in psychotherapy. Such drama is relatively rare and its appearance may be judged viscerally rather than on evaluation of lasting results. Those uncomfortable and unfamiliar with powerful emotional discharge in psychotherapy may condemn with their heads that which frightens them, while those who feel good about such ventilation may also base their positive evaluations on their feelings alone.

In the long run, the psychotherapeutic worth of catharsis can only be judged in terms of demonstrable change in patients. In evaluating this, we shall discuss research in the context of psychotherapy—studies of behavior therapy, experiencing and focusing, general reviews of curative factors, and laboratory analogues of psychotherapy. We shall also include relevant medical studies of psychosomatic disorders, and social psychological studies of aggressive behavior and of attitude change.

Catharsis In the Context of Psychotherapy

We have found only one published study in which emotional catharsis was quantified and related to therapy outcome (1). The study, conducted by M. P. Nichols, compared brief emotive psychotherapy to a more traditional approach, and specifically evaluated the impact of catharsis on improvement.

The work was conducted in a college mental health clinic and its design entailed a number of methodologically desirable features (2, 3). The 43 patients who participated were sufficiently heterogenous to permit wide generalization of the findings. Their ages ranged from 17 to 28 years, and diagnoses included: psychotics, neurotics, personality disorders, transient situational reactions, psychophysiological reactions, specific sexual symptoms, and those not warranting psychiatric diagnosis. Approximately two-thirds of the patients were male, and a slightly higher proportion were described as having an obsessive character style. The emotive and non-emotive treatment groups were evenly balanced on all of these patient variables, as well as on pretherapy criterion measures.

Six relatively experienced clinicians, four psychiatrists, and two psychologists served as therapists. All six had been trained in insight-oriented, dynamic psychotherapy, and two had prior experience using emotive psychotherapy. At the outset of the study, all six therapists received training in the techniques of emotive psychotherapy during two, two-hour training sessions.

Diverse measures of outcome were employed, including two paper-and-pencil tests (the MMPI and the Test of Emotional Styles), and two behavioral variables (behavioral target complaints, and the Personal Satisfaction Form) elicited in semi-structured interviews. In the initial interviews, patients were asked to state their goals for therapy. Generally, patients' objectives are framed in such vague terms that it is difficult to determine accurately if they are achieved. Accordingly, therapists were instructed to help their clients delineate goals in highly concrete terms. A patient who said that her goal was to be less depressed might be helped to set behavioral goals like sleeping all night, not crying during classes, spending time on her hobbies, and visiting her friends.

It was thought that some patients might set goals not particularly significant to them because they had not yet adequately conceptualized their problems, or in some cases were consciously concealing some aspects of their experience of which they were ashamed. Hence, to control for the possibility that goals defined in the first session were not the most relevant, goals were reviewed and modified if necessary during the third session. The third session was used because of the belief that after two sessions patients would be able to express themselves with greater candor and insight.

Patients were also asked to describe the degree of satisfaction they were deriving, citing specific examples, in each of eight areas of college life at the time of the initial interview (Personal Satisfaction Form). This insured a wide sampling of reported behavioral experience in areas relevant to improvement in psychotherapy, though not necessarily conceived of as primary goals. A clinical psychologist other than the therapist made diagnostic judgments as well as rating the Personal Satisfaction Form, and recorded the behavioral target complaints, based on the semistructured interviews but without knowledge of the treatment conditions.

The major treatment variable of interest was somatic-emotional discharge (laughing, crying, yelling). In an attempt to produce differential amounts of catharsis, each therapist was directed to treat half of his patients with emotive psychotherapy and the other half with traditional insight-oriented therapy. Thus, it was also possible to determine if emotive techniques like Jackins' (4) are indeed effective in generating catharsis and if there were any differences in effectiveness of emotive or traditional psychotherapy independent of the occurrence of catharsis.

Catharsis was scored by two clinically unsophisticated

judges who listened to tape recordings of every one of the 385 sessions and who did not have any knowledge of treatment conditions. After five hours of training and practice, these raters were able to record the numbers of seconds of audible crying, shouting, shaking and trembling, and laughing with a high degree of reliability (correlation coefficient .96, probability of less than 1 in 100).

Two sets of data analyses were performed. First, all patients treated with emotive therapy (22) were compared with those treated by nonemotive therapy (21) both on measures of process and of outcome. Then, the sample was divided into two extreme groups (thirds) of high and low dischargers. This split permitted a delimited test of the therapeutic value of catharsis.

Analyses based on assignment to treatment groups showed that in the emotive condition therapists used significantly more emotive techniques, and that these techniques were associated with significantly more catharsis. This finding established the potency of emotive techniques such as role-playing, repetition of affect-laden phrases, and expressive movements in stimulating catharsis.

Of the four outcome measures, change on the Personal Satisfaction Form was the only one on which the emotive groups showed directionally greater improvement ($p < .10$). Interestingly, the nonemotive group changed significantly more on the MMPI (sum of D, Pt and Sc scales). This finding was contrary to prediction, and may have been a byproduct of increased self-disclosure or sensitization in the emotive group. This interpretation was supported by the discovery of a significantly greater drop in MMPI K (social desirability) scores for the emotive group ($p < .001$).

Although the emotive group had a significantly higher mean number of seconds of discharge, this difference was largely due to the contributions of a subset of subjects in the emotive group who had extremely high levels of catharsis. In fact, some subjects in the emotive condition discharged relatively little. High dischargers improved significantly more on behavioral goals and showed a directional trend toward greater improvement on the Personal Satisfaction Form.

Preliminary follow-up data showed that the high discharge group maintained their superior achievement of goals and improved significantly more on the Personal Satisfaction Form.

Nichols interpreted these findings as definite support for the effectiveness of emotive techniques in stimulating catharsis, and partial support for the effectiveness of catharsis to produce improvement in psychotherapy.

Catharsis in Behavior Therapy

Advocates of catharsis generally adhere to a dynamic model of man, making reference to hypothetical inner states, including affects and the unconscious. Behaviorists, on the other hand, have criticized such concepts as meaningless—that is, not empirically verifiable—and have limited their analyses to observable behavior. In recent years, however, behavior theorists have begun to deal with increasingly complex events including variables thought to mediate between stimuli and responses, such as thoughts, anxiety and affects. The introduction of such subject matter into the province of behaviorism simply underlines the fact that there is no fundamental distinction in subject matter between behavioral and dynamic psychology. Rather, behavioral psychology is essentially a methodology that involves rigorous scientific analyses of any aspect of behavior, including at times so-called internal events (5) or even hypothesized events (6).

In fact, numerous reports and studies done within the framework of behavior modification tend to support the efficacy of catharsis. Wolpe and Lazarus (7) wrote that although abreaction is difficult to understand and control, it is often therapeutic. If it could be induced at will, they said, it would expedite therapy in many cases. They suggest that behaviorists have avoided catharsis, not because it doesn't produce positive results, but because of the complexity of conditions necessary. In their words, "It would seem, however, that in a certain percentage of neurotic patients the unadaptive emotional responses have been conditioned at the onset to particularly intricate stimulus compounds which cannot be adequately replaced by stimulus situations extracted from the present." Then, in cases where simpler deconditioning methods fail, abreaction may be well nigh indispensable as suggested both by Wolpe and by Costello (9).

Wolpe's (8) interpretation of the effectiveness of catharsis is that it is a function of the reciprocal inhibition of anxiety by emotional responses. Wolpe apparently refers here to somatic-emoting; he suggests that it is significant only as it interferes with anxiety, and that it is not intrinsically preferable to relaxation. As evidence, he cites two case studies in which catharsis occurred in treatment sessions and was followed by "signal improvement." In addition, he describes several cases of effective treatment by drug-induced abreaction. Noting the intensely cathartic effects of these sessions, he wrote, "Presumably the anxiety could thus be reciprocally inhibited, and the general context of high emotional arousal would make it possible for the anxiety-response habit to be largely or entirely eliminated in the course of even a single session."

Wolpe's own preferred method of treatment is systematic desensitization. This is fundamentally an emotionally calming rather than exciting technique. Instructions to relax are paired with previously anxiety-eliciting stimuli in a process thought to involve counterconditioning. However, reports of success using Wolpean desensitization without relaxation may have been due to the effects of catharsis (10). Wolpe claims that reciprocal inhibition of anxiety is the basis of all psychotherapeutic benefits. Interestingly, some of the reciprocal inhibitors of anxiety may in and of themselves produce discharge of emotional tension. If assertive responses, sexual responses, and various motor responses are simply serving counterconditioning, then when presented with the CS, patients should become aroused by these newly conditioned reactions. On the contrary, patients tend to feel indifferent when presented with the previously anxiety-provoking stimulus (11). Perhaps anxiety may have been generated by repressed anger, rather than classically conditioned. This possibility is further supported by the successful use of emotive imagery in the treatment of children's phobias (12), with emotionally expressive behavior found to be effective in dealing with fearful and anxious responses. In fact, Ullmann and Krasner (13) described interview-induced emotional responses, including abreaction and emotive imagery, as one of the basic procedures of successful behavior modification. They refer, apparently, not only to somatic, but also to cognitive-emotional catharsis.

The behavioral analysis of depression typically involves reference to lack of reinforcing behaviors in the patient's repertoire (14). The implications for treatment derived from such an interpretation often entail the shaping of behaviors that will lead to positive reinforcement. Here, too, behavioral therapists have referred to affective states as well as to overt behavior. For example, Lazarus (15) has said that affective expression, especially of anger, will dismantle the depressive equilibrium. The principle he offers is to provide powerful reinforcers to disrupt the emotional inhibitions which characterize depressed patients. The explanation of this process is open to various interpretations, but the observable behavior entails a great deal of somatic-emotional expression.

Another behavior therapist, Shoben, considered catharsis effective in therapy because it allows for symbolic reinstatement of repressed cues for anxiety within the context of a warm, permissive, nonjudgmental social relationship (16). He explained this effect in terms of counter-conditioning. The process he outlines entails reactivation of traumatic responses in order to extinguish them through catharsis. He found that catharsis provided a necessary emotional release, which must precede re-examination and re-integration of formerly traumatic experiences.

Shoben's method of reactivating traumatic responses to extinguish them through catharsis is quite similar to Thomas Stampfl's fundamentally cathartic implosive therapy. Stampfl treated his first patient with this method in 1957. Stampfl has a learning theory background, and developed his approach in accordance with principles derived from the animal laboratory. His theory of abnormal behavior is an elaboration and extension of Mowrer's (17) two-factor theory of learning which holds that learning involves both conditioning and problem solving. Thus, the development of an avoidance response involves: classical conditioning of fear, through CS=UCS pairing, followed by instrumental learning of an escape or avoidance response. With human beings, the unconditioned stimulus might be parental punishment, attack by a dog, or an automobile accident; the instrumental response learned to reduce fear and anxiety might be tantrum behavior, withdrawal, or avoidance of certain objects or situations. Though the behavior learned to reduce the anxiety or fear may become counterproductive, or "neurotic," it persists. The avoidance is sustained by reduction of unbearable anxiety or fright that results if the neurotic person attempts to overcome his fears. A stable pattern of maladaptive behavior is thus established. This mechanism is most easily applied to simple, phobic-like avoidance situations, but its implications are quite broad. Though conditioned avoidance stimuli may be simple and external, such as the sight of a rat or smell of waste products, they may be multiple, extremely complex, or even endogenous. In childhood, punishment may become associated with thoughts or images of acts; and thus a child may learn to avoid (repress) the idea as well as the behavior.

Stampfl's procedure for curing (extinguishing) maladaptive avoidance responses is to present the conditioned stimuli, not allow an avoidance response, and present no reinforcement. Forced to confront his fears, even in imagination, the patient learns that he suffers no baleful consequences, and the fear subsides (18). This sequence is described in learning theory terms, rather than as a corrective emotional experience. Stampfl neither requires nor mentions emotional discharge. In fact, however, a great deal of somatic-emotional catharsis occurs in implosive therapy sessions.

Stampfl's method (6) consists of four steps. First, two standard diagnostic interviews are conducted in which conditioned aversive stimuli, which mediate emotional responses and in turn determine symptoms, are sought. Second, patients are trained in neutral imagery, and learn to imagine cues in various sense modalities. During this process, the therapist establishes his role as director of the imagery, and the patient learns to imagine both real and fantastic scenes related to his fears. Following this, the implosive extinction sessions are conducted. The therapist describes scenes with the emotive imagery, attempting to maximize the patient's arousal while preventing his attempts at avoidance. The images presented consist both of symptom-contingent cues and hypothesized cues, deduced from psychoanalytic theory. Thus for a dirt-phobic patient, the therapist may describe scenes involving contamination with fecal matter, even though such images were not reported by the patient. After each implosive session patients are instructed to practice the procedure at home. Treatment is continued until little or no emotional arousal is forthcoming when the feared scenes are described. In addition, spaced follow-up sessions are arranged to counteract spontaneous recovery.

Affect is relevant to the hypothetical construct extinction only because dysphoric emotion is taken as a sign that the stimuli being presented are indeed the appropriate ones, and the somatic-emotional reactions are presumed to be part of the conditioned stimulus configuration. Despite the peripheral role assigned to affect in this theory, in practice emotional discharge is prominent. As Stampfl hammers his clients with melodramatic descriptions of their greatest fears and most painful fantasies, they shudder in fear, cry out in anger, and dissolve in tears. Nor does he relent when patients beseech him to stop. Instead he generates the scenes again and again, until the emotional outburst subsides.

Stampfl says that the greater the anxiety that occurs in an implosive session, the more profitable it is presumed to be. He encourages patients to "lose themselves" and to "live" the past with genuine emotion. Hogan (19) has noted that implosive sessions are replete with emotional ventilation. "The therapist is trying to elicit maximum emotional response and will use any word or description that is effective." Hogan argues that far from being incidental a violent emotional experience is necessary for the implosive therapy to be successful. Furthermore, like cathartic therapists, Hogan speaks of the importance of overcoming patients' emotional defenses and of recovering repressed material. He describes how he directs a patient to imagine expressing the anger and aggression that he feels, and abandoning himself to wildly primitive hostile impulses (20):

> As I build the emotion I have him attack the source of his frustration with bites, kicks and curses. I have him imagine a scene in which he takes a knife or hatchet and cuts out the victim's eyes and tongue, mutilates his body and destroys his sexual organs. In another sequence, the client might be required to picture himself as a wild leopard savagely ripping and clawing his victim. Underlying such a creation would be our emphasis on loss of control by the person, and the complete expression of impulse.

Fazio (21) has also characterized implosive therapy as an intensely cathartic procedure with frequent and intense crying and sobbing. Stampfl has also suggested (6) that in cases resistant to change, the implosive therapist should use hypothesized cues related to repressed anger and hostility. Stampfl is more directive and psychoanalytically oriented than Jackins or Janov; otherwise, his behavior in therapy and the catharsis he produces are strikingly similar to theirs.

Implosive therapy thus involves both cognitive- and

somatic-emotional catharsis. When the implosive therapist presents symptom-contingent cues, the patient is forced to think about things that had been either forgotten or avoided. Furthermore, these thoughts and images seem to generate physical discharge of emotion. Although Stampfl emphasizes what we have called cognitive-emotional catharsis—remembering and being exposed to painful thoughts and images—it seems that implosive therapy relies more on somatic discharge to achieve its result. Two observations support this contention. First, symptom-contingent cues are usually not difficult to remember. In fact, they are readily accessible to consciousness. Therefore it seems likely that their impact is due to the somatic-emotional results that follow from imagining them. That is, no new cognitions are discovered in this process; instead, unpleasant events of which the patient is already aware are kept in consciousness long enough to produce discharge. Secondly, it seems that hypothesized cues are extremely unlikely to generate forgotten material. Instead, these fantastic scenes are simply the sort of material uniquely suited to provoke the most intense somatic-emotional reactions in each individual patient.

Implosive therapy has some theoretical support from animal learning experiments and human learning studies. As for studies of its therapeutic effectiveness (and, by implication, that of catharsis), Morganstern (22), has reviewed the literature, and concluded that the approach remains to be validated. However, Morganstern's review itself needs to be reviewed. He correctly points out that clinical reports of success are useful only for generating hypotheses, not for drawing rigorous conclusions. He goes on, however, to lump analogue studies with studies carried out on patient populations in clinical settings. Analogue studies do offer attractive possibilities for experimental control and manipulation of variables, but they are a less decisive test of psychotherapy than are studies carried out in naturalistic settings because often they are too distant from the practice of psychotherapy to be relevant.

To date, four studies of implosive therapy in clinical settings have appeared in the literature. In the first (23), 26 hospitalized patients treated with implosive therapy improved significantly more on the MMPI than 24 patients treated with traditional psychotherapy. Furthermore, at one year follow-up,

18 of the 26 implosive patients had been discharged as opposed to only 8 of the 24 non-implosive patients. Levis and Carrera (24) found implosive therapy to produce significantly greater improvement on the MMPI than traditional treatment in an outpatient population.

The third study (25) involved flooding, which is similar to implosion, except that the imagery in flooding consists of realistic situations the patient fears, while the implosive imagery also involves unrealistic fantasies. In the case of a snake phobia, flooding scenes would typically involve visualizing a snake; implosive scenes would also include images of the snake coiling, striking, and ripping the flesh of its victim. In the flooding study, 16 phobic patients were treated with flooding and desensitization, in a cross-over design. That is, half of the patients were treated for six sessions with flooding, followed by six sessions of desensitization, while this order of treatment was reversed for the remaining half of the group. Outcome measures were made prior to therapy and again following the sixth and twelfth sessions. Both groups showed significant improvement on clinical ratings and physiological indices of anxiety, but the flooding group improved significantly more.

The fourth and most carefully designed study of the effectiveness of implosive therapy was conducted by Boudewyns and Wilson (26). Methodological strengths of this study included multiple outcome criteria, with behavioral measures and the evaluation of family members; an attention-placebo control group; process measures of anxiety during treatment; and follow-up evaluations. The treatment comparisons involved implosion, desensitization, and milieu therapy. Findings showed implosive therapy to produce significant improvement which was sustained at follow-up. The results of desensitization were equivocal, since improvement in psychological test scores was not sustained at follow-up.

Taken as a group these studies support the effectiveness of implosive therapy. Analogue studies on the other hand have not provided clearcut support. In some, implosive treatment was shown to be effective in treating phobic college students (27, 28, 29), while in others, implosive treatment did not reduce phobic avoidance responses (30), or the results of desensitization were found to be more stable over time than implosion (31, 32). Barrett concluded that implosive therapy was more efficient because it took less than half the time that desensitization required. Another study (33) showed that reality-oriented discussions about the harmlessness of snakes and the extent to which fears are shared and understood by others were associated with greater reduction of phobic behavior than implosion. A well-designed crossover study (34) compared the effectiveness of shaping, desensitization, and implosion in the treatment of phobic patients. Although shaping produced the superior results, implosion was more effective than desensitization. In this study, support for shaping is attenuated by the fact that the avoidance measure was very similar to the shaping treatment procedure.

A series of recent studies by Marks and his colleagues further supports the efficacy of implosive principles. In these carefully controlled studies (35, 36, 37), flooding was shown to be more effective than desensitization in producing improvement in both specific phobics and agoraphobics. DeMoore (38), however, found that although both desensitization and flooding led to reductions in fear, the results of desensitization were more lasting.

As is so often the case in therapy research, the evidence in support of implosive treatment is not overwhelming. Taken in sum, however, these studies generally support the effectiveness of implosion. In particular the research with actual patients strongly supports the effectiveness of implosive therapy. However, adducing these findings as evidence of the therapeutic power of catharsis is somewhat less certain. Saying that implosion achieves its results by catharsis is an hypothesis that must itself be substantiated by controlled studies. Stampfl himself is impressed by the effects of cathartic therapy, but suggests that they cannot be operationally distinguished from the process of extinction in implosive treatment.

Two studies provide data relevant to this point. In the first (39), results support the contention that the effects of implosive treatment are due to nonspecific emotional arousal and discharge, rather than to extinction of specific phobic imagery. In the second (40), equally significant improvement was obtained using imaginal flooding with phobic scenes and with scenes normally frightening to anyone. These two studies lend support to the interpretation that emotional discharge is a significant determinant of the success of implosive therapy.

Experiencing and Focusing in Psychotherapy

Another indirect source of support for catharsis in psychotherapy stems from the client-centered approach and involves emotional focusing. Carl Rogers is credited not only with developing client-centered psychotherapy, but also with pioneering in the research evaluation of therapy theory and technique. His efforts and his influence have led to a steady stream of research based on analyses derived from tape recordings and typescripts of actual therapy sessions. Consequently, the client-centered group has a wealth of data on the critical variables of successful psychotherapy. The best known of these findings have to do with conditions provided by the therapist. In a long series of studies, summarized by Truax and Carkhuff (41), accurate empathy, warmth (unconditional positive regard), and genuineness (congruence) on the part of the therapist were consistently related to positive therapeutic outcome. High levels of these three conditions lead to patients' improvement, while low levels lead to deterioration rather than no change (42). Chinsky and Rappaport (43) have challenged both the reliability of accurate empathy ratings and the precise meaning of the construct used in many of these studies, and they suggest that the findings related to accurate empathy are attenuated by the lack of rigor used to assess it.

So much for the qualities of the good therapist. Rogers has consistently maintained (44, 45) that a special kind of change in a patient's internal functioning indicates progress in successful psychotherapy. His remarks have been couched in phenomenological terms consistent with his own theory, but the ideas have wide applicability. He postulates that the ideal behavior for a patient is to focus on and express feelings, so that ultimately he can integrate affective and intellectual components of experience. Essentially, then, therapeutically productive patient behavior is emotional focusing. In Rogers' vocabulary, both *experiencing* and *focusing* are phenomenological terms, describing patients' behavior in therapy. Various scales have been devised to assess these constructs, the latest and most widely used of which is the Experiencing Scale (46). The Experiencing Scale refines and quantifies the description of the patient's behavior in therapy. Ideal patient behavior is described as a high level of experiencing, which consists of active emotional involvement and self-reference. While experiencing is not synonymous with catharsis, they are related on the same continuum, with dispassionate and abstract intellectualizing at one end, and experiencing and discharging feelings at the other. Furthermore, experiencing may be equivalent to what some emotive therapists call "involved talking" (47). This is thought to be cathartic, although the emotion displayed is intense verbal involvement and obvious affective arousal (cognitive-emotional catharsis), rather than tears or laughter (somatic-emotional catharsis). These scales measure verbal descriptions of and manner of relating feelings, rather than somatic-emotional discharge; nevertheless, it can be assumed that the vividness with which patients describe feelings is a valid index of the quantity and intensity of emotional experience and arousal. Intense focusing therefore seems to fit our description of cognitive-emotional catharsis.

Rogers and some of his co-workers first developed a scale designed to measure the ongoing process of psychotherapy (48). This scale included a total of six "strands" (factors), including a "feelings" factor which ranged on a continuum from "unrecognized, unexpressed" to "living in flow, fully experienced." In their validation study, ratings derived from the process scale were significantly correlated with ratings of progress in psychotherapy. These ratings were made independently. The implicit assumption is that a brief sample of expressive behavior can be used to assess a client's level of personality functioning and growth, and that therapy can usefully be evaluated while in progress.

Gendlin's studies of client focusing have concentrated on the physiological and personality correlates of focusing ability. Using counselors' ratings to evaluate both process and outcome variables, Gendlin, Jenney and Schlien (49) found that three items from a six item rating scale, at the end of time-limited psychotherapy with adult outpatients, related to therapeutic success. Of interest in the present context is that one of these three curative factors was described as "expressing his feelings directly instead of reporting them." Furthermore, this was the only process item on which change was significantly related to positive outcome. Unfortunately, these findings were contaminated because counselors judged both process and outcome variables. In later studies Gendlin was able to achieve better control, and eventually marshalled a great deal of support for the utility of focusing; he has summarized much of this work in a review paper (50). Though working from within the client-centered framework, Gendlin and his associates have devised process measures that are content free (51) and therefore applicable to other forms of treatment.

Gendlin points out that "intellectualizing" and "externalizing" are known to be ineffective forms of patient behavior, and that to get better, patients must work with their feelings in addition to achieving purely cognitive understanding. Working with feelings involves experiencing them, not just describing them. The client-centered therapist reflects the client's feelings in order to help the client clarify and focus on his affective experience. Gendlin uses the terms *focusing* and *experiential* to refer to the ideal psychotherapy interviews. He cites studies which show that focusing is a characteristic of successful therapy sessions, and is absent in unsuccessful sessions. Feeling (experiencing) is an essential ingredient in successfully conducted therapy.

Gendlin delineates four phases of focusing: (1) *Direct reference* entails the client's attending directly to what he feels internally. When this behavior is manifest, it leads to a shift like the yielding or release of what is concretely felt. (2) *Reference movement* is the feeling of release, or tension-reduction, following catharsis. (3) *Wide application* involves new facets of experience and their relevance to other tuations. (4) *Content mutation* consists of changes in the client's ideas about the nature and content of his feelings (insight). This process seems to involve cognitive-emotional catharsis, although it may eventuate in actual somatic-emotional discharge. Like the cathartic therapists, Gendlin is concerned more with *how* the client tells his story than with *what* he says. Talking in an emotionally aroused, deeply involved manner leads to successful outcomes.

Gendlin (50) reviews a number of studies by Tomlinson and others who used the Process Scale as a measure of levels of experiencing in therapy. The aggregate of findings demonstrate that successful clients show higher levels of focusing ("The individual is living some aspect of his problem in his experiencing") both early and late in the course of psychotherapy. This relationship was found to be true not only with outpatients, but also with hospitalized schizophrenic patients at the Mendota State Hospital in Wisconsin. "The findings establish that success depends on a certain mode of in-therapy behavior, namely that mode characterized by high levels of experiential attention and involvement."

These studies imply that success is predictable from the start of therapy and therefore, is perhaps more a function of the client's personality than of the effects of psychotherapy. Although an active therapist can teach his patients to dis-charge, Gendlin found only five of 38 cases in which there was an increase in experiential level over the course of therapy. Luborsky (52) found that patient variables are far more signifi-cant predictors of outcome in psychotherapy than therapist or treatment variables. It may be, therefore, that what the client brings to the therapy will determine his success or failure, but that he can be taught to improve effective in-therapy behavior to some extent. Furthermore, since what the patient brings to therapy is immutable and what the therapist does is not, these findings also suggest that the therapist who is not content to confine his practice to patients already at high levels of ex-periencing should expend his efforts to enhance emotional arousal.

Gendlin himself has become convinced that focusing can be taught and used as an adjunct tool in any form of psy-chotherapy. He has described (51) focusing as a bodily method that can be divided into three steps. First, clients should pause before speaking, in order to get in touch with their bodily feel-ings. Secondly, they should express these feelings. And finally, clients are taught to avoid analyzing their feelings. As Gendlin points out, "Then the bodily felt version of what the trouble is makes itself felt clearly enough." The therapist is very impor-tant in this process of deliberately zeroing in on feelings. "Therapist responses can carry the patient's experiencing forward, into experiential affects and bodily release, or they can leave his experiential bodily process stuck where it was stuck." Fresh, self-expressive relating by the therapist facilitates focusing, since feelings develop in the interpersonal interaction of the therapeutic relationship as well as in the patient's outside life.

Howard and Orlinsky found that successful psychotherapy is an intense affective experience (53, 54), and that patient and therapist tend to share a dominant mood or affect during each therapy session. Bierman (55) also has found that optimal benefit accrues with active engagement in the context of positive regard. While this observed correlation does not establish that it is the therapist who shapes the patient's mood, it seems reasonable to assume that at least some of the variance is due to the therapist's impact on the patient. If this is so, then by focusing intensely on the patient and his material (Jackins' "free attention") the therapist will influence the patient to do the same. Further support for the efficacy of affective experiencing in therapy comes from Luborsky (52), who found emotional experiencing to be a significant predictor of positive outcome, and concluded that the successful patient is capable of experiencing deeply and is reflectively aware of his feelings.

As part of his emphasis on emotional focusing, Gendlin has developed a new procedure to intensify the patient's affective experiencing (56). In addition to having the patient focus intensely on what he is saying, he uses images to vivify the experience and enhance the emotional arousal. Catharsis is presumed to result from verbal expression which releases the feelings aroused by the use of imagery in experiential focusing.

The Experiencing Scale (46) is a modification of an earlier version by Gendlin and Tomlinson (51). It is a standardized rating scale with seven stages designed to evaluate the quality of the patient's affective involvement in psychotherapy. The scale was designed for direct application to tape recordings or typescripts of therapy sessions, and has been used primarily for that purpose.

Typically, studies with the Experiencing Scale have used random sampling of four- to eight-minute segments extracted from therapy sessions. One particular advantage of this instrument is that clinically unsophisticated judges are as reliable as trained professionals. Interjudge reliabilities have generally been high. Correlation coefficients for the means of judges' ratings have varied from 0.76 to 0.91.

Kiesler (58) has summarized the results of validity studies of the Experiencing Scale. He lists four general findings: (1) Experiencing clearly differentiates between diagnostic groups, with neurotics manifesting higher levels than schizophrenics (59). (2) Level of experiencing is related to outcome, with more successful cases showing higher levels of experiencing. (3) Patients tend to show a U-shaped curve of change across therapy sessions. (4) The quality of patient experiencing is related to therapist empathy and congruence.

In summary, then, the work on focusing and experiencing

is solid research support for the therapeutic value of affective involvement and arousal in psychotherapy. Affective involvement does promote cognitive-emotional catharsis. Somatic-emotional discharge, however, has not received direct support from these studies.

Studies of Curative Factors

Rosenzweig (60) suggested many years ago that catharsis and the personality of the therapist may be the unrecognized critical factors in all forms of psychotherapy. More recently, Jerome Frank (61) emphasized the themes common to different methods of psychotherapy. He concludes from his survey of the literature that one of the six features of all forms of psychotherapy is the facilitation of emotional arousal. He also notes that abreaction is receiving a renewed emphasis in various new approaches, such as those of Janov and Jackins. Symonds (62) reviewed case reports of 68 reported changes of behavior, attitude, or feelings in psychotherapy. He found that 59 successful changes followed abreaction, seven followed interpretations, and two were related to changes in perception. On this basis, he concluded that the basic factor that promotes change in psychotherapy is abreaction. Abreaction implies a prior state of tension—dammed-up impulses or feelings—and represents a discharge or release of these accumulated tensions. Most of the abreactions in the material reviewed by Symonds were expressions of aggression. He also notes that abreaction depends on the therapist's creating an accepting and permissive atmosphere, which would seem to be particularly true with a socially proscribed behavior like aggression. Unfortunately, Symonds does not distinguish between abreaction as recall of lost memories (cognitive) and abreaction as (somatic) emotional discharge. He does say that it must be a total, fully feeling response to be effective. Furthermore, Symonds does not identify the source of the 68 reported favorable changes, and without this information, it is not safe to presume that his sample was unbiased.

Analogue Studies

When the complexity of naturally occurring events seems to defy understanding, scientists have built and tested laboratory models. It may be belaboring the obvious to point out that psychologists became interested in the variables effecting a rat's ability to negotiate a maze in order to better understand the process of human learning. Psychotherapy is an extraordinarily complex process. Each of its major dimensions, patient, therapist, treatment, and outcome, involves an intricate network of interacting attributes, such as age, sex and intelligence, as well as subtle factors, such as motivation, expectancy and attractiveness. Achieving even reasonable control over these various elements is a herculean task. One response to the complexities which make "live" psychotherapy refractory to study has been to isolate a subset of its elements under the conditions of relatively greater control that experimental models or analogues permit.

Some researchers, however, have raised penetrating questions regarding the conclusions drawn from analogue research. Thus Cooper and his colleagues (63) have challenged much of the validation of systematic desensitization. They point out that much of the evidence for the effectiveness of systematic desensitization rests on analogue studies, using nonpatient animal phobics. Volunteer subjects who are afraid of rats or snakes are easy to obtain and change is easy to define operationally; however, the various therapeutic procedures used to obtain change may be irrelevant to the "cures." Their evidence suggests that repeated contact with the experimental therapists and suggestion were enough to permit subjects to overcome their fears. Phobic subjects told that they should pretend to be unafraid were able to handle snakes following an average of eight sessions. In addition, both self-report and physiological indices of stress showed them to have mastered their fears.

This study clearly demonstrates the dangers in generalizing from analogue studies to the actual practice of psychotherapy. On the other hand, Goldstein, Heller and Sechrest (64) make a strong case for their relevance, and deny that there are research problems unique to psychotherapy. Their argument is hard to dispute; nevertheless, to have an impact on clinical practitioners, research must capture some of the essential ingredients of therapy as it is practiced. To the extent that research is removed from clinical situations, as it is in analogue studies, the risk is that some essential features of actual therapy will be obscured. The risk is worth taking, but the analogue researcher needs to be particularly careful in drawing generalizations.

Charles Keet's (66) attempt to establish a miniature therapy paradigm in a laboratory setting, for instance, raises issues relevant both to catharsis in psychotherapy and to analogue methodology. Keet's design consisted of an experimental induction of stress in volunteer subjects, followed by one of two experimental treatment procedures and an analysis of their effectiveness in alleviating the stress.

Keet began by administering the Jung word-association test to all subjects. He then selected the most disturbing word for each based on reaction time and inability to recall the word upon re-administration of the test. Twenty-five of 30 subjects were then unable to remember the traumatic word during a serial learning test. Failure to recall the traumatic word apparently made the subjects uneasy, and each of them spontaneously began to talk about this discomfort. Keet described this as a conflict situation "closely resembling a compulsion neurosis."

As the subjects spoke of their annoyance at forgetting, Keet engaged them for thirty minutes in experimental therapy. In the "expressive technique," he encouraged half of his subjects to express their frustration over their difficulty in recalling, while the experimenter clarified their feelings and encouraged catharsis. With the other half of the subjects, the experimenter used the "interpretive technique." This consisted of offering direct help in finding the missing word by suggesting that there must be personal (unconscious) meaning involved in the forgetting. The experimenter encouraged personal associations and helped subjects to interpret the meaning of these associations in terms of their relationship to forgetting.

Following experimental counseling, subjects performed a second learning experiment which required the recall of the forgotten words. This provided the criterion for the success of the counseling procedures. The results showed the interpretive method to be clearly more effective than the expressive one. Eleven of 12 subjects recalled the traumatic word following the interpretive condition, while none of the 13 in the expressive condition recalled the traumatic word.

Keet's study was regarded as significant in developing a useful method for studying psychotherapy in the laboratory; however, two attempts to replicate Keet's findings failed (67,

68); in neither study did subjects selectively forget traumatic words, and in one study (67) there was no tension observed in subjects who were unable to recall forgotten words. As a consequence Keet's paradigm has been largely abandoned. This inability of other workers to replicate Keet's findings should come as no surprise, for his project, while ambitious, was poorly conceived.

The value of Keet's paradigm rests on the assumption that the subjects' inability to recall a certain word is analogous to the presenting concerns of psychiatric patients. Clearly, it is not. Real patients seek psychotherapy for a variety of concerns which explicitly or implicitly have to do with personal maladjustment and conflict. Therapy or counseling is designed to help people change some aspect of themselves in order that they may solve problems or resolve conflicts. In Keet's study, personal maladjustment and conflict are irrelevant to the design. Operationally defined, the subjects' problem was to remember the forgotten word, and the most direct help in solving this problem would be to tell them the word. It may be that their difficulty in remembering stimulated conflict, or made the subjects unhappy or worried. These concerns *are* relevant to the process of psychotherapy, but no attempt was made to measure their resolution. The only criterion of success was recall of the forgotten words.

A second major criticism of Keet's study has to do with the description and application of the two methods of experimental therapy. The study is described as a comparison of expressive and interpretive therapy. In fact, the comparison was between an expressive procedure and a combination of expressive and interpretive procedures. In the interpretive condition, the experimenter provided subjects with the opportunity to ventilate their feelings and then made leading interpretations; he deduced what was on their minds and then told them. Thus, in the interpretive procedure the experimenter gave the subjects some direct help in solving their problem, which was nothing more than remembering a forgotten word. The study had other minor methodological flaws, such as using one experimenter to administer both therapeutic procedures, but these are not as significant as Keet's failure to establish a realistic analogue to the clinical situation.

The behaviorists' attempt to introduce scientific rigor into the analysis and modification of behavior led them to use specific responses to evaluate aspects of psychotherapy. The more discreet, phasic types of behavior, such as approaching a phobic object, were among the first objectives to be specified and measured. More tonic behavioral states, such as anxiety, have been measured by examining self-reports and physiological reactions. Anxiety as a behavioral state is associated with various somatic components of emotion, especially arousal of the sympathetic components of the autonomic nervous system. Since it is generally agreed upon that psychotherapy has as one of its goals a reduction in anxiety, the autonomic measures are therefore a suitable yardstick for outcome in therapy analogues.

Haggard (69) used shock as an analogue to minor trauma followed by three different "therapeutic" interventions. One treatment, "rest therapy," consisted of allowing subjects to relax after being shocked. The second group of subjects were given "experimental extinction," which consisted of reexposure to the CS, but with no shock. The third group was given "catharsis-information therapy," in which subjects were encouraged to express their feelings of fear and anger. Reduction in GSR served as the criterion of effectiveness of experimental treatment. Catharsis-information therapy was the most effective intervention in reducing the general level of disturbance. Unfortunately, the catharsis-information group was also allowed to ask questions about the purpose and nature of the experiment, and, if they asked, were told that no further shocks would be used. As a result of such confounding, this study cannot be viewed as analogous to actual psychotherapy, in which the therapist does not control and predict the future.

Levison, Zax and Cowen (70) did an analogue study of the effectiveness of verbalizing feelings on the reduction of experimentally induced anxiety. In this study, GSR (galvanic skin response) was used as the index of anxiety. Anxiety was induced by classical conditioning; the word *chair* served as the CS, and was paired with a loud buzzer (UCS). Following this, subjects spent 20 minutes in one of three conditions. In the first condition, subjects discussed their reactions and feelings about the experiment with a clinical psychologist. This "stimulating therapy" was designed to provide catharsis of cue-related affect. A second group merely rested for twenty minutes. A third group talked with an experimental therapist. With this group, used to control for the effects of merely relating to the therapist, any discussion related to the anxiety-producing experience was avoided. Following these three treatments, extinction trials were conducted in which subjects' GSRs were measured and compared with the conditioning trials. "Therapeutic" success was equated with a reduction in GSR. The group that discussed their feelings showed the greatest drop in anxiety, followed by the talk control group. However, these differences were not statistically significant. The authors did note that those subjects observed to have discussed their feelings most freely dropped the most in anxiety. "Thus it seems that the ability to verbalize easily and to express affect, including negative feelings and hostility, realistically prompted by the noxious experimental situation, may be a crucial factor in tension reduction as measured by GSR."

Wiener (71) induced stress in college students by implying that their Rorschach scores indicated possible maladjustment. Surprisingly, this seemingly threatening message had little effect in producing measured signs of distress. Only one of five personality test measures (the Discomfort Relief Quotient) significantly differentiated between the stressed subjects and unstressed controls. Wiener noted that the other four measures showed differences in the expected direction, and the probability of the pattern of scores coming out as it did was .02. The results do not justify Wiener's statement that the groups were adequately differentiated.

Following the attempt to induce stress, subjects were assigned to one of two experimental counseling procedures, or to one of two control groups. Wiener reported that both "reassurance-interpretation" and "catharsis-reflection" proved superior to rest or discussion of neutral topics. In fact, the differences on criterion measures between counseled and noncounseled subjects were not statistically significant. In this, as in most other analogue studies, the induced situation was not comparable to the problems for which people seek psychotherapy; furthermore, treatment procedures were complex, and confounded effective ingredients. The same experimenter who induced stress by telling subjects that they might be maladjusted also attempted to alleviate it in a 15-minute session. In the "interpretation-reassurance" group the experimenter told subjects that their thoughts and feelings were not different from those of any normal, well-adjusted person—thus directly contradicting the original stressor message. In the "catharsis-reflection" treatment, subjects were invited to talk about their feelings, but there is no indication whether they actually expressed or ventilated any feelings.

Gordon (65) used a hypnotic procedure to suggest to a group of nonpatient subjects that they had undergone a mildly upsetting experience. While under hypnosis, subjects were told that they would not be able to recall the experience when they awoke, but would spend an hour trying to figure out what was bothering them. Two forms of intervention were compared for effectiveness in helping subjects recall analogues of repressed traumatic experiences. Experimental therapists followed either a leading procedure—asking questions and making suggestions—or a following procedure—clarifying, restating, and reflecting. The results were not clear, but showed a nonsignificant trend for more recall after the leading condition.

In another study, Grossman (72) compared the impact of different therapeutic procedures without attempting to induce stress. The major question he sought to answer was, Would subjects gain more insight from therapist statements that recognized explicitly expressed feelings and attitudes (reflection), or from statements that recognized inferred or implied feelings and attitudes (interpretation)? Two groups of ten male college students, matched on various measures of personality, motivation, and verbal ability, were tested, treated, and then retested. Despite the attempt to match groups, striking differences were noted, independent of experimental treatment between groups. By chance, the group in the interpretive condition were concerned about personal problems, and discussed them much more openly than the subjects assigned to the reflection group. Effectiveness was defined in terms of increased insight, which was assessed by having subjects predict their personality test scores. The interpretation group showed directionally, but not significantly, more insight. In light of the sort of treatments being compared, it seems that Grossman selected a poor dependent variable. In the interpretive condition, therapists made leading remarks that helped subjects predict their personality test scores, whether or not they helped them feel better or change their behavior.

Autonomic nervous system activity has been shown to wax and wane with emotional intensity or arousal. However, various psychophysiological measures of arousal do not intercorrelate significantly (73). O'Kelly (74) has suggested that periodic measures of autonomic functioning be made over time in standard situations. Then when a standard stressor is applied, autonomic reactivity can be assessed. Skeletal muscle tension could provide additional data.

Studies correlating ongoing events, such as catharsis, with physiological recordings, are not common, but one investigator (75) did correlate psychophysiological measures with catharsis during the course of psychotherapeutic interviews. Goldman-Eisler related breathing activity during speech and output of speech per breath to emotional intensity and expression. She examined the fluctuation of speech output and rate of breathing, which in turn are related to changes in action potentials of muscular activity. These various changes were studied in context of clinical interviews. Goldman-Eisler concluded that her measures were indeed related to catharsis (laughing and crying), thus giving a very literal meaning to the term "emotional ventilation." Unfortunately, for technical reasons her work has never been replicated, nor has it had much influence.

Several studies have demonstrated that GSR, as an index of emotional arousal, decreases as a function of therapy. One of the earliest of these studies (76) was conducted in the context of an ongoing series of "real" psychotherapy sessions. Even so, it can be considered a laboratory analogue, because continuous recording of GSR clearly modifies the usual therapy situation. Dittes compared GSR responses accompanying the reporting of sexual behavior and wishes early in therapy to those that occurred late in therapy. Based on the premise that fear or embarrassment associated with sexual wishes would diminish upon reporting them to a therapist, his hypothesis was that GSR would drop over time. The evaluation was conducted with a case study of a single patient seen weekly for 43 sessions. The results showed a clearcut drop in the GSR accompanying embarrassing sex statements over the course of treatment ($p <$ .01). The author related these findings to the resolution of transference in therapy, and speculated that fear of thinking embarrassing thoughts may have been the important behavior that was changed. While these notions are interesting, they go far beyond the actual data, which dealt only with the emotional concomitants of reporting embarrassing material. However, the study may be misleading in suggesting that simply reporting embarrassing thoughts extinguishes the embarrassment. It is also important to learn what sort of response from the therapist—reassurance, or facilitation of catharis—is effective in producing this decrease in GSR.

Two later studies (77, 78) supported the hypothesis that discussing and expressing feelings about conflict areas is associated with less anxiety than avoiding discussion of such troublesome material. Increased approach to emotional material led to a larger decrease in basal levels of anxiety, as measured by self-report and skin conductance. Those subjects who avoided dealing with emotional material showed an increase on both measures of anxiety. Furthermore, there was a marked increase in approaching emotionally important and painful material both within and between sessions as a function of therapists' accepting, noncritical attitudes and positive reinforcement—that is like Jackins' free attention. Similar findings were obtained by Gendlin and Berlin (79) who reported that direct experiencing of troublesome feelings led to tension reduction as measured by skin conductance.

Ruesch and Prestwood (80) also found that the most successful method of abating anxiety is to share it through verbal communication. Persons who never express anxiety are heavily defended and tend to break down in emergencies, while those who discharge anxiety regularly in interpersonal situations can tolerate the anxiety engendered by emergencies. This view was supported by data showing that when anxiety is expressed overtly in therapy, its general level is reduced.

Richard Lazarus (81) has extended these findings by pointing out that those who avoid an emotional response to stressor stimuli tend to show higher levels of physiological stress as compared to emotional responders. In one study subjects were shown a film of primitive pubertal subincision rites, while autonomic indicators of stress (GSR and heart rate) were monitored. Those high in denial tendency ("repressors" on Byrnne's Repression-Sensitization Scale) showed the greatest autonomic reactivity. "High deniers refuse to admit disturbance verbally, but reveal it autonomically, while low deniers are apt to say that they are more disturbed while showing less autonomic reactivity." The implication of this work is that verbal catharsis is able to attenuate the residual effects of emotional stress.

Several of these studies discuss interventions regarded as cathartic. However, none of these interventions involve the intense emotional discharge advocated by contemporary emotive therapists. Moreover none of these studies attempt to measure the occurrence of catharsis. For these reasons, we cannot say that they demonstrate the effectiveness of cathartic therapy.

Most of the analogue studies reviewed have attempted to test either an entire theoretical approach or single components of a theory, often out of context. While testing theories of therapy—eventually with sophisticated controls—may be worthwhile, clinicians are more concerned with evaluations of therapy practice. Thus, it seems wiser to determine first which forms of therapy, as practiced clinically, are effective through outcome studies. Once an approach is demonstrated to be effective, then analogue studies would be useful to determine the specific elements contributing to success. These elements should be extracted from actual therapy practice, not extrapolated from theory. In the case of cathartic therapy it seems desirable to demonstrate its effectiveness, as practiced, in naturalistic outcome studies. If and when this is done, then analogue studies may provide sufficient control to answer such questions as: With which type of patients is cathartic therapy most useful? What are the immediate (for instance, physiological) effects of somatic-emotional discharge? What sort of patient-therapist pairing is optimal? and What are the most effective procedures in eliciting emotional discharge? At the present these questions are premature. They will become relevant only following proof that cathartic therapy is effective.

Psychosomatic Medicine

In psychosomatic medicine, mental events are said to "cause" physical symptoms. There is, of course, no such thing as mind distinct from body. Rather, there are various ways to conceptualize and describe phenomena. Physiological and anatomical explanations have proven most useful in dealing with medical problems; psychological concepts have been more fruitful in dealing with behavioral problems. Therefore, when we speak of psychosomatic illness, we are choosing to describe pathology in physical terms and etiology in mental terms. For the sake of convenience, we may speak of "emotional processes" influencing "organic illness"; in fact, though, we are only switching frames of reference.

Because psychosomatic medicine is generally the province of physicians, the descriptions of psychological antecedents are often inelegant and not rigorous. Both psychological stress and emotional inhibition have been implicated in the etiology of psychosomatic illness; however, most of the material about pernicious results of affective blunting is made up of anecdotal evidence and clinical descriptions, with little hard data. Nevertheless, it is an almost ubiquitous observation of workers in this field that suppressed emotional responding is a major pathogenic factor.

Diseases most commonly related to emotional suppression are rheumatoid arthritis, ulcerative colitis, peptic ulcer, bronchial asthma, essential hypertension, and migraine headache (82). These syndromes generally involve a single organ system ennervated by the autonomic nervous system. Organic dysfunction develops when the physiological reactions, which are part and parcel of an emotional reaction, are not terminated as a result of a somatic-emotional discharge. Somatic-emotional arousal primes the body for emotional discharge. If this reaction is inhibited, the physiological arousal persists. Instead of returning to basal levels, the physiological response mechanisms continue in activation to a point where the system is overtaxed and the eventual result may be an organic dysfunction.

Various attempts have been made to trace the influence of emotional arousal on organic disease processes by the effect on endocrine and exocrine functioning. We shall confine our discussion here, however, to behavioral descriptions of these etiologic factors.

It is a routine assumption in cases of psychosomatic syndromes that the patient has difficulty in expressing aggression, hostility, or protest in an effective, adaptive manner (83, 84). Lewis and Lewis (85), for example, describe a process whereby repressed aggressive feelings may lead to ulcerative colitis. "The colon reacts sharply to emotion. During periods of tranquility it is pale and quiet, its secretions of enzymes low. During periods of anger and resentment, however, it becomes engorged with blood and very active. Secretions increase. Spots of abnormal tissue may occur. Ulcerative colitis is thought to develop when a predisposed person fails to express chronic resentment and anger. On an unconscious level, the mucous membrane of his colon *does* respond to these repressed emotions. The ensuing engorgement and hypersensitivity produces bleeding. Enzymes secreted by the intestine further erode the membrane, leaving it open to bacterial infection."

In addition to being disinclined to express anger, a large percentage of ulcerative colitis patients experience a well-defined life crisis within the six months preceding the onset of their illness. Apparently, then, chronic emotional constraint may interact with traumatically stressful situations in the development of psychosomatic disease. However, since life crises are difficult to predict or control, attention has been focused on the predisposing personality and the style of responding to trauma.

The person who has learned a chronic pattern of emotional suppression is least likely to respond to frustration or deprivation with outbursts of temper or grief. Groen (86) has stated that man learns increasing inhibition of emotional discharge both phylogenetically and ontogenetically. Psychosomatic reactions develop from inhibited discharge, and, "The development of the cerebral connections has greatly enhanced the possibility of isolating, damping and inhibiting discharges. These mechanisms came into action under the influence of imprinting, early conditioning and learning of incorporated norms, and conscious insight. . . . "

Groen indicates that because psychosomatic patients do not express and discharge emotional reactions, their autonomic nervous system reactions are prolonged and intense. Consequently, he suggests, "This state of affairs is, for instance, most evident in patients with essential hypertension, who have been found to be at the same time hypersensitive and aggressive and yet inhibited in their aggressive discharge." Instead of ventilating hostile feelings through muscular action, such as yelling, these patients suffer a prolonged cardiovascular arousal. This response, in turn, becomes conditioned to stress and frustrations. This is similar to the psychoanalytic position (87, 88) that the physical expression of an affect occurs without the patient's being consciously aware that he is having an emotional reaction. In this way, some, but not all, of the affect is discharged; and the effect may be that the affective attitude becomes expressed chronically through somatic "affect equivalents." When the mental content of the affect is warded off, but the physical activation (arousal, not discharge) takes place, the physiological response is more chronic and thus leads to organic stress. This psychoanalytic view is supported by Schachter's dual component theory of emotions (89). In Schachter's model, an emotional reaction consists of a state of somatic arousal that is recognized and labeled in a way consistent with a concurrent cognitive image. If the cognition were not formed (that is, repressed), then the autonomic response would occur without the subjective experience of an emotional reaction.

Psychosomatic patients have been characterized as people who typically blunt their emotional reactions in particular situations. These patients do not manifest an unemotional manner because they are emotionally flat or dulled; indeed, they may even be hypersensitive to some types of affect. What is missing is the response, not the reaction.

Bastiaans (83) has suggested that the psychosomatic patient may be subject to patterns of psychological stress and affective arousal similar to the neurotic, but that he wards off the feelings because he considers them to be childish, weak, or dangerous. Bastiaans calls the psychosomatic patients "self-controlling fighters," and says, "Thus the psychosomatic patient becomes involved in a tragedy of maladaptation: while believing that he is a master of his own emotional life, in fact he becomes a victim of this supreme denial of the value of his best assistant, his psychobiological warning or arousal apparatus."

Some investigators have identified the suppression of feelings other than anger as a contributory cause of psychosomatic disorders. Groen (86), for one, noted that most of the psychosomatic patients he studied had a pattern of suppressed weeping. Miller and Baruch (90) identified a "hunger for affection" as a common feature of allergy patients—a phrase that is a simplified residue of an earlier psychoanalytic metaphor. According to Fenichel, a chronically frustrated, oral-receptive, demanding person is prone to develop gastrointestinal disorders—that is, because he is "hungry for love" the mucous membrane of his stomach begins to secrete acid which in the absence of food eats away at the stomach lining.

Actually, the most common type of emotional inhibition identified in the personalities of psychosomatic patients is suppressed anger. As Bastiaans observed, "It is a hard clinical fact that psychosomatic syndromes do not arise when activated aggression has not been suppressed or repressed beyond a certain degree." It is common to overestimate the danger of verbalizing one's hostile feelings, so modern culture fosters a rigid inhibition of aggressive impulses which sometimes leads to physiological exhaustion. In psychosomatic patients, hostility may be activated in fantasy, but verbal discharge, such as complaining, is likely to be suppressed.

The fact that suppressed emotional expression is a major contributing factor in psychosomatic illness implies that psychosomatic patients should learn to express their feelings. The question is, How? Some experts suggest insight-oriented psychotherapy, while others advocate expressive, emotive therapy. Bastiaans strongly advocates cathartic discharge of aggressive feelings in psychotherapy with psychosomatic patients. He has advised that hypnosis, narcoanalysis and LSD analysis may be useful by promoting therapeutic catharsis, and he points out that greater effort must be spent on encouraging affective expression to achieve a balance between intelligence and emotion with psychosomatic patients. He has noted a lessening in intensity of psychosomatic syndromes as soon as patients are able to discharge some of their inner tension through verbal and nonverbal expression of feelings. After patients have experienced catharsis in psychotherapy, he works to help them to express feelings more freely in their daily lives.

Even in the context of psychoanalytic therapy, catharsis of aggression may be employed. It may even be beneficial to foster cathartic discharge without analyzing the reasons for the emotional blockage (88). Lewis and Lewis (85) have pointed out that "The most common prelude to migraine is repressed rage. Psychoanalysts treating migraine patients have observed that an attack may disappear when a patient gives vent to his hostility."

Miller and Baruch (90) advise an approach that combines re-education with catharsis to achieve emotional discharge in and out of therapy. They advise therapists working with psychosomatic patients to listen carefully to discover what the patient is feeling, and then to help him understand and express his feelings. This process includes not only labeling and reflecting feelings, but also promoting discharge, especially of anger. "For a major part of treatment, the expression of repressed anger will need to be rechanneled from being directed against the self in illness to the external target against whom it is felt." Noting that anger is repressed both currently and from past situations, they advise the clinician to foster angry expressions of feeling toward present and past persons.

Ungoverned hostility can, of course, be disastrous. Psychosomatic patients may have an exaggerated fear of the consequences of their hostility, precisely because it remains buried; furthermore, their fantasies may be extremely violent. A woman who does not express her annoyance and resentment toward her husband may have fantasies of beating or murdering him. Such thoughts may frighten her, and cause a further entrenchment of her emotional rigidity. In expressive psychotherapy, patients can experience their emotions, and not only achieve discharge of tension, but also learn to recognize and deal realistically with their feelings in the future.

Catharsis and the Social Psychology of Aggression

Catharsis has also been investigated in nonclinical contexts. Social psychologists have studied catharsis in two major areas, the social psychology of aggression, and attitude change. While this work does not involve catharsis as a treatment modality, it is concerned with behavior change, which follows the same laws no matter what the context. These studies therefore do have some relevance for successful therapy.

In *Frustration and Aggression* (91), Dollard *et al.* outline the "catharsis hypothesis" of aggression, according to which, "The occurrence of any act of aggression is assumed to reduce the instigation to aggression." That means that any discharging of aggression, even displaced aggression (contrary to Freud), should lessen pent-up feelings of aggression. Aggression is not presumed to be a basic drive (again contrary to Freud), but the necessary result of frustration. The net effect of living with undischarged frustrations is to create a kind of reservoir of aggressive feelings, which can be drained only by being tapped.

Konrad Lorenz (92) applied this notion uncritically to anthropology. Members of socially isolated groups, he argued, must build up a powerful aggressive drive because they have no outsiders to attack. The best thing for them to do, he said, would be to smash a vase with a loud resounding crash. This simple-minded advice to engage in displaced somatic-emotional discharge ignores the source of the anger and frustration, as well as the feelings that the original experience engendered.

Holt (93) provides a more sophisticated version of this line of reasoning. To those who argue—with good reason—that free expression of aggressive impulses can be dangerous, Holt replies that aggression can be expressed in constructive ways, and furthermore, that not expressing anger has its own maladaptive consequences, including psychosomatic disorders. Rather than urging indiscriminate violence, however, he suggests direct expression of anger, that is, to the person who generates it, in a judicious manner. Healthy interpersonal interactions can be non-sum zero games—one member of a dyadic interaction need not come out a winner and the other a loser. Instead, both parties can win if anger is expressed directly in a socially acceptable manner. Telling someone that what he did has made you angry is quite different from punching him in the nose, and is also a happier solution than keeping the feeling submerged, festering, which can lead to later maladaptive aggressive acts. Holt presents evidence to show that unexpressed anger not only leads to a variety of psychosomatic symptoms, but also interferes with cognitive efficiency.

Some social scientists believe that catharsis of aggressive behavior leads to an increase in aggression. Leonard Berkowitz, for instance, has studied the associative determinants of impulsive violence, and attacks the popular belief that it is desirable and necessary to act on aggressive impulses (94), a position he attributes to "the ventilationists." In reviewing the data, he demonstrates clever phrasemaking and a proclivity for attacking men of straw: "Although there are small colonies scattered throughout the United States, most ventilationists are located on the East and West coasts, but particularly in California. I regard them as part of California's contribution to the American dream, along with Hollywood and Disneyland. One notable feature of this cult is its rejection of intellect." He claims that cathartic therapists, by rewarding unrestricted aggression, unwittingly, foster it outside of therapy. In place of expressive discharge of feelings, Berkowitz advises therapists to help their patients understand and control their emotions.

He does, however, misunderstand the psychoanalytic position on catharsis. He states (95) that the analytic position is that an opportunity to express hostility reduces physiological tension, and therefore is pleasurable. However, he distorts the analytic position which includes the notion that psychic energy is linked to specific mental contents (96). Those who espouse the therapeutic benefit of catharsis consistently recommend that the feelings generated by distressful experiences must be discharged, not that aggressive behavior be indulged.

Interpreting the wealth of data on the social psychology of aggression is difficult and confusing, since the term *catharsis* is used with a variety of referents. In some studies (97), subjects simply observed aggressive behavior taking place in a laboratory setting, which did not involve them directly. Another set of studies (98) involved subjects witnessing something unpleasant happening to their tormentors without the subjects doing anything aggressive themselves. In other studies subjects either have the opportunity to hurt their frustrator without actually interacting with him (99), or to express aggression in a direct and harmful manner (100). Likewise, dependent measures of the effects of catharsis have varied from feelings of general hostility or arousal (95), heart rate and systolic blood pressure (101), hostile feelings toward the frustrator (98) to aggressive behavior toward the frustrator (102).

Phillips and Wiener (103), in writing about short-term psychotherapy, point out that the catharsis hypothesis is too vague to permit prediction as to whether catharsis will reduce or increase aggressive symptomatology. This seems true, but only because catharsis is used to describe many types of behavior. They support Bandura's position (5) that direct or vicarious participation in aggressive behavior predicts later increases in the incidence of aggression. Aggressive catharsis, says Bandura, reinforces undesirable aggressive behavior in children. However, "participating in aggression" may properly be called *catharsis* only if aggressive *feelings* are directly expressed.

Berkowitz has done a number of studies which show that although hostile behavior (which he mislabels catharsis) may make a person feel better, it is likely to increase hostile behavior in the future. Subjects frustrated in a laboratory setting who were allowed to administer what they thought were electric shocks to their frustrator, felt better. (Martin Orne's cautionary comment on the Milgram shock study, that subjects do not believe researchers will allow anyone to be hurt, must be kept in mind in interpreting these findings). Substitute aggression, such as witnessing a poor performance from the frustrating agent, also made subjects feel better.

Doob and Wood (100) have shown that angered subjects

who either hurt their annoyer or even see him being hurt by someone else will subsequently choose to hurt him less. In a similar study, Konecni and Doob (104), found that aggression (administering pseudo electric shocks) directed at the frustrator or displaced to another person was "cathartic"—that is, led to a decrease in subsequent aggression. The authors concluded that catharsis may occur through either direct or displaced aggression. These findings do demonstrate one type of situation that leads to a decrement in aggressive behavior, but the independent variable is probably better described as retaliation than catharsis.

Other studies have demonstrated that aggressing toward an agent of frustration may not even reduce tension, much less reduce the likelihood of future aggression. Kahn (101), for example, subjected college students to anger-arousing experiences, after which one group expressed anger to a sympathetic "physician," while the other group sat quietly for an equivalent period of time. Following this, the catharsis group expressed dislike of the provocators significantly more than controls. Kahn interpreted these findings in terms of cognitive consistency. That is, he said that verbal catharsis does not free a person of negative feelings, but rather solidifies these feelings. Furthermore, members of the catharsis group were more physiologically aroused than controls during recovery. Unfortunately, he failed to consider the possibility that the increased physiological arousal is time-locked to the expression of anger, and is likely to fall below the level of controls (repressors) after more time passes.

When frustrated in their attempts to solve simple problems by other children acting as stooges, a group of third graders became angry and hostile (102). Allowing the frustrated children the opportunity to administer what they thought were annoying but not harmful shocks did not reduce their anger or hostility, however; nor did verbal aggression reduce angry feelings. In many cases, angry words even increased hostility. Most effective in reducing aggression was the experimenter's interpretation of the frustrator's behavior. The measure of residual aggression following the experimental procedures (direct aggression, verbal aggression, or rational explanation) was the number of pseudo electric shocks delivered to the frustrator. Instead of demonstrating that the opportunity to behave hostilely increased future aggression, however, the findings may be viewed as resulting from the initial aggression having been neither fully or directly expressed. The setting was such that the usual anxiety over aggression was assuaged (having been encouraged by an adult authority figure), and the aggressive behavior resulted neither in punishment nor in seeing the stooges suffer. Although aggressive behavior is usually attended by anxiety (105, 106), social acceptance of the reasons for aggression results in subjects feeling more comfortable about committing aggression (95).

Studies (106) have shown that level of guilt or anxiety over aggression varies significantly with individuals. Both high and low guilt subjects obtain tension-reduction (evidenced by a drop in diastolic blood pressure), although low guilt subjects show a greater effect following direct aggression (shocking the frustrator). However, only low guilt subjects show a significant decrease in blood pressure after shocking someone who was not the agent of their frustration.

In view of the inhibiting effect of anxiety over direct aggression, what are the effects of watching another person commit aggression? This question bears directly on the impact of exposure to movie and television violence. In a recent review article, Berkowitz (107) concluded that observing films of violent behavior serves to justify the behavior itself and leads to increased acts of violence on the part of spectators. He finds the same result from witnessing aggressive behavior directly. The accuracy of these findings is supported by replication in numerous settings, and their social relevance is clear. However, they are not evidence that catharsis of aggressive *feelings* leads to aggressive behavior. Berkowitz calls modeling and positive reinforcement catharsis. They are not. The effects of witnessing aggression and those of expressing—directly and appropriately—one's own aggressive feelings are quite different.

In the Baker and Schaie study (105), frustration was aroused by having subjects count backward from 99 by twos while being interrupted and harrassed. Following this, control subjects were allowed to rest, while the experimental group counteraggressed directly or by watching a vicar apply (apparent) shock, verbally attacking, responding to card 8BM of the TAT (the surgery scene), or pressing a button to signal that the frustrator was performing poorly on a task. Significant drops in systolic blood pressure were found following overt counteragression. But the effects of aggressing alone, or with another, did not differ significantly. If direct aggression arouses anxiety, then expressing aggressive feelings in a therapy session should help abate this anxiety. In the Baker and Schaie study the vicar's presence did not affect arousal. However, the parallel between a warm accepting therapist, and an experimental cohort is a weak one, and this study provides little data to suggest that a therapist cannot help to mitigate the anxiety over discussing aggressive feelings. The results suggest that some anxiety would persist even with a warm accepting therapist, but a certain level of anxiety in psychotherapy is helpful.

Berkowitz attacks the psychoanalytic energy model of motivation, which he says suggests that aggressive behavior reduces aggression. He ends by saying that an individual in whom an aggressive response sequence has been activated achieves completion of this sequence and tension-reduction when he believes the instigator has been injured, but that future aggression is thereby facilitated. The crucial distinction between this conclusion and the claims of cathartic therapists is between hurting people, and expressing (verbally) and discharging aggressive *feelings* in psychotherapy.

Catharsis and Attitude Change

Attitudes are molded by experience, and despite their relative stability they are modified by experience. Just as a therapist encounters resistance in trying to change behavior, so does a person encounter opposition when he attempts to alter the attitudes of another person. Each of us at times attempts to persuade others. In so doing, we employ various strategies, some of which are more successful than others. Students of attitude change have endeavored to discover the ingredients in effective strategies, and some of the variables influencing attitude that have been studied (108) include: the prestige and credibility of the communicator; one-sided as opposed to two-sided communications; order of presenting arguments; forewarning and distracting the audience; inoculation against counterarguments; and role-playing.

Social psychologists have also examined catharsis as a facilitator of attitude and social change. While describing resistance to social change, Zander (109) noted that catharsis is a most effective means to overcome resistance. Once again, however, Zander uses *catharsis* to refer to the verbalization of negative ideas and contrary beliefs, not to cognitive or somatic discharge of pent-up emotions. Therefore, the data presented which indicate that catharsis potentiates attitude change can be seen as only indirectly supporting the use of emotional expression in psychotherapy.

Gordon Allport (110) has described catharsis as an efficient means of reducing racial prejudice. He begins by noting that to mend an inner tube, it is first necessary to let the air out. He studied racial attitudes among public officials in an eastern city, and found that race relations improved following cathartic sessions in which hostile feelings and opinions were vented. Allport concludes that verbal release of emotional tensions can diminish rigidly held opinions and open the possibility of reeducation.

A listener, he said, who is bursting with feelings needs to express them in order that he may be free to respond to the speaker's message, instead of just his own thoughts. In other words, as a member of the audience hears the speaker's opinion, he may develop counterarguments, and if he does, he must be given an opportunity to express them before he will openly and attentively listen to the speaker's points. This, of course, is a very cognitive aspect of catharsis. It is important that the new viewpoint be presented following the expression of the old, or the audience member may simply be silently rehearsing his previously held viewpoint.

Allport's work suggests that when resistance is encountered in attempting to change attitudes it is necessary to encourage ventilation of the old opinions and feelings. After this is done, then restructuring of attitudes will be more successful.

Kurt Lewin (111) devised a most elegant model for the analysis of attitude change, called "quasi-stationary social equilibria." It includes catharsis as part of the "unfreezing" process by which old attitudes are replaced by new ones. Lewin's description of catharsis is similar to Zander's, but puts more emphasis on emotional expression.

Jerome Frank has also done some studies on the use of catharsis in attitude change. His first study (112) was a questionnaire survey of people who had been "radicalized" or committed to peace work. Questionnaires were returned from

92 respondents, the preponderance of whom were college graduates. Most were in young or middle adulthood and slightly more than half were women. In the vast majority, it was found that change in attitude (and behavior) had been preceded by intense emotional responses. It is worth noting that the criterion for inclusion in this sample may have biased the results. The term "radicalized" suggests a sudden conversion. Perhaps emotional responses are only involved in these dramatic changes in commitment, while a slow accretion of information is the more usual process.

In a later study (113), Frank and his associates studied the impact of catharsis on attitude change in psychotherapy. Attitude change in neurotic patients was investigated under conditions of high and low emotional arousal. Seven patients, aged 22 to 39, were used, and arousal was manipulated by the use of ether. All patients were encouraged to vividly re-enact the emotions of a past significant experience. Attitude change was measured using Osgood's Semantic Differential. It was found that attitude change was greater in the arousal sessions, and that the patients were more susceptible to the therapist's suggestion after the peak of arousal had passed than during or before maximal excitation. Follow up showed that four of the seven showed behavioral change compatible with the new attitude. This finding helps negate the obvious criticism that change on the Semantic Differential may have been due to compliance with the demand characteristics of the situation. The more serious problem is that arousal is not discharge. In all likelihood, discharge followed arousal in this study, but since it was not measured the support for catharsis is again only inferential.

The idea that catharsis facilitates attitude change is widely but not universally held. Arnold Goldstein for one (64) has challenged the usefulness of catharsis. Though his argument is unsupported by data, it is a penetrating one. Writing from the perspective of a social psychologist who is interested in psychotherapy, Goldstein has suggested that catharsis is counterproductive for changing attitudes or behavior because catharsis amounts to practicing undesirable responses. According to Goldstein, permitting catharsis of attitudes or feelings is analogous to letting a child who is being taught to speak French practice incorrect responses in hopes that he will eliminate them.

As applied to cathartic therapy, Goldstein's argument entails the dubious assumption that expression of dysphoric affect is an undesirable behavior. By his analogy, insight-oriented psychotherapy is also counterproductive because it involves an extended analysis of "negative" attitudes and responses. His remarks may be more germane to the field of attitude change. If catharsis of the old view consists of only the response of stating it, then it may be reinforced. However, advocates of catharsis for attitude change recommend that the catharsis be followed by exposure to the new argument.

The work on catharsis in attitude change, may be summed up as saying that strong attitudes are often anchored emotionally, so that rational argument is insufficient to produce change. Change of attitudes is facilitated by emotional arousal. As Schachter (89) demonstrated, under heightened emotional arousal people search out explanations for their feelings, and this makes them more suggestible. In this case, explanations would be likely to lead to a reduction of tension—whether or not the explanations are correct.

Summary and Analysis

As we have seen, there is only one study (1) in which catharsis (defined as somatic-emotional discharge) has been quantified and then related to measures of outcome in psychotherapy. The results of this study strongly support the effectiveness of emotive therapy techniques in generating intense emotional catharsis; however, in terms of the more crucial question of the therapeutic value of catharsis, its results were less conclusive. Some of the outcome criteria were significantly affected by catharsis, while others were not. The fact that catharsis patients improved significantly on both of the behavioral measures employed tends to confirm the beneficial impact of cathartic therapy.

Widespread indirect support for the efficacy of catharsis does exist in the many approaches that use emotional discharge. However, this indirect evidence is not consistent.

For example, findings from the study of the social psychology of aggression tend to show that acting aggressively or observing others doing so serves to reinforce further aggression. Cathartic therapy encourages expression and discharge of aggressive feelings in therapy, of course, not the commission of aggressive acts; however, some of the findings suggest that an explicit distinction between words and actions may need to be drawn for therapy patients, and also that therapists should not neglect to consider behavior that occurs outside of therapy. Should a therapist encourage vivid expression of hostile feelings, he may be seen as tacitly encouraging his patients to act on these same feelings outside of therapy. In the case of a mature patient with fairly stable defenses this may lead to his telling people off in a destructive manner. Worse still, an immature or borderline patient may feel encouraged to commit acts of violence. To prevent such undesirable consequences, the cathartic therapist must clearly state his intention of assisting his patients to explore and discharge their feelings in the therapy session, not of encouraging them to express such feelings in action outside therapy.

On the other hand, if patients are able to ventilate suppressed feelings in therapy, they may be somewhat less motivated to learn how to constructively express their feelings in an appropriate manner in the interpersonal situations that stimulate them. If a wife regularly ventilates in therapy her angry feelings toward her spouse, she may avoid confronting him with her feelings about the things that anger her. These problems can be circumvented if the cathartic therapist understands that affect tends to mobilize behavior, and if he helps his patients to consider appropriate action outside the therapy situation.

The bulk of indirect support for the utility of catharsis is merely anecdotal. Despite its promotion by students of psychosomatic medicine and by surveyors of curative factors, no one has demonstrated that catharsis alleviates or prevents psychosomatic disorders or is a critical variable in successful psychotherapy.

Support for the therapeutic potential of catharsis may be derived from reinterpretations of empirical findings on focusing and implosive therapy. However, these alternate explanations are clearly speculative and require specific testing. Studies that show that implosive therapy is equally effective with or without phobic imagery tend to support the value of catharsis. On the other hand, further studies in which emotional discharge is quantified while varying the imagery are required to confirm our hypothesis.

Alternate explanations are also possible for the effects of cathartic therapy. It can be argued that hypnotherapy and drug-induced abreaction may achieve positive results by extinction of fears or reciprocal inhibition of anxiety. These procedures could be described as repeated exposure, in the absence of reinforcement, to conditioned fear-evoking images. The fact that emotional discharge is clearly reinforced in these procedures and yet gradually abates suggests that emotional release and not extinction of conditioned fears is the operant curative factor. The finding that simple recitation of traumatic experiences produces little or no improvement, while intense emotional discharge was effective, supports this explanation. The point is that without control and quantification of the critical variables, we cannot decide.

CHAPTER 9

Summary and Implications for Clinical Practice

*T*he survey of the previous work on catharsis and behavior change has taken us on a trail that runs from as far back as ancient magic rituals, through Freud and Breuer, and to such unlikely bedfellows as primal therapy and behavior therapy. Once uncovered, the material proved resistant to ready organization and summary. To begin with, the word *catharsis* itself is used with such great inconsistency that even our simple redefinition helped resolve some of the controversy around the concept. In other cases, reexamination of the literature refuted some widely held assumptions. For example, Freud and Breuer did not try and then reject an approach like recent cathartic therapies. Their cathartic method was always a more cognitive practice than modern variants, such as primal therapy. Nor were Freud and Breuer the first to recognize the value of remembering and confessing once forgotten (or wished for) events. Despite the parochial claims of some modern emotive therapists, cathartic treatment has been used for centuries in widely diverse contexts.

Finally, we have seen that the very language employed to discuss catharsis has been confusing. Apparently, emotional experience is so divorced from intellectual understanding that in talking about it people are reduced to explanation by metaphor. Those who favor catharsis in therapy describe its effects in pleasant figurative language, while those who do not opt for hyperbolic and fatuous images. This semantic confusion, of course, impedes our understanding of catharsis. So, too, does the virtual absence of empirical research.

What we will do now is summarize what we found and then consider the implications for clinical practice of the descriptive and evaluative material presented above, including the assumptions underlying cathartic therapy, the nature of emotions, how catharsis heals, for whom cathartic therapy is useful, some limits and dangers of emotive treatment, technique, and, finally, our own conclusions.

History of Cathartic Treatment

In recent years, several innovative approaches have been advanced which rely almost exclusively on emotional catharsis for psychotherapeutic benefit. The techniques employed in these approaches are fresh and distinct from those of traditional psychotherapy, which tends to be more rational and cognitive. The cathartic approaches share the immediate aim of probing intimate feelings, rather than increasing understanding. We soon discovered, however, that these modern cathartic therapies represent a rediscovery of procedures with ancient origins.

In Chapter 2, we examined religious and magic healing rites and found catharsis, along with suggestion, to be of major importance. Some readers may remain unimpressed that catharsis was widely used in ancient healing rituals. Its association with such "mumbo jumbo" practices may imply that catharsis is just another form of useless pretense. However, although no acceptable scientific proof exists that the sort of rituals we reviewed are successful in changing behavior, it seems probable, considering their longevity, that they accomplished some changes. The ubiquity of catharsis in these ceremonies suggests that it is a basic mechanism of behavior change. There is an undeniable vitality in any procedure which has been extant for so long.

That catharsis played so integral a role in the history of hypnotism suggests an important relationship between emotional experience and states of consciousness. Apparently, emotional suppression and restraint are such constant features of everyday experience that altered states of awareness produced by hypnotism lead readily to vivid emotional experiences. Even if hypnotism is viewed as more a matter of suggestion than a unique state of consciousness, by defining the situation as a hypnotic trance, people seem somehow to be freed of some of the usual restraints over strong feelings.

We cannot merely say that emotional discharge is so natural that whenever people are relaxed by hypnotism they cathart. Instead we believe that when people are relaxed and given implicit permission to behave unusually in situations defined as hypnotic sessions, they become particularly susceptible to experiencing strong feelings that are usually held in check. However, through most of the history of hypnotherapy part of the subjects' expectations include the idea that suppressed feelings would emerge. So we can conclude that hypnotism helps to potentiate catharsis by relaxing the usual prohibitions against emotional discharge—particularly when combined with the suggestion that emotional discharge will follow.

It seems that catharsis is a reasonably natural occurrence when people are given "permission" to experience their feelings, but that powerful techniques, such as hypnotism, are often required to overcome defenses against emotional expression.

In trying to understand the apparent success of cathartic hypnotherapy for the treatment of traumatic neuroses of war, we concluded that cathartic treatment may be particularly effective for dealing with relatively recent upsetting events. If substantiated, this hypothesis would be a serious challenge to some modern theories, such as primal therapy, which maintain that early childhood traumas leave residual emotions which must be discharged before psychotherapy can be fully effective.

Although certain factors in group settings, such as modeling and restimulation, may help potentiate cathartic discharge, we believe that catharsis of past emotional experiences should play only a minor role in group treatment. The richest potential of groups entails the creation of (more or less) realistic social situations. Therefore, arousal and expression of feelings generated in the immediate context of the group is probably more valuable—though less dramatic—than catharsis of emotions carried in from outside the group.

Our discussion of the desirability of emotional expression

during bereavement underscores the point that catharsis is particularly relevant in cases of recent emotional distress. We also found the widest agreement among experts on the importance of experiencing and expressing the painful feelings accompanying the death of someone who was close. Most religious traditions and virtually all mental health experts encourage emotional catharsis during bereavement. Certainly, therapists should help their patients to grieve for a lost family member or friend. Furthermore, the logical extension of this wisdom is that catharsis is a helpful way to resolve any loss. Other losses less dramatic, such as the death of a cat or dog, or less tangible, such as the awareness of growing old, probably require catharsis for optimum resolution. However, it may be that the more remote the experience of loss, the less the need for cognitive-emotional catharsis. This conclusion follows from our skepticism that emotions are stored over a long period of time.

Melancholic preoccupation with a death that occurred long ago, may be a means of escaping and avoiding living in the present, rather than a symptom of incomplete mourning. In such instances, the cathartic therapist who dwells on memories of the lost love may only prolong the patient's avoidance of living in the present. To illustrate: A family came in for treatment three years after the father died. The "identified patient" was a depressed adolescent boy. His mother, who was still preoccupied with the death of her husband, believed that the boy was mourning his father. After a thorough family evaluation it became apparent that the prolonged concern with her husband's death was a means the mother used to avoid the difficult task of adjusting to her changed circumstances. Instead of facing her anxieties about meeting people and developing new friendships, she remained obsessed with her loss. This preoccupation with the past smothered the son and retarded his efforts to become an independent adolescent. Instead of cathartic mourning for the lost father, the therapist encouraged the mother to seek out new friends and allow her son to develop an autonomous life outside the family. The importance of catharsis for the bereaved does not extend indefinitely into the future.

Little of importance has been written as theoretical support for cathartic therapy since Reich. In fact, the writings of Janov, Jackins, Lowen and Casriel are not so much thoughtfully conceived theories as they are simplified rationales for clients of what these therapies are about. Often they are fresh, sometimes even profoundly evocative, but rarely do they provide a thoughtful explanation for catharsis.

A major assumption running through these expositions is that emotions are somehow retained indefinitely until they are discharged. We find this unlikely and cannot even imagine how this storage could be accomplished. Most of the systems reviewed are claimed to be effective for virtually all problems, even those of a characterological nature. If unexpressed emotions are stored indefinitely, then it would be reasonable to prescribe cathartic therapy for character disorders. We find the premise unlikely.

Emotional suppression may have a lasting effect on character, though not due to the accumulation of undischarged affects. Instead, the form rather than content of suppression may be the source of long-standing personality difficulties. The child who is distracted or punished for crying when hurt, learns a habit of emotional avoidance. It is not so much the affect from these early traumas that remains, as it is the learned style of denial and avoidance of feelings. Thus, cathartic therapy may be helpful for character problems, not by resolving old traumas, but by loosening defenses and freeing patients to experience and express feelings. To the extent that childhood emotional suppression exerts a baleful influence on personality by rigidifying defenses and interfering with the ability to cope with subsequent experiences, rather than by pooling affect, cathartic therapy need not uncover childhood traumatic feelings to be successful. We believe that emotional suppression in childhood exerts a pathognomic influence by forming emotionally suppressed personality styles rather than by psychological poisoning from specific incidents.

We believe that a combined emphasis on cognitive and emotional factors in the etiology of psychological disorder is preferable to treating cognition as secondary to affect. In addition, emotions should be recognized as guides to action rather than merely as energy to be drained off. All the cathartic theories reviewed share the meliorist assumption that people are basically self-actualizing and that merely scraping away the crust of emotional suppression and impulse control will enable them to grow and flourish. Because most people are so emotionally inhibited, concentrating solely on expression may be useful. However, it seems unlikely that people always opt for the best solutions when their emotions are liberated.

Evidence for the Effectiveness of Catharsis

Nichols' study demonstrated that the techniques of cathartic therapy produce dramatically high levels of somatic-emotional catharsis (crying, angry shouting, and laughing). This finding is far from trivial, because it demonstrates the extreme difference between this type of treatment and traditional forms of talking therapy in producing prolonged and intense emotional discharge. Even sessions described by therapists as being highly emotional, rarely contain more than five minutes of crying. The use of cathartic techniques, on the other hand, produced sessions in which twenty minutes of profound crying was typical.

While the Nichols study provided conclusive evidence that cathartic therapy effectively generates high levels of somatic-emotional discharge, it is only a first step in demonstrating that cathartic treatment leads to significant behavior change. Patients in both insight-oriented and emotive therapy improved over baseline. Furthermore, emotive patients showed greater improvement on some measures, and this superiority was even more pronounced when those who showed highest levels of discharge were compared with those who showed least discharge.

We found to our surprise that many behavior therapists support the claims of cathartic treatment and that this support is bolstered by some research evidence.

Implosive therapy is unquestionably the most emotive of all not specifically cathartic therapies, but research support for implosive therapy cannot be claimed as unequivocal support for catharsis in therapy. However, since there is no denying that implosive therapy is a powerful emotionally evocative approach, the evidence supports the use of emotional confrontation.

Researchers in the client-centered tradition have amassed a good deal of evidence that successful psychotherapy is an intensely emotional process. Though affective involvement probably promotes catharsis, they are clearly not synonymous. Although acceptance of the value of emotional involvement is almost universal, the same does not hold true for intense cognitive- and somatic-emotional catharsis. Thus, the work on focusing does not bridge the gulf between the many who accept emotional intensity as a key to therapy and the few who claim emotional catharsis to be important.

Catharsis is generally included in lists of the underlying curative factors common to all forms of psychotherapy. When experienced scholars and clinicians survey the field and conclude that catharsis is a basic mechanism of behavior change, we should listen. However, the problem is that in the absence of more careful definition of catharsis we cannot know precisely what is being claimed to be effective. Some writers may use the term catharsis to mean emotional intensity, while others use it to mean what we have called cognitive-emotional catharsis.

Unfortunately, the bulk of analogue studies fail to duplicate what appear to be essential ingredients of the naturalistic setting, and we urge caution in extrapolating from one situation to the other. Rarely, for example, are experimental subjects sufficiently distressed to motivate them to change significant aspects of their behavior. Lack of motivation to change, combined with the difficulty of simulating techniques as powerful as those of psychotherapy in a brief laboratory study, may be more responsible for the frequent absence of significant results than the inherent weakness of therapeutic procedures per se. At best, these analogue studies provide suggestive evidence that emotional catharsis leads to tension-reduction. But the power of sustained catharsis to produce behavior change has yet to be tested in the laboratory.

It seems clear that emotive psychotherapy can be an important part of the treatment of psychosomatic disorders. Intense somatic-emotional expression can release the tension of prolonged autonomic arousal. Though emotional release may play a useful role in the treatment of psychosomatic disorders, it seems essential that effort to relieve chronic tension be directed at its source. That is, the psychosomatic patient must learn to deal with the chronic emotional arousal that is a feature of his everyday experience.

The bulk of empirical research conducted by social psychologists on catharsis of aggression can be described as refuting the claim that catharsis reduces aggression. These findings do an invaluable service by pointing out that by watching violence on television and by playing aggressive games, children may learn to be more, rather than less, violent.

However, this research is not directly relevant to cathartic psychotherapy, because indulging in or observing aggressive behavior is quite different from encouraging cognitive- and somatic-emotional discharge of previous distressful experiences.

Although studies of attitude change seem to support catharsis, researchers on this problem employ an equally limited use of the term catharsis. Here, catharsis is generally used to describe the process of allowing subjects to verbalize beliefs that run counter to those that the experimenter is attempting to instill. Even when this process is intensely emotional, it differs from remembering and expressing feelings about important live interactions as a means of better handling such interactions in the future.

In examining both indirect and anecdotal evidence, we found a tendency to support the utility of catharsis as a vehicle of behavior change. This evidence suggests that therapists need to make explicit the distinction between cathartic discharge in therapy and behavior outside therapy. If this distinction is blurred, it is possible that patients might be unwittingly encouraged to act on their hostile fantasies, or might become so preoccupied with ventilation in therapy sessions that they fail to express angry feelings appropriately in everyday situations. Of these two unhappy possibilities, we find the latter more probable. In therapy, it is never so easy to harm patients as it is to fail to help them to learn new and more constructive ways of behaving.

A thorough review has yielded neither a satisfactory theory of the mechanics of catharsis and how they might be therapeutic, nor a systematic body of empirical research that demonstrates when, how and with whom catharsis is therapeutic.

Implications for Clinical Practice

The work of cathartic therapists is based on several assumptions implicit in the literature reviewed above. One fundamental premise shared by all cathartic therapists is that therapeutic change can be accomplished by focusing on the individual patient. This assumption has been challenged by family and systems therapists, who maintain that treating individuals outside the context of their significant social systems is often the least effective way to proceed. It does seem reasonable that the effectiveness of treatment of individuals will depend somewhat on the extent to which their family or social groups will accommodate change; so it must be said that even cathartic therapists, despite this focus on the individual, are always treating patients who are part of and must adjust to particular social systems. This focus on individuals in isolation goes hand in hand with an implicit belief in the value of inner change.

Furthermore, the theories reviewed above are rooted in psychoanalytic metaphors of inner space. Repressed emotions are thought to be stored up and to require discharge. A corollary belief shared by cathartic therapists is that people are basically good and naturally tend toward "self-actualization." Therefore, if the residue of undischarged affects is drained, they assume that patients will automatically behave in more adaptive and satisfying ways. Though all cathartic therapists share this basic value commitment, they vary in the degree to which they say behavior change will automatically follow catharsis. Harvey Jackins (1), for example, explicitly claims that catharsis alone is enough to produce the greater awareness and rationality that lead to behavior change. Following discharge (which we take to mean somatic-emotional catharsis), re-evaluation and improved adjustment are said to occur spontaneously. Fritz Perls, on the other hand, has a slightly more complex view, and emphasizes both catharsis and more effective functioning. Emotions are not viewed as something to be rid of, but as guides to action. Furthermore, Gestalt therapy balances its interest between affective and cognitive aspects of treatment and of life.

Obviously, the past is over and cannot be changed. What remains from various traumatic episodes are maladaptive avoidance patterns, and perhaps some residual physical tension in the autonomic nervous system. Patients must learn to cope with the future; this is the end to which therapy is directed. Ultimately, the changes that result from psychotherapy will also affect coping skills and ability to handle stress. Manipulation of intrapsychic entities doesn't accomplish this automatically.

We believe that focusing on memories of the past in order to produce catharsis may be a useful strategy. By temporarily ignoring the necessity to cope with present and future realities, a therapist may better be able to help clients achieve cathartic release. However, at some point, achieving behavior change requires active planning. Though catharsis may help patients to do this active readjustment themselves, therapists can usefully be involved in this process, and may help patients to avoid slipping back into old patterns and repeating errors of the past.

Finally, cathartic therapists share the belief that psychological disorder is primarily based on inhibition. Freud spoke of neurosis as "an ingrown gesture," and most cathartic therapists would agree. But even if this is so, it isn't necessary to assume that the cure must be expressive. Expressive therapy may indeed be useful for many types of problems, but there are other problems not necessarily caused by inhibition. Furthermore, cathartic treatment may even reinforce behavioral inhibition by providing an emotional release for pressure that might otherwise be used in the service of behavioral action. Yelling angrily in role-play scenes in therapy need not preclude an appropriate expression of angry feelings in the real world. But it also does not automatically follow that catharsis will stimulate such realistic and adaptive behavior.

The Nature of Emotions

Lack of understanding about the nature of emotions, with a consequent reliance on metaphor and analogy, is responsible for much of the confusion about catharsis. We must therefore briefly consider the theories of emotion to see how they shape not only our understanding, but also our experience of emotions. If emotions are considered to be concrete, then they must have a container capable of being filled and needing periodic discharge. If, on the other hand, emotions are considered to be dispositions and guides to action, they should be responded to accordingly.

One of the criticisms of cathartic treatment is that it is a byproduct of Freud's early hydraulic model of emotions, which he subsequently discarded. This theory was that undischarged affects accumulate incrementally unless they are "ventilated" or "drained off." If they aren't, pressure builds to a point where it becomes destructive. To put it another way, affects are like boiling water in a steam kettle; if they are not allowed to discharge, the kettle will eventually explode. Freud later (2) came to consider emotions to be both the perceived aspect of drives and their energizing force. Emotional expression, in this view, provides release of pressure and reduction of frustration when the object of a drive is out of reach. Catharsis, or abreaction, allows internal discharge and tension reduction when action to satisfy an instinct is impossible or dangerous.

Fenichel (3), in a modification of Freud's position, suggested that emotion breaks through only when ego control fails. Hence, vivid emotional expression, as in catharsis, is thought to be a regressive phenomenon. Furthermore, this viewpoint implies that catharsis is symptomatic of both frustration and inability to cope with it. As a child matures, Fenichel wrote, increased ego mastery should result in a modification of the nature of affect. Affect should be tamed by the ego and used as a sign to anticipate the urgings of instincts.

Implicit in all psychoanalytic discussions of emotion, as in most other views as well, is the idea that emotions are concrete entities. We speak of emotions as having substance, quantity, extension, and place. We say such things as: "She was filled with anger," "He kept his anger inside," or "He let the anger spill over." This manner of speaking also legitimizes the notion of an inner and an outer space, and implicitly assumes, furthermore, that people are passive recipients of their emotions. We speak about people "struggling with their feelings" or "suffering them." This implied passivity separates the person from the emotions, so that he is described as "coping with" them.

Although we are used to treating emotions as concrete entities, they are not. The words we use to refer to them are merely labels ascribed to a complex series of events. We do not suffer emotions passively; rather, we make and choose them through our behavior, including observing and labeling our overt actions and covert bodily reactions. People are actors; they are not passive recipients of feelings. The spatial and quantitative implications of metaphorical descriptions of emotion are both inaccurate and misleading. Anger is neither inside nor outside; we cannot be so filled with anger that we require discharge. It is not useful to think of anger as something concrete. Physiological arousal, thinking about acting hostilely, or hitting someone are concrete actions; anger *itself* is not. Nor does anger reside in any place, or persist indefinitely.

But if emotions are not entities, do not exist in some place, do not increase in quantity, and are not stored over time, then cathartic discharging of emotion is strictly speaking not possible, since most ideas about expressing or discharging emotion rest on the idea that emotion is a substance and persons are containers. Descriptions of cathartic therapy usually include—and seem to be predicated on—the notion of accumulating and storing up old feelings. "The patient," we say, "finally ventilated the grief she had kept inside for ten years since her husband died." But if emotions are not substances, they cannot be stored and preserved. There are no such things as ancient feelings, and grief is not something that can be kept inside.

Instead of saying that the patient repressed, stored up, and finally ventilated her grief, we can say that at the time of her husband's death, she avoided thinking about it and thus avoided realizing, with feeling, the full significance of her loss. Now she is less defensive, and able to acknowledge frankly and consciously the reality of the death. Therefore she remembers it emotionally. In this version, it is the event that is old, and the memory that is stored, not the feeling. Feelings only seem to be stored with memories because, as memories are recalled, feelings are restimulated.

The reader may be inclined to disagree. The idea of stored feelings is firmly entrenched in our experience and in our vocabulary of emotional events. This is true not only because we tend to concretize all mental events, but also because as we remember past events we are apt to feel precisely as we did when the event first occurred. Indeed, in some instances—cases of repressed emotion—our feelings may be even stronger when we recall an event than they were when the event took place. We think this proves that repressed feelings are stored; however, we can describe these sequences very adequately without using metaphors at all.

Take, for example, what is frequently described as "venting old anger" in therapy. When a husband begins to yell at his wife for the first time in cathartic therapy, it seems as though his anger has long been stored up. The fact is that people often do things more feelingly when they have long delayed doing them or avoided thinking about them. This husband, let us say, had long been continually provoked, but restrained. His feeling of anger is current, even though we speak of it as having accumulated. His anger has a cognitive aspect—he thinks about his wife and how unfair she is and how much he resents her for it. He has previously avoided these thoughts. Only when he finally begins to think rather than avoid them, does the anger begin. Furthermore, even thinking these thoughts may not stimulate other aspects of anger, such as denouncing her, yelling at her, or being viscerally stirred up. Metaphorical statements such as, "He was so filled with anger that he finally exploded" are therefore inaccurate, however common.

How then, can catharsis be described without resorting to concretizing emotions? Catharsis is part of an emotional action sequence. It involves remembering something with feeling, communicating that feeling, and vigorously carrying out the bodily actions that are part of what is meant by "having" the feeling. Catharsis does not mean uncovering and discharging quantities of psychic energy. It is an emotional action sequence appropriate to changed subjective circumstances. Crying, for example, is part of what happens when we think about an event or circumstance that we deeply regret. To "repress the sadness" means to avoid focusing on the thoughts and memories. To "uncover and discharge the sadness" means to think about what happened, and not hold back the tears. We thus have a concrete choice: we can avoid thinking about the event; or, we can think about the event and act sadly.

We must also differentiate between the view that emotions are descriptions of an action sequence, and a strictly behavioristic explanation. Emotions are not descriptions of only observable behavior. One can think of something angrily without showing anger. Emotional actions include private aspects of feeling (thoughts, memories, rumblings in the stomach) that are potentially reportable or observable, as well as public actions that express feeling. Furthermore, emotional actions can include what seems from a behaviorist perception like lack of action. "Not behaving sadly," or "keeping sadness inside," can better be described as avoiding thinking about events or holding back tears. Keeping secrets from others (suppression) is also action, as is keeping secrets from oneself (repression).

If a patient denies or avoids acting sadly, we may say that the feelings are suppressed or repressed, but what is actually happening is not that some *thing* is stored, but that part of the natural action sequence (crying) is being avoided. Catharsis, then, is part of completing the action sequence. By finishing it, the patient may become clearer about the experience, less tense, and more able to become involved with current events.

As we showed in Chapter 8, enough clinical material,

laboratory analogue studies, extrapolations from other contexts, and controlled investigations of catharsis in psychotherapy exist to provide reason for continued interest in catharsis, although they may not actually confirm its value. It does remain to be demonstrated that catharsis cures; nonetheless, it is worth speculating how it operates therapeutically.

As we have said, catharsis is not a simple, unitary phenomenon, but a complex process, involving two related, but separate, components: one, cognitive-emotional, the other somatic-emotional. The former consists of the contents of consciousness during the re-experiencing of an emotional event. The latter consists of the physical discharge of emotion, such as the tears and sobbing of grief, or the trembling and sweating of fear. Furthermore, each of these components may serve more than one function in therapy. For example, cognitive-emotional catharsis may serve both to increase self-awareness on the part of the patient and also to help him tell his memories to the therapist. This distinction between cognitive-emotional and somatic-emotional catharsis will be used here to explain how catharsis works in therapy.

Cognitive-Emotional Catharsis

In the early development of psychoanalysis, when catharsis was the major focus, Freud was more interested in cognitive events than somatic ones. Although he spoke of giving energetic expression to emotions, his main concern was bringing repressed traumatic memories into awareness. Later, Freud came to believe that this emotional process of remembering was not enough, and that catharsis was of lasting value only when the memories led to understanding of how past events revealed hidden impulses that play a role in current behavior. Not only did his emphasis shift from remembering, as a means of cleaning out the unconscious, to insight, he also began to conceive that the critical material was unconscious drives and motives, rather than traumatic events.

Freud's procedure was to have patients speak their thoughts freely and follow the memories and associations until they recalled early, repressed, painful experiences. This remembering was said to be accompanied by a re-experiencing of the feelings involved, and followed by a feeling of release.

Freud's original explanation for the way this cathartic remembering relieved symptoms was based on the hydraulic model; he viewed the brain as made up of neurons that fill up with stimuli, or "cathect." When filled, neurons reflexively discharge. Thus catharsis was said to be useful because it discharged and cleansed the nervous system. Although we reject this model, it remains true that Freud found remembering to be effective for removing at least certain symptoms. How are we to explain this?

Looking primarily at what happens "within" the individual patient, it seems that traumatic events involve stimuli that are associated with pain, and therefore predispose to withdrawal, defensiveness, and avoidance. As the patient remembers the painful situation and describes it in a therapeutic setting where no punishment is forthcoming, feelings of avoidance and withdrawal begin to abate. In short, an extinction of avoidance responses occurs. Symbolic repetition of the original traumatic event with no negative consequences may help to diminish the fears and avoidance associated not only with the original situation, but also with others similar to it. Catharsis, as remembering, operates partially by weakening maladaptive response patterns. However, even though it does weaken maladaptive response patterns, nothing is done to build in new and more adequate responses. Therefore, as an extinction mechanism, catharsis may be useful in some cases, but only as part of the therapeutic procedure.

In fact, as a simple process of extinction, catharsis seems to be useful in only a limited group of problems. A person who is frightened to the point where he avoids dogs can be helped by cathartic remembering of a past distressing experience with dogs. However, the significance of this extinction process may be greater. It may enable patients to differentiate better between events that are truly threatening, and those whose threat derives not from real consequences but from association with early upsetting events. A person who is continually seeking out other people's approval may, following cognitive-emotional catharsis, begin to differentiate those situations where other's approval has direct and real consequences from those where it is simply reminiscent of previously forgotten experiences.

Extinction and subsequent enhanced stimulus differentiation can occur with cognitive-emotional catharsis even in the absence of a therapist. The presence of a therapist and the patient's relationship with him or her adds another dimension.

One of the most important features of the patient-therapist relationship is that it should be an intimate, trusting one, in which both parties concentrate on the patient's productions and exert effort to produce significant material. What is considered significant varies with the type of therapy. In any case, cognitive-emotional catharsis requires that an intimate, trusting relationship has been established. To recall and describe painful experiences, the patient must feel safe enough to relax defenses against remembering, and trusting enough to reveal potentially threatening material. An additional feature of cognitive-emotional catharsis that affects the patient-therapist relationship is that there is often an element of confession in describing emotionally-laden material. Forgotten events often turn out to be embarrassing or threatening. By relating such experiences to the therapist, the patient is, in effect, saying "I am now willing to let you in on some of my most private and guarded secrets; I trust you with this disclosure." By risking vulnerability, the patient is in a position to be supported and confirmed at a more profound level by the therapist. The therapist's acceptance and valuing of the patient takes on a more significant meaning after the patient has revealed private, emotional experiences from the past.

If it is not handled correctly, cognitive-emotional catharsis may also become a destructive element in the patient-therapist relationship. When a patient reveals a series of troubles and painful experiences, the therapist listens in a warm, accepting manner intended to relax the patient who can then produce more material. If the patient simply retells a series of previously rehearsed observations involving both feelings and attributions, and if the therapist does not differentiate between the two, the attributions as well as the feelings will be supported. The patient, for example, may blame others for his troubles and wallow in feelings of powerlessness. If the therapist accepts all this, he may strengthen the patient's projections and ways of avoiding responsibility. The therapist has to demonstrate acceptance of feelings without necessarily accepting the patient's attribution of blame to other people and implied powerlessness. This is, in fact, one of the trickiest aspects of dealing with catharsis in therapy. It is not therapeutic simply to have patients speak freely and have everything they say accepted and seemingly validated by the therapist. Cathartic therapy involves urging the patient to re-experience emotionally distressing events; the therapist then accepts the feelings and encourages further exploration without getting into the issue of who is at fault. Following catharsis, however, it is important to discuss this material rationally, and for the therapist to suggest alternative ways of perceiving and acting.

Somatic-Emotional Catharsis

The physical expression of feelings in therapy affects the patient directly and indirectly by influencing his relationship with the therapist. Most writers on catharsis focus on its direct effects on the patient, and underemphasize indirect effects it has on the patient-therapist relationship.

The most obvious direct impact of somatic-emotional catharsis, though often a trivial one, is tension relief. Although trivial when conceived as an end in itself, the reduction in tension produced by somatic-emotional expression may have some important benefits in psychotherapy. If a patient remembers anxiety-provoking experiences and is able to experience somatic-emotional catharsis, the attendant release of tension may countercondition some of the feelings of anxiety. Furthermore, a reduction of tension may lead to a progressive relaxation of the muscular aspects of psychological defenses, permitting further exploration of emotional experience and further cognitive-emotional catharsis.

One of the most profoundly therapeutic aspects of somatic-emotional discharge is that it expands the patient's repertoire of emotional experiencing and expression. Most of us have learned too well to limit, suppress, and delay impulses and emotional reactions.

Take crying, for example. The observation that infants cry when hurt or frustrated leads to the position taken by some cathartic therapists, namely, that crying is an innate reaction serving primarily to relieve tension. "If a baby is frustrated (and all babies are frustrated many times every day in the course of the usual handling) he will discharge the frustration and get it out of his system if he is allowed to do so" (4). Crying may be innate, but it seems more likely that it is first an uncon-ditioned response to frustration that becomes an operant by which the infant manipulates the environment—that is, it becomes the major way in which the infant asks to be taken care of. Thus, as crying is superseded by language, it is used less and less.

The idea that crying is an operant, as well as a form of tension release, complicates the reasons why parents discourage it in their children. Some writers maintain that parents teach their children not to cry because they are anxious in the face of distressing affect. The more threatened parents are by affective display, the more difficult it is for them to allow free affective expression from the children. Only after they have transmitted their anxiety about emotion can they live with their children. This may be true, but it is not the entire explanation. Crying is ignored, not only because it generates anxiety in the parents, but also because it is inconvenient always to have to respond to a baby's operant crying. As Jules Henry (5) put it, "In our culture the illegality of crying focuses on two ideas: that the child will be spoiled and that the parent will be exploited." Nevertheless, even when the parents are attempting not to be manipulated by the operant crying, they may be inadvertently but effectively interfering with tension-release. In addition to teaching self-reliance, the parents may also be teaching emotional inhibition.

This analysis of the genesis of crying shows us why catharsis in psychotherapy is viewed as regression. By crying, the patient is saying, in effect, "I hurt like a little child; care for me." By giving vent to unhappy feelings through crying, the patient temporarily abandons his resistance to asking for nurturance, and needless to say, also becomes acutely vulnerable to disappointment. Depending upon the therapist's response, such an experience may be either rewarding or punishing. If the therapist becomes anxious or communicates disapproval, the patient mobilizes defenses and redoubles efforts to conceal weakness and need. If, on the other hand, the therapist is comfortable in the presence of strong feelings and communicates warmth, acceptance, and respect, the patient learns that even though he hurts and needs help, he is still a worthy person.

The British psychoanalyst, Harry Guntrip (6) considers regression to be an essential feature of psychotherapy. He notes that the desire to return to the safe position of infantile passivity and dependence is most extreme in schizoid individuals, but is present in us all. "The evidence provided by regressive behavior, regressive symptoms and regressive dreams and fantasies, shows that this most deeply withdrawn ego feels and fantasies a return to the womb, safe inside the 'fortress' from which it probably still has some dim memory of having emerged." All patients probably wish to regress; indeed, everyone, patient or not, retains a degree of passive longing, and some wish to return to a state of absolute passive dependent security. The safety and quiet of a temporary therapeutic regression may therefore offer an opportunity to experience and explore private thoughts and feelings, and to recuperate and become revitalized.

Usually patients struggle to contain their regressive needs, including the need to cry and be held. They resist giving way to feelings. As one patient put it, "If I were to allow you to see my painful feelings, I'd feel like a little girl; and I'm not sure that I could grow up again at the end of the hour." This resistance is adaptive, because it protects the patient from allowing herself to become vulnerable when it is not safe to do so. However, the defense becomes maladaptive if it is so pervasive that it never permits indulgence of "childish" wishes for passivity and dependence. The therapist must make it safe for the patient to achieve a controlled and constructive regression.

For Guntrip, the feeling of ego weakness and resistance to dependence is the root cause of psychopathology and the core problem of psychotherapy. The experience of regression can therefore be restful and restorative. As he puts it, "This must result from the regressed ego finding for the first time an object-relationship of understanding acceptance and safeguarding of its rights, with a therapist who does not seek to force on the patient his preconceived views of what must be done, but who realizes that deep down the patient knows his own business best, if we can understand his language." We all have the same feeling, however buried, of being a child facing a life that is too big and frightening. "Our fear and intolerance of weakness is naturally great, and is so embedded in our culture pattern, and is so additionally stimulated in the infant by the adults who handle him, that he is driven to a premature pseudo-adult self." This pseudo-adult self characteristically denies the weaker aspects of the self. It is part of a social facade, a mask of sham strength behind which the "real" self is trapped and barred from the opportunity to mature. A false pretense of strength thus develops from distrust built upon intolerable feelings of vulnerability. The psychotherapist's office is a place where it is safe to drop the mask; and catharsis can help the patient to do it. Catharsis is certainly not the only means by which to regress temporarily and accept (and be accepted in) a position of infantile dependence; but its preverbal nature enhances its usefulness in this project.

In addition to helping regression to a denied weak self, somatic-emotional catharsis also serves to uncover forgotten or culturally forbidden emotions. In our culture, chief among these is anger.

In Pathways to Madness, Jules Henry (5) points out that anger is both felt and expressed in very different ways depending upon cultural and individual factors. Further, he believes that emotions are far more complex than is generally believed and that linguistic and perceptual poverty leads us to treat them as simple. Anger is generally part of an amalgam of feelings, such as "anger-fear" or "anger-hate." Henry details how culture affects the expression of anger. Anger, is related to status in all cultures, and in our own, to be "refined" means not to express anger. In Henry's words, "When quarreling is perceived as degrading, anxious withdrawal derives not so much from the hostility of the attacker as from expectation of shame deriving from the degradation implicit in merely quarreling." In other cultures, the expression of anger may be related to potency as a warrior, and therefore is sanctioned. Furthermore, anticipating the consequences of anger may further complicate the situation and make expression all the less likely.

> When quarrels become entangled with feelings about the self, the quarrel becomes a contest, and people fight back and force the issue. Then the anger that started the quarrel is blended with fear of losing the quarrel and anticipatory shame lies beneath the surface, sustaining fear and egging anger on. At the very bottom is sorrow, waiting to burst into tears, to go into mourning and even to push for suicide (as in the Trobriand Islands) if the self is destroyed in the battle. This capacity to anticipate what one will feel often makes anger disproportionate.

The tendency to see the object of our anger as more, or other than he or she is, also exaggerates the fear of anger. Thus, when someone angers us who reminds us of our father, the anger may expand and become intense.

Henry is well aware of the undesirable effects of holding anger in, as in the case of the unassertive person who rarely expresses his anger, "Then inner rage produces secret blame; they store up resentment on the basis of their distorted perceptions, while the secret enemy—husband, wife, child—is aware only of a growing coldness, sullenness, tendencies to sudden outburst triggered by petty, almost invisible accidents." Quarreling provides the opportunity for affective release, but holds the threat of bad relationships. Thus anger is a particularly ripe subject for catharsis in psychotherapy. In addition to ventilating anger in therapy, the patient may learn when and how to allow such "dangerous" feelings to emerge in everyday relationships.

Somatic-emotional expressions generally lead to tension reduction in the patient. No reduction occurs, however, if feelings are aroused but not permitted expression, or if the expression is cut short. To put it another way, catharsis reduces anxiety, at least temporarily, because the subjective experience of anxiety is associated with tension of autonomic arousal that does not lead to vigorous activity. Physical ventilation of feelings reduces some of this tension and, therefore, lessens anxiety. Unfortunately, while this formulation is probably true, it certainly does not tell the whole story. If catharsis lessens anxiety because it involves physical exertion, running a mile or playing a game of tennis should be more efficacious for reducing autonomic tension than catharsis—assuming that extraneous factors, such as performance anxiety are held constant. Catharsis thus includes but goes beyond tension reduction. At the end of a mile run, a person showers and goes about his business. At the end of a cathartic experience, the patient is still in the therapist's office *and* is in a very different state. It is what happens at this point that seems crucial.

Much of what goes on need not be explicit, nor is the therapist necessarily required to "do something" in an active, interpretive manner. The therapeutic gain that follows catharsis can come largely as a result of the patient's own efforts.

Catharsis involves something that most patients fear very much, which is losing control. Patients with insight about some of the turbulent forces within them may fear that they will go mad. Others, with the same basic fear but with more rigid defenses and less insight, so successfully maintain their facade of composure that losing control is not consciously a concern for them. Nevertheless, they devote a great deal of energy to maintaining control. With the right combination of intense feelings and the sense that it is safe to shed defenses, the patient will experience emotional discharge. This amounts to a loss of some control. Someone who is sobbing intensely or shouting in anger has abandoned many of the usual restraints placed on affective display. An experience of losing control and learning that the self behind the defenses is worthwhile and solid can be very reassuring, however. This experience may simply confirm one's already established basic faith, or it may be a dramatic revelation, having the quality of a conversion. In either case, it helps to solidify what transactional analysts refer to as the I'm OK position. The therapist's warmth and acceptance can facilitate this process, but it is something that the patient must experience rather than merely be told.

There are diverse opinions among clinicians as to how safe it is for patients to lose control. The modal point of view among clinicians is that patients need a certain amount of ego strength before it is wise to risk (or encourage) their losing control. This certain amount of ego strength is roughly equivalent to the patient's not being psychotic. For those who are neurotic it is generally thought to be possible (though not necessarily therapeutic) to risk a direct assault on defenses. On the other hand, most clinicians (7) believe that it is dangerous to tamper with the defenses of a psychotic patient, for fear that he will lose, and be unable to regain, control. Thus, psychotic patients are most often treated with supportive therapy and drugs.

At the other end of the continuum are those who believe that therapy can be the same for all patients, and specifically that it is safe for all patients to experience loss of control (4, 8, 9). Harvey Jackins is a steadfast exponent of this position. Although the bulk of his clientele is relatively normal, he has worked with some severely psychotic patients. Jackins believes that psychotics are people with more stored up pain, who simply are more in need than neurotics of opportunities to discharge. It is interesting to note, however, that with "heavily distressed persons" Jackins makes more effort to draw the person's attention to the present time than to the (past) distressful experiences. Nevertheless, this effort is still directed at encouraging the client to lose control and discharge feelings.

Laing, as is well known, also believes that the schizophrenic must give up control (his "false self system") and experience madness in order to grow into a healthier, more integrated person. "Indeed, what is called psychosis is sometimes simply the sudden removal of the veil of the false self, which had been serving to maintain an outer behavioral normality that may, long ago, have failed to be any reflection of the state of affairs in the secret self."

Probably neither Jackin's nor Laing's positions are wholly accurate, but both contain a certain merit. Psychotics are not simply people who have a lot of stored-up pain, as Jackins asserts. Rather, they experience much pain, because they are basically and deeply marked in a way that leads to pathological interactions with people and with the environment. Emotional discharge may help to relieve some of the pain, but it is unlikely to alter the flaws. Nor will emotional discharge reverse fifteen or thirty years of learning to relate in unhappy ways.

On the other hand losing control in cathartic therapy will probably not fracture as many egos as is commonly presumed. Extremely distressed persons often have their most rigid defenses around their private emotions. Once these secrets are exposed, they may not easily be sealed over and reconstituted. Cathartic techniques with psychotics may therefore require a great deal of skill and available time, such as was supplied by Laing at Kingsley Hall. Cathartic therapy conducted by a novice for one hour is certainly not appropriate for psychotic patients. But if a skilled clinician, in a protective environment, can spend a great deal of time with patients, there may be no contraindication for emotive techniques. Experience may eventually teach, but has not yet taught, otherwise.

Learning that it is safe to lose control is doubtless not the only, or even the major benefit to be derived from catharsis. Again, if it were, there are more potent means available, for instance, taking LSD. Perhaps the most profound consequences of catharsis are the rational explanations the patient arrives at afterward. Cathartic therapy is a highly charged experience that overstimulates the patient and upsets rigid beliefs about the self and behavior. This leads him to strive for new explanations, both about the self and about the experience. At this point, the patient is extremely suggestible, or open to reformulating fundamental notions about himself. If the patient is able to use this prepotent opportunity for introspection, and/or if the therapist suggests insightful ways of dealing with behavior, the experience can be richly therapeutic.

A felicitous definition of psychotherapy offered by Jules Henry is that it is healing by revealing the concealed within us. Catharsis not only reveals concealed affect, but has been found to facilitate the impact of interpretations. Greenson (10) says that when a patient is in the grip of emotion, "Very often the best technique is to wait, giving the patient an opportunity to discharge his feelings as fully as possible." While the patient is immersed in emotional turbulence, his ability to reason is temporarily inaccessible. However, if the discharge is allowed to proceed, the patient is unusually receptive to interpretation, precisely because he has undergone a profound and unsettling experience.

A peripheral, but perhaps important point is that catharsis may satisfy the demand characteristics of certain therapeutic situations. Because it is so tangible, emotional expression clearly indicates to the patient that "something is happening." If this something has been extolled as therapeutic, the patient may take it as a sign that therapy is progressing. Discharge for a Jackinsian or Janovian patient is manifest evidence that he or she is a good patient and is getting well. From a communications standpoint, an appropriate strategy is to maximize the impression that the therapist is in charge and that what happens is evidence of this. Thus, when the patient discharges it is appropriate to underscore both the patient's faith that something is happening, and the idea that it is therapeutic. If catharsis is considered therapeutic, this becomes less of a deceptive ploy to demonstrate control of the therapy relationship.

Increased suggestibility may potentiate evil as well as good, however, and catharsis can be misused in therapy. An appropriate axiom to keep in mind is that strong medicine requires strong control.

How much catharsis is valuable, and for whom is it valuable? In order to discuss these important questions, we must distinguish between catharsis as an adjunct to treatment and intense catharsis as the major focus of treatment.

Catharsis as an Adjunct to Treatment

Most psychotherapists agree that emotional intensity is a useful if not necessary component of successful treatment sessions. Furthermore, most also agree that therapists should help their patients learn to recognize, accept, and express their feelings. However, it seems that emotional suppression is so ingrained in most of us that we are uncomfortable in the face of emotional display, and we inadvertently tend to suppress it. This discomfort is particularly apt to be felt in the face of intense emotional discharge, or in cases where there is some confusion between discharge and demand. When patients cry a little, therapists tend to be pleased and think of it as a breakthrough. But when patients wail and sob intensely, therapists are liable to think them overwrought and try to calm them down—especially in cases of serious depression.

Another instance in which therapists are not liable to support emotional discharge is when the patient appears to be manipulative. If, for example, a patient first shouts angrily at a therapist and then begins to cry when he is told that no extra sessions are available, the therapist may feel that permitting the expression of anger and disappointment is tantamount to reopening negotiations about extra sessions. Of course it is not. The problem comes from confusing the expressive or cathartic functions of emotional discharge with the negotiative or operant functions. Once it is understood that accepting feelings is not the same as negotiating to "do something" to ameliorate them, it becomes easier to tolerate a wider range of cathartic emotional expression.

In general, we believe therapists ought to accept cathartic emotional expression in almost any therapeutic context. Even if catharsis is not a central feature of the therapy, it is generally a good idea to permit patients to cry, laugh, or say angry things whenever these feelings emerge. Thus, although group therapy may be less useful when it is devoted exclusively to catharsis, group members should be permitted to cry when they are upset. Saying that patients ought to be permitted to laugh or cry or say angry things when their feelings are aroused may seem to be stating the obvious. In fact, although most therapists endorse the value of occasional cathartic expression, it has been our experience that many need to be reminded not to interfere with it. Making the distinction between the expressive and the demand aspects of emotional expression may help therapists to accept the former without fear of being manipulated by the latter.

Catharsis as the Major Focus of Therapy

While there is much agreement that occasional cathartic expression is a useful adjunct to therapy, there is much disagreement about the value of catharsis as the major focus of treatment. Thus there are two extreme positions on this matter: never or always. We believe that cathartic therapy may be a useful form of treatment, but not for everyone—more because we believe that other approaches are probably more useful in some cases than because we fear that cathartic therapy is likely to be dangerous or destructive. There are some ways, however, in which intensely cathartic therapy is apt to be dangerous. Pillow-pounding, shouting, and sobbing may be unwise for cardiac patients, pregnant women, and epileptics. Also, we suspect that the regressive features of this type of therapy make it unsuitable for the outpatient treatment of persons who have serious trouble remembering what is real and what is not.

Cathartic therapy is most likely to be useful in the individual treatment of persons who have experienced recent distressing experiences. Catharsis is useful primarily for intrapsychic change, whether this change be described in metaphors of inner space or in action and behavioral terms, because cathartic therapy isolates the individual from his social context. In treating social units such as groups or families, therapists should attend to the functioning of the system and the genuine interaction of its members. Though it is often helpful to encourage members of a family or group to support and comfort a member who is upset and crying, an exclusive focus on this type of interaction vitiates the therapeutic potential of working with the system.

Perhaps our most serious disagreement with current cathartic therapists is that we doubt the validity of somatic-emotional catharsis of early childhood experiences. For this to be considered helpful—or even possible—the therapist has to believe that undischarged affect is stored indefinitely. We don't think it is. In fact, we think that when patients cry over events from their infancy, they are merely symbolizing more recent pains, in the same way as people who cry at the movies. It does seem likely that patients frequently overreact emotionally to events in the present that remind them of events in the past. They are restimulated emotionally through a process that can be called displacement or stimulus generalization. No quantities of affect persist from early traumas; but since similar feelings may be reactivated in the present, it may be useful to remember past events and learn to distinguish them from present ones. However, we don't believe that feelings are stored or that all patients are restimulated by events similar to those that occurred in infancy. In sum, we do not think it necessary for cathartic therapists to exert relentless pressure on their patients to relive old feelings from a series of childhood events. However, it is often, though not always, helpful to help patients remember childhood upsets as a means of helping them to differentiate between their current circumstances and those of childhood.

Cathartic therapy may indeed be useful for the treatment of longstanding problems or character disorders, but not by liberating ancient affects. Instead, its usefulness lies in disrupting long held and rigid defenses against emotional expression and discharge. Thus, intense cathartic therapy may be a powerful technique for relaxing the ingrained attitude of deliberateness that characterizes obsessional persons.

Our suggestion that emotional defenses persist from childhood, though affects do not, has practical implications beyond the selection of patients for treatment, for it implies that not only is it not critical to uncover early childhood traumas, but also that it may not matter what images are used to elicit discharge. If a patient has suffered recent trauma, the content of this experience may be important. Otherwise, the content may be less important than the somatic-emotional discharge. In fact, "remembering" and crying about early childhood experiences may be effective for paradoxical reasons. Instead of actually recalling themselves and their experiences, patients may be thinking about appealing children who only symbolize themselves. Most of us learn that it is not proper to indulge in self-pity, but that of course it is quite acceptable to feel sorry for a small child. Therefore, what is thought of as remembering early childhood scenes may instead involve substituting a culturally acceptable object of pity—the image of a little child who is unhappy—for an unacceptable one—an adult who is unhappy. If breaking down defenses against emotional experience and expression is truly more important than the content of catharsis, therapists should permit and encourage any imagery which evokes discharge and not try to guide patients to any pre-conceived goals.

To recapitulate: catharsis may be virtually always useful as an adjunct to psychotherapy. If patients are aroused by feelings, and a distinction is made between the expressive and demand implications of emotional expression, brief catharsis is nearly always appropriate. As the major focus of therapy, catharsis may be most useful for persons who have suffered recent trauma or for those with overcontrolled and rigidly defensive character styles.

Not all therapists, however, should do cathartic therapy. We reject the idea that any single therapeutic approach is demonstrably superior to others. Cathartic therapy seems to be an effective approach, but people can learn about themselves and change their behavior without catharsis. Not everyone is suited to conduct cathartic therapy. Inducing or restimulating distress and painful feelings in persons who are already anxious and unhappy can make some therapists terribly uncomfortable. Therapists may simply be too apprehensive about temporarily increasing feelings of upset in patients who want to be helped to feel less upset. The therapist who is apprehensive about restimulating suffering is unlikely to be successful at doing so. Cathartic therapy can be difficult to learn, even for the therapist who feels comfortable with strong feelings. It entails a certain looseness, a willingness to experiment, and a flair for the dramatic. The powerful techniques necessary to overcome emotional defenses are unconventional enough to create difficulties in getting started.

Limits and Dangers of Cathartic Therapy

Like other avant garde forms of therapy that have come into vogue, cathartic therapy has both zealous adherents and harsh critics. Perhaps the most serious of the criticisms about intense cathartic therapy is that it is dangerous and destructive. There is no question but that emotional abreaction can be a powerful and frightening experience. In fact, it is the powerful nature of the experience that makes change—for better or worse—possible.

Some of the potential dangers for cathartic therapy stem not from the theory or technique involved, but from their mis-application. Such hazards are common to many forms of treatment, but particularly to new approaches that develop without a tradition of careful training and supervision. The hydra-headed growth of the human potential movement offers a myriad of possibilities for psychological mishaps. Untrained, and at times insensitive, persons are put in positions of responsibility at workshops, weekends, and weekly group meetings, where they must support others who are exposed and vulnerable. The potential for harm is increased by the development of powerful procedures such as those associated with cathartic therapy. But ill-trained and poorly supervised therapists may also harm patients by running encounter groups, doing marriage counseling, or by engaging in operant conditioning, since all these approaches use in common a potentially powerful influence which can be applied wisely or unwisely. Whether cathartic treatment is generally effective is still moot, but the opinion that intensely cathartic sessions and the disruption of psychological defenses are potentially destructive is widely held.

Cathartic therapy involves dramatic and somewhat radical procedures. The potency of these procedures requires that they be used judiciously. Careful training of therapists and close supervision of their work by trained and experienced workers is essential. So too are conscientious screening of patients or workshop participants, and follow-up contact. The lack of professional training of many workers in the human potential movement increases the possibility of mistreatment, but the abuse in the name of therapy is by no means limited to non-professionals. Many professionals dabble in these new techniques without training and supervision. The techniques are generally simple and easy to apply, and it seems possible to read, or observe someone else's work, or listen to a lecture on cathartic techniques, and then try them out. Actually, most people's defenses are so rigid that this sort of dabbling is unlikely to produce intense catharsis. There are, however, exceptions. Patients with tenuous defenses, for instance, may regress easily and open up poorly protected inner feelings. Or, a dilettante cathartic therapist may promote intense catharsis in a group where modeling, social tension, and emotional contagion may facilitate strong emotional discharge. The danger in these situations is not that catharsis is inherently destructive, but that exposing deep emotions leaves a person in a very vulnerable position. If intense catharsis occurs in a situation where the client does not feel safe and reassured, it can be a shameful or upsetting experience.

Some therapists believe that individuals have built-in safety valves that keep them from becoming more emotionally aroused or venting more feeling than they can easily handle in a given situation—that is, they believe that cathartic discharge will not occur unless the patient's defenses are relaxed by being in circumstances he considers safe. There is certainly some truth to this. Any psychotherapist who has labored mightily to relax and reassure a patient enough to promote catharsis can attest to how well-guarded most people's emotions are. Unfortunately, the idea that patients will only cathart if it is safe to do so is a dangerous half-truth. Some people simply are inadequately defended. Therefore, it is critical that the therapist who aims for catharsis be able to provide a very safe and protective atmosphere in order to relax the defenses of the normally defended person, and to protect the less well-defended person who too easily exposes private feelings.

In addition to the misapplication of cathartic techniques by improperly trained therapists, there may be limits and dangers inherent in the basic approach. Some critics (7) describe catharsis in therapy as generally countertherapeutic, while others have said that catharsis is only occasionally useful in treatment. The latter position is based on the conviction that psychotherapy patients often need to get some distance from their emotions so that they can more accurately perceive and understand their experiences. We agree that distance is sometimes important; however, suppressing feelings, or discussing them intellectually is usually a less effective way to get distance than is cathartic discharge. Accurate perception and clear thinking are enhanced following emotional discharge, because catharsis is more effective than suppression for distinguishing between thoughts and feelings. When patients are so stirred by feelings that it is difficult for them to consider their circumstances rationally, we believe that it is generally wiser to encourage discharge of feelings in order to free the patient from their sway.

Engel's work on the phenomenon he calls "conservation

withdrawal'' (11) has been used to suggest that catharsis may be inappropriate for patients who are very upset by their feelings. He drew together (12) observations from descriptive psychiatry, laboratory research with humans and lower animals, and the work of naturalists to support his idea that at times of extreme stress all organisms respond by becoming quiescent. He says that this natural response provides the organism with a chance to avoid overstimulation and to perform certain restitutive functions. Applied to psychotherapy, this idea implies that there are times when it is important for a person to suppress feeling, withdraw, and rest. However, Engel overgeneralizes when he says that all organisms respond to extreme stress with behavioral paralysis. Actually, some animals respond with desperate violence—for example, dominant male rhesus monkeys react to terrifying shocks in an avoidance paradigm with repeated and frantic attack, even though it is maladaptive to do so. Although it may be common for animals to withdraw from extreme stress, it is not a universal tendency. A second and more critical point has to do with the fact that most people already tend to withdraw even without intense stress. One of the reasons that catharsis is so useful in psychotherapy is precisely because it does occur so infrequently in daily life. Consequently it is more often helpful for therapists to encourage patients to confront, rather than withdraw, from their feelings.

Most people in our culture learn to avoid expressions of some, if not all, varieties of strong feeling. Women are likely to be condemned if they express angry feelings, and men who cry are liable to be thought unmasculine. Indeed, any strong display of affect renders one liable to criticism; consequently, most people develop a facade of emotional impassivity. Children learn from their parents to hide many of their real feelings. They learn to smile when they'd rather not, and to be somber when they'd rather laugh. Concealment of emotions is a social obligation, expanding in proportion as we move away from our closest circle of intimates. The psychotherapist's office is a place where this sham can be dropped, where the emotions that make us vulnerable can be exposed because there is nothing to fear. If the therapist is afraid of strong emotional display, or convinced of the importance of hiding pain, he will act, knowingly or unknowingly, to suppress feelings. The patient who is thus robbed of the opportunity to discharge feelings in therapy may come to believe that it is never safe to express them.

Some therapists think that catharsis implies a hydraulic model of the mind, and since this is an incorrect model, therefore catharsis is not useful. Lowy (7) is someone who takes this point of view. McDougall (13) maintains a similar position, challenging the worth of catharsis which, he argues, rests on the false belief that emotions consist of packets of energy capable of being opened and drained off. Both condemn the expression of affect when it is considered an end in itself, claiming rather that it should only be considered a byproduct of the (cognitive) resolution of conflict.

Lowy grossly misuses the term *catharsis* by equating it with the unrestrained expression of drives. Not only does Lowy argue that catharsis is generally not useful, he goes on to say that it may be decidedly dangerous. The danger, as he sees it, is that the patient's defenses may be overrun, so that catharsis may lead to prolonged regression including paranoid or schizoid symptoms. By defining catharsis so idiosyncratically, and by making such exaggerated claims of the dangers involved, Lowy dulls the point of his criticism. Had he challenged the adherents of catharsis to demonstrate that they do not rely on a hydraulic model of emotions, his argument would have been more difficult to refute.

Actually, we believe that one of the dangers of cathartic therapy is not that it promotes unrestrained and impulsive behavior, but that it fosters inactivity. There is a tendency among cathartic therapists to use static equilibrium as a model of behavior. Thus, for example Janov's description of post-primal patients emphasizes their passive contentment. When practiced in such a framework, cathartic treatment can stress getting rid of feelings rather than using them as guides for action. Some of the current interest in cathartic therapy is related to a cultural revolt against the repressive forces in family and culture. But by promoting ventilation, instead of gratification of impulses, cathartic therapy may be a counterrevolutionary force. We believe that catharsis, by freeing patients from the unrecognized influence of feelings, can improve their ability to think and act rationally. However, those cathartic therapists who do not engage in discussions of coping strategies waste a valuable opportunity, and such neglect of the ego functions of coping and social relations is particularly unfortunate in view of the potential that catharsis has for promoting clarity of thought. This is one of the major shortcomings inherent in cathartic therapy. Delving into the past to uncover emotional memories does not preclude additional efforts to clarify the meaning of these memories in relation to present reality, however, many cathartic therapists seem to neglect the second step. They omit the rational re-evaluation because they are convinced that people naturally tend toward self-actualization once they are liberated from the influence of emotional repression.

One of the great dangers of any form of psychotherapy is that it may not work. Most patients enter treatment in order to be cured of some problem. Because talking therapy is both complicated and vague, patients often learn from their therapists to lose sight of the presenting problem. It may become redefined from a specific problem in living, such as loneliness, to one of the therapist's etiological constructs, such as emotional repression. In addition, therapists and patients often forget about cure and look for something elusive such as growth or happiness. It is all too easy to practice therapy without any clear focus on accomplishing what the patient came in for. Instead of outcome, process (what goes on in the sessions) comes to be prized. This is particularly liable to happen in cathartic therapy. Because catharsis is so tangible and exciting, it may be valued for itself, even in the absence of behavior change. This is very much like what happened when encounter groups first became popular. They were so exhilirating and participants felt so good about their involvement, that no one bothered to notice that they had not changed as a result of the group experience.

Another potentially destructive tenet of cathartic therapy is the assumption that psychological defenses are always limiting in a maladaptive way. These mechanisms of restraint develop early in life to delay impulses. Later they may be used to avoid and deny feelings as well as the impulses behind them. Most of us learn to put off impulses and avoid feelings all too well. We become stultified and rigid. Because most people are heavily defended, cathartic therapists stress the need to break through defenses and liberate feelings long held in check. In preparing patients for cathartic treatment it probably does no harm to speak as though psychological defenses are mainly an impediment to uncovering feelings. However, therapists should recognize the utility of defenses, and in some cases, and at various points in treatment, the value of defenses should be made clear to patients.

Social reality does not countenance either unchecked expression of feelings or immediate gratification of wishes. Patients with severe problems in relating or with the potential for explosive acting on impulse need help to restrain themselves outside of therapy. Treating such patients with cathartic therapy without the safeguard of a protective environment may be unwise. The most important consideration is whether or not the distinction can be made between what is acceptable in therapy sessions and what is acceptable in the community. Actually, raising this issue in reference to seriously disturbed or impulsive patients is only a dramatic way to make a point. Most therapists would not accept these patients for cathartic treatment. But they do treat better adjusted persons without proper appreciation of the fact that most people may need to maintain a certain amount of defensiveness in order to continue living with their families and working with their associates. Defenses suggest danger. In therapy sessions, there is little danger from expressing feelings, so defenses are seen as resistance. But therapists should guard against suggesting to patients that they should no longer avoid expressing feelings in their daily lives. Therapists should not assume that all patients will discharge their feelings only in therapy until they have learned to do so appropriately in their everyday lives.

The danger is that after patients have begun to feel the exhilaration of becoming open and free with their feelings in the therapist's office, some may be too hasty about carrying this freedom of expression back home. Such increased expressiveness may be adaptive in the long run, but newly expressive converts to cathartic therapy, by suddenly becoming assertive or demanding, may produce consequences that they aren't prepared to deal with. This danger need not be a problem in cathartic therapy. Ideally, a demanding spouse will become less so after remembering and crying about childhood deprivations. Problems may arise, however, in early phases of therapy if the demanding spouse begins to feel these deprivations more keenly and becomes more demanding at home. By unwittingly upsetting the balance of tension in the marriage, the cathartic therapist may precipitate open fighting or even increased suppression of feelings.

Promoting ill-considered emotional expression outside of therapy should not and need not be a consequence of cathartic treatment. The problem arises—as it may in any form of individual psychotherapy—if there is inadequate recognition of the realities of the patient's social context. Most people have built their lives on a pattern that includes a certain amount of emotional dishonesty. Cathartic psychotherapy may be extremely useful by helping people learn to experience and express their feelings. Most of the efforts in this direction may be to loosen defenses in the artificial and relatively protected context of treatment sessions. Our point is simply that at some point the freedom from past emotional hangups must be translated into everyday living. Unfortunately, we think it likely that patients will be harmed if they use feelings only as something to be discharged in therapy sessions; or if they hastily begin to unload feelings toward the people in their lives who may not respond as supportively as therapists.

Conclusion

There is a venerable tradition in our culture of treating emotions as noxious entities which should be suppressed. Quite a bit of philosophy and religion is devoted to condemning emotions as part of our base, animal nature, while extolling the intellect as one of our uniquely human characteristics. In everyday life we are surrounded by reminders that most people learn to mistrust and suppress many of their emotional reactions and certainly most strong displays of sorrow, anger and even joy. We are taught the virtues of "restraint", "emotional maturity" and "being cool"—all of which indicate emotional suppression.

Coexisting with the custom of criticizing and restraining feelings is a longstanding tradition of catharsis in healing and therapy. For centuries, there have been healers who have advocated strong displays of emotion as part of a curative and self-actualization process. Ancient religious and magic rituals have in common with a host of contemporary approaches to psychotherapy, a basic emphasis on the curative value of remembering significant past events and fully experiencing and expressing the feelings stimulated by these events.

Ironically, both of these traditions mistake emotions for concrete things and things that should be gotten rid of—either by suppression or by expulsive discharge. Although we find much that is of value in cathartic treatment, we do not believe feelings are things to be uncovered and gotten rid of. Instead emotions are labels we use to describe a process of activation related to mobilization for action. In part, this distinction is an academic one, for even conceiving of emotions as excretia to be dug up and expelled probably results in effective therapy. Vivid expressions of emotion probably interrupt an unhappy cycle of continually being poised for but avoiding actions and therefore unrealistically overestimating their consequences.

If cathartic therapy is successful, it should lead neither to suppressing nor reflexively discharging emotions, but recognizing—in realistic proportions—the actions that they predispose. In this way, actions can be chosen and planned wisely. The outcome of cathartic therapy affects the future, not the past. Changes will alter situations, or the subjective experience of them, that patients encounter following treatment. Understanding that emotions are active—what one does and how one does it—not passive—effects caused by external circumstances—may clarify the facts of experience and enable successful patients to choose to behave in more satisfying ways.

Emotions involve the activities of anticipating, remembering, judging, and interpreting. In the so-called emotionally repressed patient, emotions may have been absent at times where they were expected, not because they were hidden or buried but because the person's estimation of the situation was different from an observer's (or therapist's). For example, the patient may have judged that it would have been immature, unwise, or pathological to cry and mourn a loss. Furthermore, such choices seem to become ingrained habits involving muscular and psychological rigidities that are exceedingly difficult to modify. Successful cathartic therapy can alter these habits with the consequences that patients become freer to choose to behave either expressively or defensively and to engage in effective action in emotional situations.

Instead of responding to emotional situations in a passive, conditioned defensive manner, patients may be able to respond actively with unique reactions to new situations. The ability to respond actively in ways appropriate to present not past circumstances can be a major force in increasing feelings of competence and enjoyment of living.

This increased freedom of expressivity and action is the brightest prospect of cathartic therapy.

References

Chapter 1

1. Aristotle. *The Art of Poetry*. New York: Odyssey Press, 1951.
2. S. Freud, and J. Breuer. *Studies on Hysteria*. New York: Avon Books, 1966.
3. S. Freud. *The Origins of Psycho-analysis*. New York: Basic Books, 1954.
4. R. Rabkin. *Inner and Outer Space*. New York: Norton, 1970.
5. S. Freud. *A General Introduction to Psychoanalysis*. New York: Washington Square Press, 1960.
6. O. Fenichel. *The Psychoanalytic Theory of Neuroses*. New York: Norton, 1945.
7. M. B. Arnold. *Emotion and Personality*. New York: Columbia University Press, 1960, 178–79.
8. A. Janov. *The Primal Scream*. New York: Dell, 1970, 88.
9. J. G. Watkins. "The Affect Bridge: A Hypnoanalytic Technique," *International Journal of Clinical and Experimental Hypnosis*, 19(1971), 21–27.
10. H. Jackins. *Elementary Counselor's Manual*. Seattle: Personal Counselors, Inc., 1962.
11. E. R. John. *Mechanisms of Memory*. New York: Academic Press, 1967.
12. W. Penfield. *The Excitable Cortex in Conscious Man*. Springfield, Illinois: C. C. Thomas, 1958.
13. T. A. Harris. *I'm OK—You're OK*. New York: Harper & Row, 1969.
14. H. Grayson. "Grief Reactions to Relinquishing of Unfulfilled Wishes," *American Journal of Psychiatry*, 24(1970), 287–95.
15. H. Jackins. *The Human Side of Human Beings*. Seattle: Rational Island Publishers, 1965.
16. R. R. Greenson. *The Technique and Practice of Psychoanalysis*, *Vol. I*. New York: International Universities Press, 1967.

Chapter 2

1. E. E. Evans-Pritchard. *Theories of Primitive Religion.* London: Oxford University Press, 1965, 34.

2. B. Malinowski. "Magic, Science and Religion," in J. Needham (Ed.), *Science, Religion and Reality.* New York: George Braziller, 1955, 25−88.

3. H. J. Shorvon, and M. B. Sargant. "Excitatory Abreaction: With Special Reference to its Mechanism and the Use of Ether," *Journal of Mental Science,* 93(1947), 709−32.

4. G. Zilboorg. *A History of Medical Psychology.* New York: Norton, 1941.

5. R. A. Levine. "Witchcraft and Sorcery in a Gusii Community," in J. Middleton and E. H. Winter (eds.), *Witchcraft and Sorcery in East Africa.* New York: Frederick A. Praenger, 1963, 221−55.

6. J. Beattie. "Sorcery in Bunyoro," in J. Middleton and E. H. Winter (eds.), *Witchcraft and Sorcery in East Africa.* New York: Frederick A. Praenger, 1963, 27−55.

7. P. Ghalioungui. *Magic and Medical Science in Ancient Egypt.* London: Hodder and Stoughton, 1963.

8. J. Gillin. "Magical fright," in Lessa and Vogt (eds.), *Reader in Comparative Religion.* Evanston, Ill.: Row, Peterson, 1958, 353−62.

9. W. LaBarre. "Confession as Cathartic Therapy in American Indian Tribes," in A. Kiev (ed.), *Magic Faith and Healing.* New York: Free Press of Glencoe, 1964, 36−49.

10. K. Rasmussen. "An Eskimo Shaman Purifies a Sick Person," in Lessa and Vogt (eds.), *Reader in Compartive Religion.* Evanston, Ill.:Row, Peterson, 1958, 362−67.

11. M. Eliade. *Shamanism. Archaic Technique of Ecstasy.* London: Routledge & Kegan Paul, 1964.

12. R. Winstadt. *The Malay Magician.* London: Routledge & Kegan Paul, 1951.

13. J. D. Frank. *Persuasion and Healing.* Baltimore: Johns Hopkins Press, 1961.

14. L. D. Weatherhead. *Psychology, Religion and Healing.* New York: Abingdon-Cokesbury Press, 1951.

15. K. M. Calestro. "Psychotherapy, Faith Healing and Suggestion," *International Journal of Psychiatry,* 10, 2 (1972), 83−113.

16. A. Metraux. *Voodoo in Haiti.* New York: Oxford University Press, 1959.

17. G. Rosen. "Psychopathology in the Social Process: 1. A Study of

the Persecution of Witches in Europe as a Contribution to the Understanding of Mass Delusions and Psychic Epidemics," *Journal of Health and Human Behavior*, 1(1960), 200−11.

18. W. G. McLoughlin, Jr. *Modern Revivalism*. New York:Ronald Press, 1959, 87.
19. W. Sargent. *Battle for the Mind*. Garden City, New York: Doubleday & Company, 1957.
20. G. C. Loud. *Evangelized America*. New York: Dial Press, 1928.
21. W. T. Ellis. *"Billy Sunday"*, *The Man and His Message*. Philadelphia: Universal Book and Bible House, 1914, 138.
22. J. B. Boles. *The Great Revival, 1787−1805*. Lexington, Kentucky: The University Press of Kentucky, 1972.
23. F. M. Davenport. *Primitive Traits in Religious Revivals*. New York: Macmillan Company, 1917.
24. W. W. Wood. *Culture and Personality Aspects of the Pentecostal Holiness Religion*. The Hague: Mouton & Co., 1965.
25. W. James. *The Varieties of Religious Experience*. London: Longmans Green & Co., 1914.

Chapter 3

1. S. Freud, and J. Breuer. *Studies on Hysteria*. New York: Avon Books, 1966.
2. S. Freud. "On Psychotherapy," *Collected Papers*, Vol. I. London: The Hogarth Press, 1956, 249−63.
3. O. Fenichel. *The Psychoanalytic Theory of Neurosis*. New York: W. W. Norton & Co., 1945.
4. S. Ferenczi. "The Principle of Relaxation and Neocatharsis," *The International Journal of Psychoanalysis*, 11(1930), 428−43.
5. S. Freud. *Collected Papers*, Vol. I, London: The Hogarth Press, 1956, 264−71.
6. R. R. Greenson. *The Technique and Practice of Psychoanalysis*. New York: International Universities Press, 1967.

Chapter 4

1. A. Moll. *Hypnotism*. London:Walter Scott, 1901.
2. G. C. Kingsbury. *The Practice of Hypnotic Suggestion*. Briston, Great Britain: John Wright & Co., 1891.
3. P. Janet. *Psychological Healing: A Historical and Clinical Study*, Vols. I & II. New York: Macmillan, 1925.

4. E. G. Boring. *A History of Experimental Psychology*. New York: Appleton-Century-Crofts, 1950.

5. J. Ehrenwald. *Psychotherapy: Myth and Method*. New York: Grune & Stratton, 1966.

6. F. A. Mesmer. *Memoirs sur la decouverte du magnetisme animal*. Paris: Didot, 1779.

7. R. Darnton. *Mesmerism and the End of the Enlightenment in France*. Cambridge, Mass.: Harvard University Press, 1968.

8. F. Alexander, and S. T. Selesnick. *The History of Psychiatry*. New York: Harper & Row, 1966.

9. J. P. F. Deleuze. *Practical Instruction in Animal Magnetism*. New York: Samuel R. Wells, 1879.

10. J. Braid. *Neurypnology: or, The Rationale of Nervous Sleep, Considered in Relation with Animal Magnetism*. London: Churchill, 1843.

11. C. L. Tuckey. *Treatment by Hypnotism and Suggestion*. New York: G. P. Putnam's Sons, 1914.

12. J. M. Charcot. *Oeuvres completes, Lecons sur les maladies du systeme nerveux*. Paris: Progress Medical, 1890.

13. A. Zilboorg. *A History of Medical Psychology*. New York: Norton, 1941.

14. S. Freud. *The Origins of Psychoanalysis*. New York: Basic Books, 1954.

15. W. Brown. "The Revival of Emotional Memories and its Therapeutic Value," *British Journal of Medical Psychology*, 1(1920),.16−19.

16. W. Brown. *Psychology and Psychotherapy*. London: Edward Arnold, 1921.

17. E. Simmel. "War Neurosis," in S. Lorand (ed.), *Psychoanalysis Today*. New York: International University Press, 1944, 227−48.

18. M. Brenman, and M. M. Gill. *Hypnotherapy*. New York: International Universities Press, 1947.

19. J. H. Conn. "Hypnosynthesis III. Hypnotherapy of Chronic War Neuroses with a Discussion of the Value of Abreaction, Regression, and Revivication," *Journal of Clinical and Experimental Hypnosis*, 1(1953), 27−43.

20. J. G. Watkins. *Hypnotherapy of War Neuroses*. New York: Ronald Press, 1949, 244−45.

21. R. R. Grinker, and J. P. Spiegel. *Men Under Stress*. Philadelphia: Blackston, 1945.

22. A. Hordern. "The Response of the Neurotic Personality to Abreaction," *Journal of Mental Science*, 98(1952), 630−39.

23. H. J. Shorvon, and M. B. Sargant. "Excitatory Abreaction: With

Special Reference to its Mechanism and the Use of Ether," *Journal of Mental Science*, 93(1947), 709–32.

24. W. McDougall. "The Revival of Emotional Memories and its Therapeutic Value," *British Journal of Medical Psychology*, 1(1920), 23–29.

25. J. G. Watkins. "The Affect Bridge: A Hypnoanalytic Technique," *International Journal of Clinical and Experimental Hypnosis*, 19(1971), 21–27.

26. K. Lipshitz, and J. H. Blair. "The Polygraphic Recording of a Repeated Hypnotic Abreaction with Comments on Abreactive Psychotherapy," *Journal of Nervous and Mental Diseases*, 130(1960), 246–52.

Chapter 5

1. J. H. Pratt. The Tuberculosis Class: An Experiment in Home Treatment. *Proceedings, New York Conference on Hospital Social Service, Vol. IV*, 1917, 49–68.

2. Z. T. Moreno. "Evolution and Dynamics of the Group Psychotherapy Movement," in J. L. Moreno (ed.), *International Handbook of Group Psychotherapy*. New York: Philosophical Library, 1966, 27–125.

3. M. Rosenbaum, and M. Berger (eds.). *Group Psychotherapy and Group Function*. New York: Basic Books, 1963.

4. T. Burrow. "The Group Method of Analysis." *Psychoanalytic Review*, 14(1927), 268–80.

5. A. M. Freedman, H. I. Kaplan, and B. J. Sadlock. *Modern Synopsis of Comprehensive Textbook of Psychiatry*. Baltimore: Williams & Wilkins, 1972.

6. S. R. Slavson. "Some elements in activity group therapy," *American Journal of Orthopsychiatry*, 14(1944), 578–88.

7. S. R. Slavson. "Catharsis in Group Psychotherapy," *Psychoanalytic Review*, 38(1951), 39–52.

8. E. J. Anthony. "The History of Group Psychotherapy," in H. I. Kaplan and B. J. Sadock (eds.), *Comprehensive Group Psychotherapy*. Baltimore: Williams & Wilkins, 1971, 4–31.

9. L. Wender. "The Dynamics of Group Psychotherapy and its Application," *Journal of Nervous and Mental Diseases*, 84(1936), 54–60.

10. R. J. Corsini, and B. Rosenberg. "Mechanisms of Group Psychotherapy: Process and Dynamics," *Journal of Abnormal and Social Psychology*, 51(1955), 406–11.

11. I. D. Yalom. *The Theory and Practice of Group Psychotherapy.* New York: Basic Books, 1970.

12. B. Berzon, C. Pious, and R. Parson. "The Therapeutic Event in Group Psychotherapy: A Study of Subjective Reports by Group Members," *Journal of Individual Psychology,* 19(1963), 204–14.

13. D. W. Baruch. "Description of a Project in Group Therapy," *Journal of Consulting Psychology,* 9(1945), 271–80.

14. C. Goldberg. *Encounter: Group Sensitivity Training Experience.* New York: Science House, 1970.

15. J. Y. Gonen. "The Use of Psychodrama Combined with Videotape Playback on an Inpatient Floor," *Psychiatry,* 34(1971), 198–213.

16. M. Karp. "Directional Catharsis: Fact or Fantasy?" *Group Psychotherapy,* 21(1968), 137–39.

17. J. L. Moreno. *Psychodrama,* Vol. II. Beacon, New York: Beacon House, 1958.

18. J. L. Moreno. "Psychodrama," in S. Arieti (ed.), *American Handbook of Psychiatry,* Vol. II. New York: Basic Books, 1959.

19. N. A. Polanski, and E. B. Harkins. "Psychodrama as an Element in Hospital Treatment," *Psychiatry,* 32(1969), 74–87.

20. J. L. Moreno. "Psychodrama," in H. I. Kaplan and B. J. Sadock (eds.), *Comprehensive Group Psychotherapy.* Baltimore: Williams & Wilkins, 1971, 460–500.

21. J. L. Moreno. *Psychodrama,* Vol. I. Beacon, New York: Beacon House, 1946.

22. Z. T. Moreno. "Beyond Aristotle, Breuer and Freud: Moreno's Contribution to the Concept of Catharsis," *Group Psychotherapy and Psychodrama,* 24(1971), 34–43.

23. L. Yablonsky, and J. M. Enneis. "Psychodrama Theory and Practice," in F. Fromm-Reichmann and J. L. Moreno (eds.), *Progress in Psychotherapy,* Vol. I. New York: Grune & Stratton, 1956, 149–61.

24. H. Jackins. *The Human Side of Human Beings.* Seattle: Rational Island Publishers, 1965.

25. K. D. Benne. "History of the T-group in the Laboratory Setting," in L. P. Bradford, J. R. Gibb, and K. D. Benne (eds.), *T-group Theory and Laboratory Method.* New York: Wiley, 1964, 80–135.

26. C. Rogers "The Group Comes of Age," *Psychology Today,* 3, 7(1969), 27–61.

27. B. Maliver. "Encounter Groupers Up Against the Wall," *New York Times Magazine,* Jan. 3(1971), 4–43.

28. J. R. Gibb. "The Effects of Human Relations Training," in A. E.

Bergin and S. L. Garfield (eds.), *Handbook of Psychotherapy and Behavior Change.* New York: Wiley, 1971, 838−62.

29. P. B. Smith. "Controlled Studies of the Outcome of Sensitivity Training," *Psychological Bulletin,* 82(1975), 597−622.

30. M. A. Lieberman, I. D. Yalom, and M. B. Miles. *Encounter Groups: First Facts.* New York: Basic Books, 1973.

Chapter 6

1. S. Freud. "Mourning and Melancholia," *Standard Edition of the Complete Psychological Works of Sigmund Freud.* London: Hogarth Press, 1937, 243−58.

2. H. Deutsch. "Absence of Grief," *Psychoanalytic Quarterly,* 6(1937), 12−22.

3. O. Fenichel. *The Psychoanalytic Theory of Neurosis.* New York: Norton, 1945.

4. J. W. Mason. "A Review of Psychoendocrine Research on the Pituitary-adrenal Cortical System," *Psychosomatic Medicine,* 30(1968), 576−607.

5. E. L. Giusto, K. Cairncross, and M. G. King. "Hormonal Influence on Fear-motivated Responses." *Psychological Bulletin,* 75(1971), 432−44.

6. C. A. Keele, and E. Neil. *Samson Wright's Applied Physiology.* London: Oxford University Press, 1965.

7. E. J. Sachar. "Corticosteroids in Depressive Illness I. A Reevaluation of Control Issues and the Literature," *Archives of General Psychiatry,* 17(1967a), 544−53.

8. E. J. Sacher. "A Longitudinal Psychoendocrine Study," *Archives of General Psychiatry,* 17(1967b), 554−67.

9. E. J. Sacher, J. M. Mackenzie, W. J. Binstock, and J. E. Mack. "Corticosteroid Responses to Psychotherapy of Depressions," *Archives of General Psychiatry,* 16(1967), 461−70.

10. C. Anderson. "Aspects of Pathological Grief and Mourning," *International Journal of Psycho-Analysis,* 30(1949), 48−55.

11. S. R. Edelson, and P. H. Warren, "Catatonic Schizophrenia as a Mourning Process," *Diseases of the Nervous System,* 24(1963), 527−34.

12. M. Klein. "Mourning and its Relation to Manic-Depressive States," *International Journal of Psycho-Analysis,* 21(1940), 125−53.

13. R. J. Wetmore. "The Role of Grief in Psycho-Analysis," *International Journal of Psychoanalysis,* 44(1963), 97−103.

14. J. Bowlby. "Grief and Mourning in Infancy and Early Childhood," *Psychoanalytic Study of the Child*, 15(1960), 9—52.

15. J. Bowlby. "Processes of Mourning," *International Journal of Psycho-Analysis*, 42(1961), 317—40.

16. K. Lorenz. *King Solomon's Ring*. London: Methuen, 1954.

17. E. Lindemann. "Symptomatology and Management of Acute Grief," *American Journal of Psychiatry*, 101(1944), 141—48.

18. O. Cope. "Management of the Coconut Grove Burns at the Massachusetts General Hospital," *Annals of Surgery*, 117(1943), 801—02.

19. S. Cobb, and E. Lindemann. "Neuropsychiatric Observations," *Annals of Surgery*, 117(1943), 814—24.

20. G. L. Engel. "Grief and Grieving," *American Journal of Nursing*, 64(1964), 993—98.

21. A. Rosell. "Lindemann's Pioneer Studies of Reactions to Grief," in A. H. Kutsher (ed.), *Death and Bereavement*. Springfield, Illinois: Charles C. Thomas, 1969, 163—65.

22. H. J. Heimlich, and A. H. Kutscher. "The Family's Reaction to Terminal Illness," in B. Schoenberg, A. C. Carr, D. Peretz, and A. H. Kutscher (eds.), *Loss and Grief: Psychological Management in Medical Practice*. New York: Columbia University Press, 1970, 270—79.

23. N. L. Paul. "Psychiatry: Its Role in the Resolution of Grief," in A. H. Kutscher (ed.), *Death and Bereavement*. Springfield, Ill.: Charles C. Thomas, 1969, 179—95.

24. C. H. Barnacle. "Grief Reactions and Their Treatment," *Diseases of the Nervous System*, 10(1949), 173—76.

25. H. Grayson. "Grief Reactions to the Relinquishing of Unfulfilled Wishes," *American Journal of Psychotherapy*, 24(1970), 287—95.

26. P. Guerin, and T. F. Fogarty. "The Family Therapist's Own Family," *International Journal of Psychiatry*, 10(1972), 6—22.

27. H. Jackins. *The Human Side of Human Beings*. Seattle: Rational Island Publishers, 1965.

28. A. Janov. *The Primal Scream*. New York: Dell, 1970.

29. L. M. Brammer, and E. L. Shostrom. *Therapeutic Psychology*. Englewood Cliffs, New Jersey: Prentice-Hall, 1968.

30. N. L. Paul, and G. H. Grosser. "Operational Mourning and its Role in Conjoint Family Therapy," *Community Mental Health Journal*, 1(1965), 339—45.

31. F. H. Lowy. "The Abuse of Abreaction: An Unhappy Legacy of

Freud's Cathartic Method," *Canadian Psychiatric Association Journal*, 15(1970), 557–66.

32. E. S. Shneidman. "You and Death," *Psychology Today*, 5, 1(1971), 43–80.

33. G. Gorer. *Death, Grief, and Mourning in Contemporary Britain.* London: Cresset Press, 1965.

34. P. Marris. *Widows and Their Families.* London: Routledge & Kegan Paul, 1958.

35. E. A. Grollman. "The Ritualistic and Theological Approach of the Jew," in E. A. Grollman (ed.), *Explaining Death to Children.* Boston: Beacon Press, 1967, 223–48.

Chapter 7

1. A. Janov. *The Primal Scream.* New York: Dell, 1970.
2. W. Reich. *Selected Writings.* New York: Noonday Press, 1960.
3. W. Reich. *Character-Analysis.* New York: Noonday Press, 1949.
4. O. Bean. *Me and the Orgone.* Greenwich, Conn.: Fawcett Publications, 1971.
5. E. Baker. *Man in the Trap.* New York: Macmillan, 1967.
6. H. Jackins. *Elementary Counselors Manual.* Seattle: Personal Counselors, Inc., 1962.
7. A. Lowen. *Physical Dynamics of Character Structure.* New York: Grune & Stratton, 1958.
8. A. Lowen. *The Betrayal of the Body.* New York: Macmillan, 1967.
9. S. Keleman. *Sexuality, Self & Survival.* San Francisco: Lodestar Press, 1971.
10. S. Keen. "Sing the Body Electric," *Psychology Today*, 4(1970), 56–88; 5(1970), 59–61.
11. W. C. Schutz. *Here Comes Everybody.* New York: Harper & Row, 1971.
12. F. M. Alexander. *The Resurrection of the Body.* New York: University Books, 1969.
13. M. Feldenkrais. *Body and Mature Behavior.* London: Routledge & Kegan Paul, 1949.
14. F. S. Perls. *Gestalt Therapy Verbatim.* LaFayette, Calif.: Real People Press, 1969.
15. F. S. Perls. *Ego, Hunger and Aggression.* New York: Vintage Books, 1969.
16. F. Perls, R. E. Hefferline, and P. Goodman, *Gestalt-Therapy.* New York: Delta, 1951.

17. C. Naranjo. "Present-centeredness: Technique, Prescription, and Ideal," in J. Fagan and I. L. Shepherd (eds.), *Gestalt Therapy Now*. Palo Alto, Calif.: Science and Behavior Books, 1970, 47–69.

18. F. S. Perls. "Four Lectures," in J. Fagan and I. L. Shepherd (eds.), *Gestalt Therapy Now*. Palo Alto, Calif.: Science and Behavior Books, 1970, 14–38.

19. J. B. Enright. "An Introduction to Gestalt Techniques," in J. Fagan and I. L. Shepherd (eds.), *Gestalt Therapy Now*. Palo Alto, Calif.: Science and Behavior Books, 1970, 107–24.

20. R. Wallen. "Gestalt Therapy and Gestalt Psychology," in J. Fagan and I. L. Shepherd (eds.), *Gestalt Therapy Now*. Palo Alto, Calif.: Science and Behavior Books, 1970, 8–13.

21. E. Polster. "Sensory Functioning in Psychotherapy," in J. Fagan and I. L. Shepherd (eds.), *Gestalt Therapy Now*. Palo Alto, Calif.: Science and Behavior Books, 1970, 70–76.

22. J. Fagan. "The Tasks of the Therapist," in J. Fagan and I. L. Shepherd (eds.), *Gestalt Therapy Now*. Palo Alto, Calif.: Science and Behavior Books, 1970, 88–106.

23. I. L. Shepherd. "Limitations and Cautions in the Gestalt Approach," in J. Fagan and I. L. Shepherd (eds.), *Gestalt Therapy Now*. Palo Alto, Calif.: Science and Behavior Books, 1970, 234–38.

24. H. Jackins. *The Human Side of Human Beings*. Seattle: Rational Island Publishers, 1965.

25. B. J. Somers. "Reevaluation Therapy: Theoretical Framework," *Journal of Humanistic Psychology*, 12(1972), 42–57.

26. F. Riessman. "The 'Helper' Therapy Principle," *Social Work*, 10(1965), 27–32.

27. A. Janov. *The Anatomy of Mental Illness*. New York: G. P. Putnam's Sons, 1971.

28. W. Kaufman. "An Anatomy of the Primal Revolution," *Journal of Humanistic Psychology*, 14(1974), 49–62.

29. D. Casriel. *A Scream Away From Happiness*. New York: Grosset & Dunlap, 1972.

30. R. D. Laing. *The Divided Self*. London: Penguin Books, 1960.

Chapter 8

1. M. P. Nichols. "Outcome of Brief Cathartic Psychotherapy," *Journal of Consulting and Clinical Psychology*, 42(1974), 403–10.

2. M. P. Nichols, and C. B. Reifler. "The Study of Brief Psychotherapy in a College Health Setting," *Journal of the American College Health Association*, 22(1973), 128–133.

3. A. E. Bergin. "The Evaluation of Therapeutic Outcomes," in A. E. Bergin and S. L. Garfield (eds.), *Handbook of Psychotherapy and Behavior Change*. New York: Wiley, 1971, 217–70.

4. H. Jackins. *Elementary Counselor's Manual*. Seattle: Rational Island Publishers, 1962.

5. A. Bandura. *Principles of Behavior Modification*. New York: Holt, Rinehart, & Winston, 1969.

6. T. G. Stampfl, and D. J. Levis. "Essentials of Implosive Therapy: A Learning Theory Based Psychodynamic Behavioral Therapy," *Journal of Abnormal Psychology*, 72(1967), 496–503.

7. J. Wolpe, and A. A. Lazarus. *Behavior Therapy Techniques*. New York: Pergamon, 1966.

8. J. Wolpe, *Psychotherapy by Reciprocal Inhibition*. Stanford, Calif.: Stanford University Press, 1958.

9. C. G. Costello. "Behavior Therapy: Criticisms and Confusions," *Behavior Research and Therapy*, 1(1963), 159–61.

10. E. T. Gendlin, and J. F. Rychalak. "Psychotherapeutic Process," *Annual Review of Psychology*, 21(1970), 155–90.

11. A. P. Goldstein, M. Serber, and G. Piaget. "Induced Anger as a Reciprocal Inhibition of Fear," *Journal of Behavior Therapy and Experimental Psychiatry*, 1(1970), 67–70.

12. A. A. Lazarus, and A. Abramovitz. "The Use of Emotive Imagery in the Treatment of Children's Phobias," *Journal of Mental Science*, 108(1962), 109–95.

13. L. P. Ullmann, and L. Krasner. (Eds.) *Case Studies in Behavior Modification*. New York: Holt, Rinehart & Winston, 1965.

14. C. B. Ferster. "A Functional Analysis of Depression," *American Psychologist*, 28(1973), 857–70.

15. A. A. Lazarus. "Learning Theory and the Treatment of Depression," *Behavior Research and Therapy*. 6(1968), 83–89.

16. E. J. Shoben, Jr. "Psychotherapy as a Problem in Learning Theory," in H. J. Eysenck (ed.), *Behavior Therapy and the Neuroses*. New York: Pergamon Press, 1960.

17. O. H. Mowrer. "On the Dual Nature of Learning—A Reinterpretation of Conditioning and Problem-solving," *Harvard Educational Review*, 17(1947), 102–48.

18. T. G. Stampfl, and D. J. Levis. *Implosive Therapy: Theory and*

Technique. Morristown, New Jersey: General Learning Corporation, 1973.

19. R. A. Hogan. "The Implosive Technique," *Behavior Research and Therapy,* 6(1968), 423—31.

20. R. A. Hogan. "Implosively Oriented Behavior Modification: Therapy Considerations," *Behavior Research and Therapy,* 7(1969), 177—83.

21. A. F. Fazio. "Implosive Therapy in the Treatment of a Phobic Disorder," *Psychotherapy: Theory, Research and Practice,* 7(1970), 228—32.

22. K. P. Morganstern. "Implosive Therapy and Flooding Procedures: A Critical Review," *Psychological Bulletin,* 79(1973), 318—34.

23. R. A. Hogan. "Implosive Therapy in the Short Term Treatment of Psychotics," *Psychotherapy: Theory, Research and Practice,* 3 (1966), 25—31.

24. O. J. Levis and R. N. Carrera. "Effects of Ten Hours of Implosive Therapy in the Treatment of Outpatients: A Preliminary Report," *Journal of Abnormal Psychology,* 72(1967), 504—08.

25. J. C. Boulougouris, I. M. Marks, and P. Marset. "Superiority of Flooding (Implosion) to Desensitization for Reducing Pathological Fear," *Behavior Research and Therapy,* 9(1971), 7—16.

26. P. A. Boudewyns, and A. E. Wilson. "Implosive Therapy and Desensitization Therapy Using Free Association in the Treatment of Inpatients," *Journal of Abnormal Psychology,* 79(1972), 259—68.

27. J. H. Kirchner, and R. A. Hogan. "The Therapist Variable in the Implosion of Phobias," *Psychotherapy: Theory, Research and Practice,* 3(1966), 102—04.

28. R. A. Hogan, and J. H. Kirchner. "Preliminary Report of the Extinction of Learned Fears via Short-term Implosive Therapy," *Journal of Abnormal Psychology,* 72 (1967), 106—09.

29. R. A. Hogan, and J. H. Kirchner. "Implosive, Eclectic Verbal and Biblio-therapy in the Treatment of Fears of Snakes," *Behavior Research and Therapy,* 6(1968), 167—71.

30. A. F. Fazio. "Treatment Components in Implosive Therapy," *Journal of Abnormal Psychology,* 76(1970), 211—19.

31. S. Rachman. "Studies in Desensitization II: Flooding," *Behavior Research and Therapy,* 4(1966), 1—6.

32. C. L. Barrett. "Systematic Desensitization Versus Implosive

Therapy," *Journal of Abnormal Psychology*, 74(1969), 587–92.

33. W. L. Mealiea. "The Comparative Effectiveness of Systematic Desensitization and Implosive Therapy in the Elimination of Snake Phobia." (Doctoral Dissertations, University of Missouri). Ann Arbor, Mich.: University Microfilms, 1968, No. 68–3636.

34. M. J. Crowe, I. M. Marks, W. S. Agras, and H. Leitenberg. "Time-limited Desensitization, Implosion and Shaping for Phobic Patients: A Crossover Study," *Behavior Research and Therapy*, 10(1972), 319–28.

35. S. Rachman, R. Hodgson, and I. M. Marks. "Treatment of Chronic Obsessive-compulsive Neurosis," *Behavior Research and Therapy*, 9(1971), 237–47.

36. J. P. Watson, R. Gaind, and I. M. Marks. "Prolonged Exposure: A Rapid Treatment for Phobias," *British Medical Journal*, 1(1971), 13–15.

37. J. P. Watson, R. Gaind, and I. M. Marks. "Physiological Habituation to Continuous Phobic Stimulation," *Behavior Research and Therapy*, 10(1972), 269–78.

38. W. DeMoor. "Systematic Desensitization Versus Prolonged High Intensity Stimulation (Flooding)," *Journal of Behavior Therapy and Experimental Psychiatry*, 1(1970), 45–52.

39. R. J. Hodgson, and S. Rachman. "An Experimental Investigation of the Implosion Technique," *Behavior Research and Therapy*, 8(1970), 21–27.

40. J. P. Watson, and I. M. Marks. "Relevant and Irrelevant Fear in Flooding—A Crossover Study of Phobic Patients," *Behavior Therapy*, 2(1971), 275–93.

41. C. B. Truax, and R. R. Carkhuff. *Toward Effective Counseling and Psychotherapy: Training and Practice*. Chicago: Aldine, 1967.

42. C. B. Truax. "Effective Ingredients of Psychotherapy," *Journal of Counseling Psychology*, 10(1963), 256–63.

43. J. M. Chinsky, and J. Rappaport. "Brief Critique of the Meaning and Reliability of 'Accurate Empathy' Ratings," *Psychological Bulletin*, 73(1970), 379–81.

44. C. R. Rogers. *Cleint-centered Therapy*. Boston: Houghton Mifflin, 1951.

45. C. R. Rogers. "A Process Conception of Psychotherapy," *American Psychologist*, 13(1958), 142–49.

46. M. H. Klein, P. L. Mathieu, E. T. Gendlin, and D. J. Kiesler. *The Experiencing Scale: A Research and Training Manual*.

Madison, Wisc.: Bureau of Audio-Visual Instruction, University of Wisconsin Extension, 1970.

47. H. Jackins. *The Human Side of Human Beings*. Seattle: Rational Island Publishers, 1965.

48. A. M. Walker, R. A. Rablen, and C. R. Rogers. "Development of a Scale to Measure Process Changes in Psychotherapy," *Journal of Clinical Psychology*, 16(1960), 79—85.

49. E. T. Gendlin, R. H. Jenney, and J. M. Schlien. "Counselor Ratings of Process and Outcome in Client-centered Therapy," *Journal of Clinical Psychology*, 16(1960), 210—13.

50. E. T. Gendlin, J. Beebe III, J. Cassens, M. Klein, and M. Oberlander. "Focussing Ability in Psychotherapy, Personality and Creativity," in J. M. Schlien (ed.), *Research in Psychotherapy, Vol. III*. Washington, D.C.: American Psychological Association, 1968, 217—41.

51. E. T. Gendlin. "Focussing," *Psychotherapy: Theory, Research and Practice*, 6(1969), 4—15.

52. L. Luborsky, M. Chandler, A. H. Auerbach, H. Cohen, and H. M. Bachrach. "Factors Influencing the Outcome of Psychotherapy: A Review of the Quantitative Research," *Psychological Bulletin*, 75(1971), 145—85.

53. K. I. Howard, M. S. Krause, and A. E. Orlinsky. "Direction of Affective Influence in Psychotherapy," *Journal of Consulting and Clinical Psychology*, 33(1969), 614—20.

54. K. I. Howard, D. E. Orlinsky, and J. A. Hill. "Affective Experience in Psychotherapy," *Journal of Abnormal Psychology*, 75(1970), 267—75.

55. R. I. Bierman. "Dimensions of Interpersonal Facilitation in Psychhotherapy and Child Development," *Psychological Bulletin*, 72(1969), 338—52.

56. E. T. Gendlin, and L. Olsen. "The Use of Imagery in Experiential Focussing," *Psychotherapy: Theory, Research and Practice*, 7(1970), 221—23.

57. E. T. Gendlin, and T. M. Tomlinson. "Psychotherapy Process Rating Scale: Experiencing (EXP) Scale." Unpublished Manuscript, University of Wisconsin, 1961.

58. D. J. Kiesler. *The Process of Psychotherapy*. Chicago: Aldine, 1973.

59. D. J. Kiesler. "Patient Experiencing and Successful Outcome in Individual Psychotherapy of Schizophrenics and Psychoneurotics," *Journal of Consulting and Clinical Psychology*, 37(1971), 370—85.

60. S. Rosenzweig. "Some Implicit Common Factors in Diverse Methods of Psychotherapy," *American Journal of Orthopsychiatry*, 6(1936), 412—15.

61. J. D. Frank. "Therapeutic Factors in Psychotherapy," *American Journal of Psychotherapy*, 25(1971), 350—61.

62. P. H. Symonds. "A Comprehensive Theory of Psychotherapy," *American Journal of Orthopsychiatry*, 1954, 697—714.

63. A. Cooper, J. B. Furst, and W. H. Bridger. "A Brief Commentary on the Usefulness of Studying Fears of Snakes," *Journal of Abnormal Psychology*, 74(1969), 413—14.

64. A. P. Goldstein, K. Heller, and L. B. Sechrest. *Psychotherapy and the Psychology of Behavior Change*. New York: Wiley, 1966.

65. J. E. Gordon. "Leading and Following Psychotherapeutic Techniques with Hypnotically Induced Repression and Hostility," *Journal of Abnormal and Social Psychology*, 54(1957), 405—10.

66. C. D. Keet. "Two Verbal Techniques in a Miniature Counseling Situation," *Psychological Monographs*, 62(1948) No. 294.

67. R. M. Merrill. "Critiques and Notes on Keet's Study, Two Verbal Techniques in a Miniature Counseling Situation," *Journal of Abnormal and Social Psychology*, 47(1952), 722.

68. D. L. Grummon, and J. M. Butler. "Another Failure to Replicate Keet's Study. Two Verbal Techniques in a Miniature Counseling Situation," *Journal of Abnormal and Social Psychology*, 48(1953), 597.

69. E. A. Haggard. "Some Conditions Determining Adjustment During and Readjustment Following Experimentally Induced Stress," in S. S. Tomkins (ed.), *Contemporary Psychopathology*. Cambridge, Mass.: Harvard University Press, 1943, 529—44.

70. P. K. Levison, M. Zax, and E. L. Cowen. "An Experimental Analogue of Psychotherapy for Anxiety Reduction," *Psychological Reports*, 8(1961), 171—78.

71. M. Wiener. "The Effects of Two Experimental Counseling Techniques on Performance Impaired by Induced Stress," *Journal of Abnormal and Social Psychology*, 51(1955), 565—72.

72. D. Grossman. "An Experimental Investigation of a Psychotherapeutic Technique," *Journal of Consulting Psychology*, 16(1952), 325—331.

73. I. Marks, P. Marset, J. Boulougouris, and J. Huson. "Physiological Accompaniments of Neutral and Phobic Imagery," *Psychological Medicine*, 1(1971), 299—307.

74. L. I. O Kelly. "Physiological Changes During Psychotherapy," in O. H. Mowrer (ed.), *Psychotherapy Theory and Research*. New York: Ronald Press, 1953, 641–656.

75. F. Goldman-Eisler. "A Contribution to the Objective Measurement of the Cathartic Process," *Journal of Mental Science*, 102(1956), 78–95.

76. J. E. Dittes. "Extinction During Psychotherapy of GSR Accompanying 'Embarrassing' Statements," *Journal of Abnormal and Social Psychology*, 54(1957), 187–91.

77. J. E. Gordon, B. Martin, and R. M. Lundy. "GSRs During Repression Suppression and Verbalization in Psychotherapeutic Interviews," *Journal of Consulting Psychology*, 23(1959), 243–51.

78. B. Martin, R. M. Lundy, and M. H. Lewin. "Verbal and GSR Responses in Experimental Interviews as a Function of Three Degrees of Therapist Communication," *Journal of Abnormal and Social Psychology*, 60(1960), 234–40.

79. E. T. Gendlin, and J. I. Berlin. "Galvanic Skin Correlates of Different Modes of Experiencing," *Journal of Clinical Psychology*, 17(1961), 73–77.

80. J. Ruesch, and A. R. Prestwood. "Anxiety: Its Initiation, Communication and Interpersonal Management," *Archives of Neurology and Psychiatry*, 62(1949), 527–50.

81. R. S. Lazarus, and E. Alpert. "Short-circuiting of Threat by Experimentally Altering Cognitive Appraisal," *Journal of Abnormal and Social Psychology*, 69(1964), 195–205.

82. Z. J. Lipowski. "Review of Consultation Psychiatry and Psychosomatic Medicine: III Theoretical Issues," *Psychosomatic Medicine*, 30(1968), 395–422.

83. J. Bastiaans. "The Role of Aggression in the Genesis of Psychosomatic Disease," *Journal of Psychosomatic Research*, 13(1969), 307–14.

84. M. Gitelson. "A Critique of Current Concepts in Psychosomatic Medicine," *Bulletin of the Menninger Clinic*, 23(1959), 165–78.

85. H. R. Lewis, and M. E. Lewis. *Psychosomatics*. New York: Viking Press, 1972.

86. J. Groen. "Psychosomatic Disturbances as a Form of Substituted Behavior," *Journal of Psychosomatic Research*, 2(1957), 85–96.

87. F. Alexander. "Fundamental Concepts of Psychosomatic Research: Psychogenesis, Conversion, Specificity," *Psychosomatic Medicine*, 5(1943).

88. O. Fenichel. *The Psychoanalytic Theory of Neurosis*. New York: Norton, 1945.

89. S. Schachter, and J. Singer. "Cognitive, Social and Physiological Determinants of Emotional State," *Psychological Review*, 69(1962), 379−99.

90. H. Miller and D. W. Baruch. *The Practice of Psychosomatic Medicine*. New York: McGraw-Hill, 1956.

91. J. Dollard, L. W. Doob, N. E. Miller, O. H. Mowrer, and R. R. Sears. *Frustration and Aggression*. New Haven: Yale University Press, 1939.

92. K. Lorenz. *On Aggression*. New York: Harcourt, Brace and World, 1966.

93. R. R. Holt. "On the Interpersonal and Intrapersonal Consequences of Expressing or Not Expressing Anger," *Journal of Consulting and Clinical Psychology*, 35(1970), 8−12.

94. L. Berkowitz. "The Case for Bottling up Rage," *Psychology Today*, 7, 2(1973), 24−31.

95. L. Berkowitz, J. Green, and J. R. Macaulay. "Hostility Catharsis as the Reduction of Tension," *Psychiatry*, 25(1962), 23−31.

96. R. Schafer. "Requirements for a Critique of the Theory of Catharsis," *Journal of Consulting and Clinical Psychology*, 35(1970), 13−17.

97. R. G. Green, and L. Berkowitz. "Some Conditions Facilitating the Occurrence of Aggression after the Observation of Violence," *Journal of Personality*, 35(1967), 666−76.

98. D. Bramel, B. Taub, and B. Blum. "An Observer's Reaction to the Suffering of His Enemy," *Journal of Personality and Social Psychology*, 8(1968), 384−92.

99. S. Feshback. "The Drive-reduction Function of Fantasy Behavior," *Journal of Abnormal and Social Psychology*, 50(1955), 3−11.

100. A. N. Doob, and L. E. Wood. "Catharsis and Aggression: Effects of Annoyance and Retaliation on Aggressive Behavior," *Journal of Personality and Social Psychology*, 22(1972), 156−62.

101. M. Kahn. "The Physiology of Catharsis," *Journal of Personality and Social Psychology*, 3(1966), 278−86.

102. S. K. Mallick, and B. R. McCandless. "A Study of Catharsis of Aggression," *Journal of Personality and Social Psychology*, 41(1966), 591−96.

103. E. L. Phillips, and D. N. Wiener. *Short-term Psychotherapy and Structured Behavior Change*. New York: McGraw Hill, 1966.

104. V. J. Konecni, and A. N. Doob. "Catharsis Through Displacement of Aggression," *Journal of Personality and Social Psychology*, 23(1972), 379–87.

105. J. S. Baker, and K. W. Schaie. "Effects of Aggressing 'Alone' or 'With Another' on Physiological Arousal," *Journal of Personality and Social Psychology*, 12(1969), 80–86.

106. S. Gambaro, and A. I. Rabin. "Diastolic Blood Pressure Responses Following Direct and Displaced Aggression After Anger Arousal in High- and Low-guilt Subjects," *Journal of Personality and Social Psychology*, 12(1969), 87–94.

107. L. Berkowitz. "Experimental Investigations of Hostility Catharsis," *Journal of Consulting and Clinical Psychology*, 35(1970), 1–7.

108. E. E. Jones, and H. B. Gerard. *Foundations of Social Psychology*. New York: Wiley, 1967.

109. A. Zander. "Resistance to Change—Its Analysis and Prevention," in W. G. Bennis, K. O. Benne, and R. Chin (eds.), *The Planning of Change*. New York: Holt, Rinehart and Winston, 1964, 543–48.

110. G. W. Allport. "Catharsis and the Reduction of Prejudice," *Journal of Social Issues*, 1, 3(1945), 3–10.

111. K. Lewin. "Quasi-stationary Social Equilibria and the Problem of Permanent Change," in W. G. Bennis, K. D. Benne, and R. Chin (eds.), *The Planning of Change*. New York: Holt, Rinehart and Winston, 1964, 235–38.

112. J. D. Frank, and E. H. Nash. "Commitment to Peace Work: A Preliminary Study of the Determinants and Sustainers of Behavior Change," *American Journal of Orthopsychiatry*, 35(1965), 106–19.

113. R. Hoehn-Saric, J. D. Frank, and B. J. Gurland. "Focussed Attitude Change in Neurotic Patients," *Journal of Nervous Mental Disease*, 147(1968), 124–33.

Chapter 9

1. H. Jackins. *Elementary Counselor's Manual*. Seattle: Rational Island Publishers, 1962.

2. S. Freud. "New Introductory Lectures on Psycho-analysis," *Standard Edition*, Vol. 22. London: Hogarth Press, 1933.

3. O. Fenichel. *The Psychoanalytic Theory of Neurosis*. New York: W. W. Norton & Co., 1945.

4. H. Jackins. *The Human Side of Human Beings*. Seattle: Rational Island Publishers, 1965.

5. J. Henry. *Pathways to Madness*. New York: Random House, 1971.

6. H. Guntrip. *Schizoid Phenomena, Object-Relations and the Self*. New York: International Universities Press, 1969.

7. F. H. Lowy. "The Abuse of Abreaction: An Unhappy Legacy of Freud's Cathartic Method," *Canadian Psychiatric Journal*, 15(1970), 557−65.

8. A. Janov. *The Primal Scream*. New York: Dell, 1970.

9. R. D. Laing. *The Divided Self*. Baltimore: Penguin Books, 1960.

10. R. R. Greenson. *The Technique and Practice of Psychoanalysis*. New York: International Universities Press, Inc., 1967.

11. G. L. Engel, and F. Reichsman. "Spontaneous and Experimentally Induced Depressions in an Infant with a Gastric Fistula," *Journal of the American Psychoanalytic Association*, 4(1956), 428−52.

12. G. L. Engel, and A. H. Schmale. "Conservation-withdrawal: A Primary Regulatory Process for Organismic Homeostasis," in R. Porter and J. Knight (eds.), *Physiology, Emotion, and Psychosomatic Illness*. Ciba Foundation Symposium 8 (n.S.). Amsterdam: Elsevier-Excerpta Medica, 1972, 57−85.

13. W. McDougall. "The Revival of Emotional Memories and its Therapeutic Value," *British Journal of Medical Psychology*, 1(1920), 23−29.

Index

Academy of Sciences, 48
Adler, A., 120
Affect bridge, 10
Aggression, 1. 186–191
Alexander, F. M. 121
Alexander technique, 120–122
Allen, J., viii
Allport, G., 192
Altered state of consciousness, 63
Anger, 70, 207
Animal magnetism, 43
Anna, O., 8, 29
Anxiety, 59, 106, 137
Aristotle, 2
Arnold, M., 4
Arousal, 207
Attitude, 191–194

Baker, E., 107, 112
Baker, J. S., 190
Bandura, W., 1
Baquet, 42
Barnacle, C. H., 96
Barrett, C. L., 165
Baruch, D. W., 184
Bastiaans, J., 184
Bean, O., 110
Beattie, J., 15
Behavior modification, 159, 175
Behavior therapy, 159
Benne, K., 79
Berkowitz, L., 1, 187
Berlin, J. I., 180
Bernheim, H., 48
Bereavement, 89–102, 135
Berzon, B., 72
Bierman, R. I., 170
Binet, A., 49
Bioenergetic Analysis and Therapy, 115
Blair, J. H., 62
Boudewyns, P. A., 165
Bowlby, J., 93
Bradford, L., 79
Braid, J., 47
Brammer, L. M., 97

Breuer, J., 2, 29, 197
British Medical Association, 49
Brown, W., 53
Burrow, T., 67

Calestro, K. M., 21
Carkhuff, R. R., 167
Casriel, D., 144–151
Casriel Institute, 147
Catalepsy, 48
Catharsis, vii, 1–12, 70, 74, 188
    and psychoanalysis, 29–38
    cognitive-emotional, 8, 74, 168, 210
    effectiveness, 202
    evaluation, 155
    group-, 74
    group treatment, 65–72
    history of treatment, 198–202
    hypnotically induced, 56
    hypothesis, 186
    in behavior therapy, 111
    individual-, 74
    limits of therapy, 224
    mental-, 74
    neo-, 37
    somatic-, 74
    somatic-emotional, 8, 213
    therapy, 14, 68, 209
Charcot, J. M., 48
Child, 11
Chinsky, J. M., 167
Client-centered therapy, 167
Conditioned Emotional Reaction (CER), 5
Conditioned Stimulus (CS), 62
Confession, 18
Confrontation, 80
Cooper, A., 173
Corybantes, 15
Costello, C. G., 159
Cowen, E. L., 176
Crying, 69, 103, 110, 129, 184, 209, 222
Curative factors, 172–181

Darwin, C., 4, 93
Daytop Village, 145

Death, 89, 98
Delson, C., 44
DeMoore, W., 166
Depressants, 57
Depression, 36, 59, 71, 90, 92
Deutsch, H., 90
Discharge, 79, 103
Discomfort Relief Quotient, 177
Dittes, J. E., 178
Dollard, J., 186
Doob, A. N., 188
DuBrin, J., viii
Dysfunction, 182

EEG, 141
Efran, J., viii
Ego, 74, 77
Eliade, M., 19
Elliotson, J., 47
Emotion, 4, 184, 206
Encounter groups, 79—87
Encounter group attitudes, 84
Engel, G., 94, 227
Esalen, 83
Esdaile, J., 47
Evans-Pritchard, E. E., 14
Experiencing Scale, 167, 171
Extinction, 62

Fagan, J., 127
Fair Employment Practices Act, 79
Fantasy, 29
Fazio, A. F., 163
Feedback, 80
Feldenkrais, Moshé, 120
Fenichel, O., 4, 36, 184, 207
Ferenczi, S., 36
Finney, C., 24
FIRO-B, 84
Fletcher, J., viii
Flooding, 165
Focusing, 169
Fogarty, T., 98
Forgetting, 31
Frank, J. D., 23, 172, 192
Frau Emmy von N., 32
Freides, I., viii
Freud, S., 1, 3, 4, 29, 34, 49, 56, 90, 121,
    142, 197, 207
Fried, B., viii
Friendship Questionnaire, 84

Gendlin, E. T., 168, 180
Gestalt, 82
    therapy, 123—130, 205
Gibb, J. R., 83

Gillin, J., 17
Goldman-Eisler, F., 179
Goldstein, A. P., 173, 193
Goldstein, K., 123
Gordon, J. E., 178
Gorer, G., 99
Grayson, H., 12, 96
Greenson, R. R., 36, 120
Grief, 90, 97
Grinker, R. R., 58
Groen, J., 183
Grosser, G. H., 97
Grossman, D., 178
Group therapy, 65—72
    adolescent, 68
    Adult, 68
    child, 67
    encounter, 79—87
    T-, 79
Guerin, P., 98
Guilt, 69
Guntrip, Harry, 214

Haggard, E. A., 176
Hallucination, 54
Hart, J., 142
Heidegger, M., 89
Heller, K., 173
Henry, J., 214
Heroin, 138
Hogan, R. A., 163
Holt, R. R., 187
Hordern, A., 58
Hostility, 70
Howard, K. I., 170
Humanistic psychology, 132
Hypercathexis, 3
Hypnosis, 47, 53, 178, 185, 199
Hypnotherapy, 10, 39—64
Hysteria, 31

Implosion, 103, 125, 163
Indian Ghost Dance, 40
Individual therapy, 64
Intervention, 91

Jackins, H., 10, 47, 103, 131—137, 157,
    180, 205, 218
James, W., 27
Janet, P., 39, 49
Janov, A., 9, 47, 103, 112, 137—144
Jenney, R. H., 168
Jung, C., 174

Kaddish, 102
Kahn, M., 189

Karle, W., 142
Katharsis, 2
Keet, C., 174
Keleman, S., 118–120
Kiesler, D. J., 171
Kircher, A., 41
Klein, M., 92
Kraepelin, E., 49
Krassner, L., 160

LSD, 219
Laing, R., 153, 219
Language, 109
Lazarus, A. A., 159, 161
Lazarus, R., 180
Lazell, E., 67
Lebarre, W., 18
Lethargy, 48
Levine, R. A., 15
Lewin, K., 79, 192
Lewis, H. R., 185
Lewis, M. E., 185
Liberman, M. A., 83
Life-Space Questionnaire, 84
Lindemann, E., 93
Lippitt, R., 79
Lipshitz, K., 62
Lorenz, K., 93, 186
Loud, G. C., 25
Lourdes, 23
Lowen, A., 1, 115–118
Lowy, F. H., 228
Luborsky, L., 170

McDougall, L., 4
Magic, 13
Magnetism, 40
Malinowski, B., 14
Maliver, B., 83
Marijuana, 138
Marks, I. M., 166
Marris, P., 100
Marsh, L. C., 67
Mason, J. W., 91
Massage, 110
Maxwell, W., 40
Medicine men, 16
Melancholia, 90, 92
Members of This Group, 84
Mendota State Hospital, 169
Mesmer, A., 40–48
Metraux, A., 22
Miles, M. B., 83
Milieu therapy, 165
Miller, H., 184
MMPI, 157, 164

Moody, D. L., 25
Mourning, 90
Moreno, J. L., 67, 73
Moreno, Z., 67, 75
Morganstern, K. P., 164
Mowrer, O. H., 161

Nancy School, 48
Narcosynthesis, 59
Neurons, 3, 57
Neurosis, 39–64
    sexual, 53
    symptoms of, 137
Nichols, M. P., 156, 202
Nonagression, 15
Naranjo, C., 125
Northfield Center, 71
Nowicki, S., viii

O'Kelly, L. I., 178
Openness, 80
Orgone therapy, 110
Orlinsky, A. E., 170
Orne, M., 188

Pain, 137
Parson, R., 72
Paul, N. L., 97
Penfield, W., 11
Pentothal, 59
    sodium-, 96
Perls, F. S., 123
Personal Anticipation, 84
Personal Description Questionnaire, 84
Personal Dilemma Questionnaire, 84
Personal Satisfaction Form, 157
Phobia, 160
Physiotherapy, 62
Pierce, R., viii
Pious, C., 72
Pratt, J. H., 66
Prestwood, A. R., 180
Primal therapy, 103, 137–144
Process Scale, 169
Psychodrama, 73–79
Psychodramatist, 76
Psychoneurosis, 53
Psychopathology, 49
Psychosomatic medicine, 181–186
Psychotherapy, 65–72, 172

Q, 3

Rappaport, J., 167
Rasmussan, K., 19
Re-enactment, 79

Re-Evaluation Counseling, 10, 103, 131—136
Reich, W., 105—114, 142, 200
Release, 100
Repression, 54, 59, 70
Revivalism, 24
Rituals, 13
   religious, 13—29
   magic healing, 13—29
Rogers, C., 83, 167
Role, 58, 78
Rolf, I., 121
Rolfing, 120—122
Rosenberg Scales, 84
Rosenzweig, S., 172
Ruesch, J., 180

Sachar, E. J., 91
Sargant, M. B., 57
Sargant, W., 25
Satre, J., 89
Schacter, S., 184, 194
Schaie, K. W., 190
Schilder, P., 67
Schizophrenia, 219
Schlein, J. M., 168
Schutz, W., 122
Scream, 139, 144, 150
Sechrest, L. B., 173
Self-actualization, 119, 205
Self-disclosure, 80
Semantic Differential, 193
Shaman, 16
Shell shock, 53
Shiveh, 102
Shoben, E. J., Jr., 161
Shorvon, H. J., 57
Shostrom, E. L., 97
Shouting, 69
Simmerl, E., 55
Slavson, S., 68
Smith, J. F., viii
Smith, P. B. 83
Smith, J., 142
Social psychology, 186—191
Somer, B. J., 132
Somatic therapy, z21
Somnambulism, 48
Sorcery, 15
Soubirous, B., 23
Spiegel, J. P., 58
Stampfl, T. G., 162
Stress, 59
Structural Integration, 121
Suicide, 95
Sullivan, H. S., 137
Sunday, "Billy", 25

Supernatural, 13
Symonds, P. H., 172
Symptomatology, 35
Synanon, 83, 145

T-groups, 79
Theater of Spontaneity *(Stegreiftheater)*, 73
Therapy, 1
   abreactive hypnotic, 53
   behavior-, 159
   body, 130
   catharsis-information, 176
   client-centered, 167
   Gestalt, 104
   group, 65—88
   individual, 65
   milieu, 165
   New Identity, 158
   orgone, 106, 108
   primal, 104, 137—144
   psychoanalytic, 185
   vego-, 106
Thomas, R., viii
Transactional Analysis, 83
Transient situational reaction, 52
Trauma, 55, 63, 223
Truax, C. B., 167

Ullman, L. P., 160
Unconditioned Response (UCR), 62
Unconditioned Stimulus (UCS), 62

Vegotherapy, 106
Ventilation, 71
Violence, 15
Voodoo, 21

Watkins, J. G., 10, 58
Weatherhead, L. D., 23
Weiner, M., 177
Welch Army Hospital, 59
Wender, L., 67, 71
Wesley, J., 25
Wheelock, E., 25
Widow, 100
Wilson, A. E., 165
Witchcraft, 15, 23
Wolpe, J., 159
Wood, L. E., 188
World War I, 39, 52
World War II, 52, 57, 70

Yalolm, I. D., 71, 83

Zander, A., 191
Zax, M., 176